CHARLOTTE, THE SLUGGER, AND ME

A Coming-of-Age Story of a Southern City and Two Tenacious Brothers

JACK CLAIBORNE

SPARK Publications
Charlotte, North Carolina

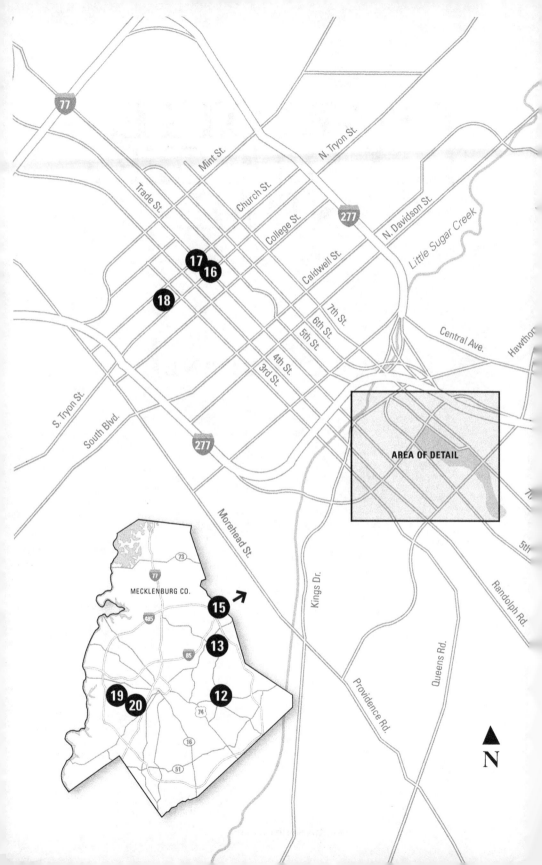

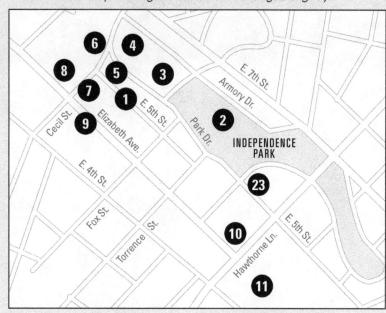

These numbers represent locations referenced in this book. Because the setting of this book spans several decades, some streets may no longer exist or have changed slightly.

1. 1235 East Fifth Street
2. Independence Park
3. Memorial Stadium
4. Armory Auditorium
5. 1200 Park Drive
   (first boarding house)
6. Central High Athletic Field
7. 214 Cecil Street
8. Central High School
9. 1217 Elizabeth Avenue
10. Andersons Restaurant
11. Presbyterian Hospital

12. Jackass Lane *(11 miles)*
13. UNC Charlotte *(13 miles)*
14. Barclay Cafeteria *(3 miles)*
15. Chapel Hill *(139 miles)*
16. Independence Square *(1.5 miles)*
17. City Club *(1.5 miles)*
18. Charlotte Observer *(1.7 miles)*
19. Douglas Airport *(18 miles)*
20. Griffith Park *(3 miles)*
21. Mint Museum *(3.5 miles)*
22. 2305 East Fifth Street
    (Jack's home since 2009)
23. Caldwell Presbyterian Church

Charlotte, the Slugger, and Me
A Coming-of-Age Story of a Southern City and Two Tenacious Brothers
Jack Claiborne

Designed, produced, and published by
SPARK Publications
SPARKpublications.com
Charlotte, North Carolina

Stock Image Credit: sath aporn

Printed in the United States of America

Paperback, November 2023, ISBN: 978-1-953555-64-9
Library of Congress Control Number: 2023919891

DEDICATION

This book is dedicated to the memory of our courageous mother, Minnie Harton Claiborne, and to the generous spirit of our older brother, Harold Goode Claiborne, each of whom worked selflessly to hold our family together, opening doors of opportunity that enabled Slug and me to flourish.

TABLE OF CONTENTS

PART TWO:

PROLOGUE

This is the story of a pushy little Southern town that threw off some of its Old South inclinations to emerge as one of the nation's newest big cities. It is also the story of how two fatherless boys from a Depression-depleted family rose with pluck—and occasional audacity—to positions of distinction within it.

Told through the eyes and adventures of those two boys, it is an American story of government investments that inspired hope, self-discovery, and upward mobility. It portrays an era of family solidarity, community collaboration, and focused activity that brought goals within reach. It is a story of optimism and community spirit.

In a time of national division and mistrust, it is also an antidote to the poisonous rancor and suspicion that often paralyzes progress. Further, by extension the story hints at the South's gradual integration into the culture of the rest of the United States, thanks to New Deal projects, World War II military encampments, and manufacturing establishments, plus the enlightenment accompanying civil rights advances of the 1950s, '60s, and '70s.

The two fatherless boys were Jack and Jimmy Claiborne, though from age six onward Jimmy became "Slug" or "the Slugger." As the town grew, we boys grew with it, sharing its excitement and inhaling its ambition. Having been shaped by the town, we grew up to shape it in some important ways, the Slugger through trend-setting restaurants, genial hospitality, and community service, and I through prize-winning journalism, research into local history, and reflective newspaper editorials.

As the youngest of our mother's six children, we became the family favorites. Lumped within the household as "the boys" and within the neighborhood as "the Claiborne boys," we were about as opposite as brothers could be. I was tall and skinny and looked like our father. Jimmy was short and stout and looked like our mother. I was wary and withdrawn; he was ebullient and outgoing. But we fed off each other's attributes.

Our birthdays were only 359 days apart, meaning that for six days a year we were the same age. On the seventh day I nudged a year ahead. That seniority was never lost on either of us. It goaded my brother to do all he could to prove himself my better and drove me to invent ways of staying ahead. Throughout our lives that competition was a spur to each of us. Fortunately, we didn't often get in each other's way. I was more interested in understanding the past while he was impatient to explore the future.

The pushy little Southern town was Charlotte, North Carolina, once insignificant but now one of the nation's busiest urban centers. Though many newcomers look on it as a new place fresh out of the box, Charlotte has a long and memorable past. At its founding in 1768, it was hardly a dot on the map, yet in 1780 when British Redcoats invaded, their commander, Lord Charles Cornwallis, condemned it as a "hornet's nest" of rebellion.

Without a distinctive physical feature—a river or harbor or mountain peak—it began as the crossing of two Native American paths. That committed it to a life of trade and commerce astride the Carolina boundaries. In the 1850s the Native American paths were replaced by two railroads, one from South Carolina and another from North Carolina. Their junction made Charlotte a transportation and supply center for much of the two states. When the railroads gave way to automobiles and air travel, Charlotte became the junction for two interstate highways and its airport grew into one of the world's busiest.

Extravagantly named for Queen Charlotte, the wife of Britain's King George III, the town bred ambition. In time it became the "Queen City," a welcoming place where you didn't need a fortune or a pedigree to make friends or find favor. It encouraged its citizens to think big. From its earliest days it was led by forward-looking people, most of them from elsewhere, men and women who were attracted by the city's entrepreneurial spirit.

Among them were the Oates brothers, J. B. and Robert, from Shelby, who in the 1850s ran the cotton wharf that made Charlotte a cotton shipping point and later built the city's first cotton mill; William Henry Belk of Monroe and J. B. Ivey of Shelby, both builders of extensive department store chains that made Charlotte the shopping center for much of the Carolinas; James B. Duke of Durham, who electrified the Catawba River valley in creating a power company that brought a cadre of experts to Charlotte and later established a foundation with headquarters in the city; lawyer Cameron Morrison of Rockingham, who became North Carolina's good roads governor and built a model dairy farm that is now almost a city unto itself around SouthPark Shopping Mall; Rush S. Dickson of Grover, whose investment banking taught Charlotteans to accumulate wealth; Ben Douglas, a funeral director from Gastonia who as mayor led Charlotte out of the Great Depression; Herbert Baxter of Boston, who as a city council member and mayor was Charlotte's leading progressive and idea man; C. A. "Pete" McKnight of Shelby, who became editor of the *Charlotte News* and later of the *Charlotte Observer* and turned both into progressive forces; A. G. Odell from Concord, whose architecture helped to modernize the post-war city; Stanford R. Brookshire from Iredell County, who led Charlotte through the threatening 1960s racial protests; and Cliff Cameron of Raleigh and Ed Crutchfield of Stanly County, who built First Union National into a financial powerhouse.

A remarkable number came from South Carolina, including D. A. Tompkins of Edgefield who showed Charlotteans how to build, finance, and equip textile mills; E. D. Latta of Pendleton who developed Dilworth as a near-town neighborhood and installed the streetcar system; William States Lee of Anderson who persuaded James B. Duke to create a power company with headquarters in Charlotte; Bonnie Cone of Walterboro who created Charlotte College, which became the University of North Carolina at Charlotte; Hugh McColl Jr. of Bennettsville who in leading

Bank of America to the highest ranks of the nation's financial institutions also pushed Charlotte to reach new artistic and cultural heights; and architect Harvey B. Gantt of Charleston who after desegregating Clemson College (now Clemson University) became Charlotte's first Black mayor.

Those and hundreds of other newcomers supported progressive goals that encouraged Charlotteans to provide better amenities and invest in people. The city taxed itself to build better schools, a teaching hospital, large parks and playgrounds, and after World War II three public colleges. In the background, the South, often following Charlotte's lead, was grudgingly relaxing its Jim Crow barriers and conforming to the nation's biracial culture.

Our story reflects a time that no longer exists, a slower-paced period when people in our town, survivors of the Great Depression and later of World War II, regarded each other as neighbors, pulled together, and offered helping hands. Undergirding that communal spirit was an entrepreneurial spirit and a promotional verve that rubbed off on us. We watched as Charlotte shed the dust of its gold-mining and cotton-milling past to become one of America's celebrated cities.

Positioning us to play roles in Charlotte's emergence is the focus of our story. Along the way are landmark moments in the city's evolution and the sights and sounds of what it was like to live through some of the most tumultuous times in American history—the Great Depression, World War II, and the racial and gender revolutions that brought wider opportunities to a more open South.

The narrative spans eighty years of accelerating change resulting from a steady migration of Americans from rural to urban environments and a steady shift from brawn to brains in the workplace. Within those eighty years, many other middling American cities—Atlanta, Denver, Phoenix, Nashville, Seattle—also rose to prominence.

Across North Carolina the urban population exploded, rising from 970,000 in 1940 to more than six million in 2010. Previously a state of small farms and small towns, North Carolina saw the emergence of a half dozen significant cities. As Charlotte's population grew from 85,000 to 850,000, Raleigh's rose from 40,000 to 400,000; Greensboro's from 55,000 to 264,000, Winston-Salem's from 75,000 to 229,000; and Durham's from 80,244 to 228,330.

As boys and young men, we witnessed astonishing advances that added television to radio; brought air conditioning to theaters, offices, and homes, opening the South to more comfortable summers; and snuffed out kerosene lamps in favor of incandescent lights, which in time were replaced by LED lamps. We saw typewriters give way to computer keyboards and propeller-driven airplanes succumb to jet propulsion that carried men to the moon. Further, the period included unrest over issues of religious, racial, and gender equality. Slug and I were there to witness and learn from all those changes.

PART ONE

"The Boys"

Jack (left) and Slug at about ages five and four

"We had been living in strained, sometimes desperate circumstances and needed all the help we could get. The rainbow lifted our spirits and led us to think better days might be ahead."

CHAPTER

1

A Reason to Hope

Our very first visit to Charlotte with the family proved providential. It was September 10, 1936, when the Great Depression still hung like an angry cloud over American life. The city was aflutter over the impending arrival of Franklin Roosevelt, the first American president to visit since Woodrow Wilson in 1916. Roosevelt was regarded as something of a political savior charged with lifting the country out of the deepest economic catastrophe in American history. Many Carolinians had heard his reassuring voice over the radio but had never seen him. Before television, opportunities to see an American president were rare. Even at ages four and five, Jimmy and I could feel the throb of anticipation.

The town was bedecked in flags and bunting, welcoming visitors from miles away. The event was billed as Roosevelt's only campaign appearance this far south, giving down-the-ballot Democratic candidates an opportunity to be photographed with him. Democratic leaders from seven states were invited. Hotels and rooming houses were bulging with guests. More than one hundred thousand people—enough to overwhelm Charlotte's eighty-five thousand residents—lined the President's route from the city's western gateway through the center of town and eastward to the new stadium where he was to speak.

In efforts to energize the national economy, Roosevelt had launched job-creation programs all across the land, including more than a dozen in Charlotte. Funded through the Works Progress Administration (WPA), those ventures were changing the city's landscape by expanding the post office and federal courthouse, relocating a century-old US Mint, improving the city's street system, creating new parks and playgrounds, and, most importantly, grading gullied, red-clay land on the town's western outskirts for a public airport, only the second one in the state.

Our mother, recently widowed and struggling to maintain a ninety-acre cotton farm ten miles north of town, had seen Roosevelt's New Deal revive hopes among millions of American farmers. To make sure her six children experienced this once-in-a-lifetime opportunity, she went to extraordinary efforts to give us a glimpse of the great man. She roused us early that morning and walked us about a mile from our farmhouse to the nearest railroad depot. There she bought us tickets on the Southern Railway to its soot-stained terminal on Charlotte's West Trade Street, five blocks from midtown. Beyond the terminal we boarded an electric streetcar that rumbled through the heart of town and a mile or more east to the Elizabeth neighborhood. We got off at what was then Fox Street, a narrow little lane later to become traffic-laden Independence Boulevard.

As we exited the streetcar and began our walk toward newly completed American Legion Memorial Stadium, itself a WPA project, a rainstorm broke, forcing us to dash under the awning of a small grocery at the mouth of East Fifth Street. From other shelter-seekers huddled there we learned that just down the way was an alley that would lead us into the path of the President's motorcade. We found the alley and soon were standing in an ivy-bordered yard waiting for motorcycle police to roar past, followed by the President's long, black limousine.

Heavy rain had disrupted the President's schedule, causing him to run about an hour late. Even worse, during the hundred-mile drive from Asheville the President's open car had been in and out of rainstorms. His black suit was sodden and the brim of his black hat was turned down on all sides, allowing water to run off in rivulets. Yet, under the hat was the famous face and radiant smile that looked like sunshine. As he passed, he waved and nodded as throngs lining the street responded with cheers.

Once the motorcade passed, we crossed Park Drive and entered the jam-packed stadium to hear the President speak. Mother squeezed us into the grandstand's very back row, hard against a white concrete wall. We saw the President's long black car enter the stadium and stop at a freshly built wooden platform on the grassy playing field. With the help of his son John and a Secret Service agent, the paralyzed President "walked" to a lectern, steadied himself, and smoothed the text of his prepared remarks. As he was about to speak, the clouds parted and the sun burst through.

"My friends...," he began in that warm, soothing voice people had often heard on the radio. Then abruptly he stopped. "Look!" he exclaimed, gesturing toward the far end of the stadium. "I see a rainbow in the sky!"

Sure enough, arching across the heavens were bands of red, green, blue, and gold, just the promise to offset the gloom of an otherwise inclement afternoon. The crowd roared its approval.

Drawing on references from the twenty-third psalm to "green pastures" and "still waters," Roosevelt talked of restoring the South's soul through a variety of programs for soil and water conservation and price supports for cotton, tobacco, and other crops that would produce a living wage.

Afterward, the President stopped at an uptown hotel to be photographed with party principals and then caught a train to Washington, DC. But the rainbow proved to be a good omen. He won lusty applause for his speech and went on to win reelection in a landslide.

The rainbow was a good omen for the Claiborne family too. Since the stock market crash of 1929 and the calamitous death of our father the previous January, we had been living in strained, sometimes desperate circumstances and needed all the help we could get. The rainbow lifted our spirits and led us to think better days might be ahead.

Though we couldn't know it at the time, the rainbow was also a positive sign for Jimmy and me. Despite our humble origins and boyish fears, it gave us reason to hope good things might happen to us. The first of those good things occurred almost immediately. As our family returned from the stadium, we retraced our steps through the alley back to East Fifth Street. There our oldest sister Alice noticed a house for rent and called Mother's attention to it. She, our sister Phyllis, and Mother went on the porch to look in the windows and scan its interior. After a brief conference, Mother made a brave decision. Without knowing how it might be accomplished, she authorized Alice to go to the real estate agent listed on the "For Rent" sign, determine the price, and rent the place if we could afford it, which Alice did the next day.

The extraordinary effort to hear the President speak, the sudden rainstorm that drove us under the grocery awning, and our discovery of the Fifth Street alley and the rental house all proved beneficial. From that house at 1235 East Fifth Street Mother could earn money cooking, sewing, and upholstering. Our sister Alice, a recent graduate of Newell High School, could walk to her job at a hosiery mill at Ninth and Brevard Streets in uptown Charlotte, saving train and trolley fares and contributing more to the family's support. Our sister Phyllis could work part time while entering the twelfth grade at nearby Central High to learn secretarial skills that would qualify her for better-paying jobs using brains rather than hands. For the rest of us—our brother Harold, our sister Anne, Jimmy, and me—the Fifth Street house would position us to get better educations in Charlotte's public schools and explore an urban environment. We could also earn money by doing odd jobs in the neighborhood.

From President Roosevelt's visit onward, instead of struggling to survive on subsistence farming, the Claiborne family would gradually regain the middle-class comforts it had once enjoyed. The ascent was long and precarious, but Charlotte, and especially the bustling Elizabeth neighborhood, about a mile from the center of town, gave us opportunities to succeed.

Jack beside the playhouse at about age four

CHAPTER

2

The Fall from Comfort

The severity of our climb out of poverty can be measured by the depths of our fall from middle-class comfort. During the decade before Jimmy and I were born, our father and mother, Henry and Minnie Claiborne, and their four children lived in relative ease on the rolling hills of Derita, a rural community about eight miles north of Charlotte. In later years on separate occasions my brother Harold and my sister Phyllis walked me over the homesite, pointing out where the white-framed, one-story house had stood, surrounded by fruit trees, grape arbors, and wisteria trellises. The house was laced with steam heat, powered by electricity, and equipped with indoor plumbing. Beyond the house stretched pastures and grain fields to serve a dairy farm that produced milk, cream, and butter for delivery to homes across Charlotte. With a bull and three cows, our father had developed a herd of twenty milkers. He built a barn with stalls for each and equipped it with electric lights and milking machines.

Further, our father built an elaborate playhouse in the backyard for his daughters. A stickler for precise joints and smooth finishes, he built it to exacting standards. It stood on a brick foundation, had a covered front porch with columns, a large inner room with working windows, plaster walls, and hardwood floors. It also had electricity. He applied the same exacting standards to making furniture for the big house. He built beds, desks, cupboards, and a kitchen table with benches attached. He furnished the living room with a black, store-bought player piano, on which our sisters Alice and Phyllis learned to play and around which the family often gathered to sing such songs as "There's a Long, Long Trail."

In a corner of the backyard stood an apiary of beehives from which our parents, wearing hats, veils, gloves, and smokers, robbed the bees of honey, which Mother put up in jars sealed with wax and stored in the pantry. In those days the Claibornes lived well.

When our father wasn't overseeing the dairy farm, he was building houses in Charlotte for the Sherrill Company. He built many of the houses still standing along the eastern edge of the Dilworth neighborhood on what are now Harding Place and Kenilworth Avenue, about a mile from the center of town.

Like many Americans in the 1920s, Henry Claiborne acquired much of his land and improvements on credit, assuming the prosperity of the Roaring Twenties would endure. Such optimism was contagious in the 1920s. Stock market prices had doubled and quintupled during the decade. Much of America was enjoying a new Gilded Age.

The market crash of 1929 changed all that. Businesses failed, mills shut down, unemployment soared, and banks began closing. The Great Depression had begun. Without a steady income, our father, like farmers and businessmen everywhere, could not pay the bills. He soon lost the farm and the comfortable life. In 1930 he moved the family to more humble surroundings on ninety-three acres of rented land at Newell, a ragged hamlet straddling the Old Concord Road about ten miles north of Charlotte.

In many ways the move was a retreat to the nineteenth century. The farmhouse was a framed, two-story dwelling weathered to a dingy gray. Supported by brick piers, it stood on a bluff overlooking a long, sloping yard that tumbled unevenly into a red-clay drainage ditch. Beyond the ditch was a dirt road known in the neighborhood as "Jackass Lane," later to be named Rocky River Road. It drew its colorful nickname from the male donkeys that J. A. Newell kept in his backyard at the lane's entrance. He bred his jacks with mares to produce mules, a staple of Depression-era farming.

J. A. Newell was a county commissioner and the village justice of the peace, entitling him to use the honorific "Squire." With a build like Burl Ives and the manner of Andy Griffith, Squire Newell was highly visible in the village. Dressed in blue denim overalls and a flannel shirt, his bald pate glistening over a green eyeshade, he made daily rounds, from his home to the Post Office, the hardware store and the railroad depot, greeting villagers and often offering sage advice. You knew you were approaching the Squire's place before you got there because you could hear those jacks honking and braying in his backyard.

In the move to Newell our father brought along a tractor, a Model-T Ford, a mule, and a remnant of his dairy herd. He also brought the big, black player piano, and the backyard playhouse.

As soon as he arrived, he set out to improve the new surroundings. He built a big red barn, a milk house for processing each day's dairy production, and began clearing woods across Jackass Lane for cotton fields, gambling that cotton prices, which had spiraled downward for a decade, would soon spiral up again. After President Roosevelt's election in 1932, he, like millions of other American farmers, had reason to hope.

The church in Skipwith, Virginia

CHAPTER

3

Hard-Scrabble Lives

The early 1930s were desperate times for most Americans. For the Claibornes, the move to Newell was a descent down the economic ladder. It meant renting instead of buying and often living from hand to mouth. Our mother did her best to make the drafty, two-story house a home without the conveniences she had earlier enjoyed. Instead of electric lights she relied on candles and kerosene lamps. She heated the house with wood fires in a living room fireplace and a big, black, cast-iron stove in the kitchen. In winter she and her children jumped out of bed, hurried downstairs to bathe and dress in front of the fireplace or within the warmth of the kitchen stove.

Without household appliances, she drew water from a hand-operated pump in the backyard. She washed clothes outside in a black washpot heated by a fire below. She scrubbed them on a washboard, rinsed them in galvanized tubs of bluing, then hung them on a line to dry. Later she starched some of them and smoothed them with flat irons heated on the kitchen stove. Having grown up in a farm family, she was equal to all that. She bore the hardships with good humor and strove to make the home a happy place.

Her oldest girls, Alice and Phyllis, who had begun school in Derita, transferred to Newell School two miles away, as did their six-year-old brother, Harold. The school offered instruction in grades one through eleven, with heavy emphasis on agriculture and home economics. Without milking machines, Harold and his older sisters joined their father in milking the cows before school each morning and again in the evening. With our father, our sister Phyllis continued to make a few milk deliveries in Charlotte. Wearing white bib overalls, she ran fresh milk to doorsteps and brought back empty bottles.

For our father, having to move to inferior quarters was a bitter defeat. He had been a better provider. Born in 1878, he had grown up in middle-class comfort in Mecklenburg County, Virginia, on the Virginia-North Carolina line. His father had been a farmer and builder and had taught his son those skills. As a teenager he helped his father build a big, white-framed church, in which his family and the surrounding community worshipped.

In addition to the church, they built two large, framed houses that still stand on a country road near Skipwith, Virginia. As evidence of the family's standing in the community, a paved road still bears the name Claiborne Circle. Jimmy and I knew none of that. We knew only the poverty we saw around us at Newell.

We knew little of our mother's ancestry. She was born in October 1898 as Minnie Priscilla Harton, the eldest child of Sallie Bet and James H. Harton, a farmer-logger in Warren County, North Carolina, just across the state line from our father's birthplace in Mecklenburg County, Virginia. She had an eighth-grade education, the most that North Carolina public schools offered in those days. With a mother who was almost constantly pregnant—she gave birth to ten more children—Minnie learned early to cook and clean and care for her siblings.

It was her cooking that brought her to our father's attention. According to our aunt known as "Sis Ora," in the fall of 1913, after the failure of his first marriage, our father had moved to a rooming house in Chase City, Virginia, where he was running a sawmill. A logging crew headed by James Harton, our mother's father, was supplying timber for the mill. One morning, hearing our father complain about the food at his rooming house, James Harton suggested that Henry Claiborne dine with him, bragging, "I've got a great cook at home." Our father accepted the invitation, sampled our mother's cooking, and moved from his rooming house into a spare room at James Harton's place.

In the spring of 1914 Henry Claiborne offered our mother, known to her siblings as "Sis Min," and her next oldest sister, Sis Ora, a ride to a Wednesday night prayer meeting. As Minnie climbed into his buggy, Henry Claiborne noticed ugly welts on her lower leg. When he asked how she got them, Sis Min said she had fallen, an answer that brought giggles from Sis Ora. Gradually Henry Claiborne wheedled the truth from the two girls. The sisters said their father had accused Minnie of welcoming Henry Claiborne into her bedroom, and in a fury their father had beaten her.

Henry Claiborne knew the charge was false. Though he admired Minnie, he hadn't been near the bedroom she shared with several sisters. He made up his mind to rescue Minnie from that abusive environment. He told her to pack her bags, that he was coming for her in a few days. He sold the sawmill, bought a car, settled his accounts, and at about midnight on April 27, 1914, picked up Minnie. They eloped to Washington, where the next day they were married in a civil ceremony. Henry Claiborne had just turned thirty-six. Minnie was fifteen.

In selling the sawmill and whisking away our mother, Henry Claiborne had deeply offended our mother's father. Not only had James Harton lost his chief cook and housekeeper, but he also had lost his job. The sawmill's new owners found other suppliers of timber. Wanting to put significant distance between his ex-wife in Mecklenburg County, Virginia, and his aggrieved father-in-law in Warren County, North Carolina, our father took Minnie Claiborne to Charlotte, near the South Carolina border, a full state away. Charlotte was enjoying a building boom. A model neighborhood named Myers Park, designed by the famous John Nolen, was being developed, and a rival neighborhood, known as Dilworth, designed by the Olmsted brothers, was breaking ground in the hills around a ravine that is now Latta Park. Henry and Minnie Claiborne took rooms in uptown Charlotte's Fourth Ward, then one of the city's respected neighborhoods.

Our father got work at local construction sites and in 1917 became foreman of a crew helping to build Camp Greene, a US Army training base just outside Charlotte's western boundary. The camp trained soldiers to fight in World War I. The camp's forty thousand men exceeded the population of Charlotte, changing the face and pace of the town, and touching off an economic expansion that lasted twelve years.

In the summer of 1917, with his wife expecting their first child, Henry Claiborne rented a house on Liddell Street, nine blocks north of the town square. There in August they welcomed the birth of our sister Alice, who was born at home, as were all of Mother's children. Shortly afterward the family moved several miles north to a village called Derita and began dairy farming. Our second sister Phyllis was born there in 1920 and our brother Harold in 1923. Our sister Anne was born there in 1928. Jimmy and I were the only children born in the farmhouse at Newell.

The move to Newell and work on the house and grounds took a toll on our father, a hard-working, task-oriented man. Once slim and handsome, with a thick mustache and a full head of dark hair, he had become bald, clean-shaven, and jowly. His love of our mother's cooking, especially biscuits sopped in honey, had given him a bay window that strained the fabric of his blue denim bib overalls. With age, though, had come a softening of his voice, a gentling of his touch, and a cooling of his volcanic temper. After supper, he often retired to his little library at the front of the Newell house and read from his prized set of leather-bound carpentry books.

Our mother was short—about five feet five—and plump. Everything about her was round—her face, her hands, her arms, and her fingers. She had dark, curly hair, gray-green eyes, a strong chin, and a mellow contralto voice. She liked to sing and to this day, when we stand in church to sing the Doxology, I can almost hear her beside me warbling a throaty "Praise God from whom all blessings flow..."

Though her eyes were sad, they disguised a lively sense of humor. She liked to tell stories about her many brothers and sisters, with whom she remained close. Over the years all but one of her ten siblings came to live with her temporarily. She was not only a good cook but also a skilled seamstress. She made our clothes, curtains, quilts, and slipcovers. But as she entered her thirties, she began to lose her hearing. Over her last dozen years she wore a hearing aid.

Mother gave birth to me on October 19, 1931, the year the Great Depression hit bottom. In an effort to emphasize upbeat events, Charlotte newspapers were heralding an exhibition of "All-Southern Aeroplanes" at the privately owned Cannon Airport, a gravel landing strip off Tuckaseegee Road that had once been the parade grounds for Camp Greene. Cannon Airport later went bankrupt, a victim of the Depression, which made WPA funding for a public airport all the more important.

My birth early on a Monday morning discomfited my fourteen-year-old sister Alice. In addition to milking chores, she had to substitute for Mother in cooking for the family, a burden she blamed on me. According to family lore, at about age two I partially redeemed myself. In keeping with the nursery rhyme "Monday's child is fair of face," she took me by train to Ivey's department store at Tryon and Fifth Streets, then a popular Charlotte emporium, and entered me in a "prettiest baby" competition. I didn't win first place but brought home several prizes. In later years, when that distinction was recalled at family gatherings, my brother Jimmy would roll his eyes and walk away. The possibility of my winning anything in a "pretty baby" contest was more than he could bear.

Jimmy was born on October 13, 1932, the year national unemployment hit twenty-four percent. Banks were failing across the country. Franklin Roosevelt was campaigning for president and promising to lift America out of despair. Being born on the thirteenth never bothered Jimmy. What mattered more was his birth on a Tuesday. He took to heart the nursery rhyme's warning: "Tuesday's child has far to go." Throughout his life he set high goals for himself, as if determined to go as far as he could.

We didn't know it until much later, but our births in 1931 and 1932 proved to be a great advantage. In those Depression years fewer families chose to have babies, dropping birthrates to record lows. That meant that as we grew older, we would have fewer cohorts against whom to compete when it came to school, college, and employment.

Both of us inherited our mother's quick mind, sunny disposition, and collaborative, can-do spirit. But the surrounding poverty inspired in us a will to seek better lives. When we saw opportunities for improving our lot, we worked to make the most of them.

Henry and Minnie after their move to Charlotte

CHAPTER

4

A Great Distress

The routine at Newell had a rhythm and sameness about it, but as boys just beginning to explore the world, we found marvels all around us and delighted in exploring them. We had no inkling of the disaster awaiting us.

The backyard had a large vegetable garden and in one corner a fenced chicken coop. Sometimes Harold would let Jimmy and me sprinkle kernels of corn on the barren ground to bring the chicks scurrying. It was Harold's job to collect eggs from the hens' nests that were elevated, he said, to deter poaching by snakes, raccoons, and other pests.

Farther off was an enclosed hog pen where a wobbly old sow and a litter of grunting piglets wallowed in muck. Sometimes Harold let us go with him as he poured a swill of kitchen waste into a feeding trough, bringing the piglets squealing in delight. Nearby was an outdoor privy, an unpainted, wooden closet sitting over a deep pit. Like all things related to toileting, it was a fascination for us boys. We'd do our business then peer into the dark bottom to see what happened to it. Surprisingly, the privy's odor was less offensive than the stench from the hog pen.

Almost from birth Jimmy and I were rivals. My sisters said I once threw him from a wing chair into the fireplace, from which he emerged unscathed. Our brother Harold liked to tell how, as I was being weaned from the bottle,

I offended Jimmy. As our father was splitting wood in the yard, he said, I went down to watch and set my bottle on a nearby stump. When a slice of log our father had split sailed over and smashed my bottle, my father said, "Well, that ends that. You'll drink from a cup from now on." But as naptime came Jimmy was heard wailing from his upstairs crib. I had sneaked in and stolen *his* bottle.

As we got older Jimmy and I had cause to pull together. On Saturday mornings our father occasionally would take us in his boxy black Model-T to the Newell general store on Old Concord Road. We would wait in the car until he returned with his supplies. Sometimes he would hand one of us a pair of red-spiraled peppermint sticks and say, "Here, share these with your brother."

He also loved ice cream and often made it in a hand-cranked freezer. Once the cranking was done, he would remove the dashers and let Jimmy and me lick the wooden paddles and laugh at our smeared faces. Our father also was fond of watermelon and would call us over as he plunged a butcher knife into the dark rind of a cannonball melon, eliciting an audible "ker-ack" as the melon split into bright red halves. With a grin he'd scoop out a chunk of the glistening melon's heart and hand it to us, making sure his small sons got a taste of the sweetest, juiciest part.

In summer we would venture down to Toby Creek, which flowed across the western edge of our farm. There we grasped for squirmy tadpoles to imprison in glass jars or picked ripe blackberries that grew along the creek bank. Downstream our older siblings had dammed the muddy orange water to create a swimming hole, but Jimmy and I were too young for that.

Late one afternoon on our way home we passed the barn and stopped to watch the evening milking. It was there amid the zing-zings of warm milk hitting the tin pails that the mischievous Harold squirted my face full of sticky milk straight from the cow's teat, souring forever my taste for milk.

As the Depression eased, our father resumed building houses. One summer morning our sister Alice took us by train into Charlotte and by streetcar to Kenilworth Avenue where he was framing a large, two-story structure. With the sweet scent of raw pine piercing our nostrils, we scrambled up and down the crude stairs and in and out of exposed studding, much to our father's annoyance. He was forever saying, "Get away from that," "Leave those alone."

"Get back from there," and, "Put that down." Peace came briefly when we discovered curled wooden shavings from a carpenter's plane and tried hanging them from our hair. In time our father put us to work. He gave each of us a brick and a hammer and told us to straighten all the bent nails we could find. When the workday ended, he took us home in his tweedling Model-T.

Though he could be stern, our father took special delight in Jimmy and me. One night he pulled me into his big wing chair beside the fireplace, slipped his gold pocket watch—what he called a "railroad watch"—from his waistband and showed it to me. He said if I promised not to smoke until I was twenty-one, he'd give me the watch. He also promised to give Jimmy a collapsible, silver drinking cup he carried in a brown leather case. Though I began smoking at age sixteen, I still got the watch. Jimmy also got the drinking cup.

Beyond running the Newell farm, our father sought other ways to make money. He was skilled at harvesting and threshing wheat and often would bring in a crop for a neighboring farmer for a share of the profit. He also was good at harvesting sorghum for cattle feed and squeezing the juice from the stalks to be boiled into molasses, which my mother bottled and sold. I can still smell the bittersweet steam rising as Mother stirred the brown liquid bubbling on the rendering table. The memory of sorghum molasses on a hot, buttered biscuit is still a delight.

Despite those extra efforts, money was scarce. Our father had been building a house on North Tryon Street for a Charlotte woman who had not paid him for the materials or his labor, though the house was nearly finished. That meant the Christmas of 1935 was going to be lean. Mother made clothes for the older children and a doll for my sister Anne. Our father made wooden "kiddie carts" for Jimmy and me. The carts were like tricycles without pedals. The rider sat on a pear-shaped wooden seat and propelled the cart by pushing his feet against the floor. On Christmas morning we found the bright red carts hidden under the tall cedar Christmas tree, gifts from Santa Claus.

When our father finished the house for the Charlotte woman, she paid him for the materials and labor but refused to pay for change orders that amounted to extra costs. Toward the middle of the month he began to look pale. He was short of breath and complained of tiredness in his arms and legs. To improve his rest, Mother moved his bed downstairs and told Jimmy and me to play quietly. On January 21 he made another effort to collect back bills from the Charlotte woman but came away frustrated and angry. The next morning, he complained of chest pains. Mother borrowed a neighbor's telephone to call her brother Bill Harton, who worked as a mechanic at a nearby service station and had a car. Uncle Bill drove our father to see a doctor in the Independence Building on Charlotte's midtown square. By the time they got there our father was too weak to go inside. Uncle Bill parked at the curb and summoned the doctor, who came down to the sidewalk. There, amid passing pedestrians and street traffic, the doctor heard our father's complaints, listened to his heart, noted his shortness of breath, and gave him what Mother described as "a hypodermic." He advised Uncle Bill to take our father home and put him to bed. Uncle Bill followed those orders.

Mother cautioned Jimmy and me to play upstairs. Our father went right to sleep and slept through the noon meal. About two in the afternoon, Mother crept in to check on him and found him without breath or pulse. His big heart had stopped—three months short of his fifty-eighth birthday.

Jimmy and I heard Mother's shriek and came running. She was crying and walking about aimlessly. "Your father's dead," she said. We were numbed by the news. In the minds of preschool boys, death was a difficult idea to grasp. When two men from the mortuary came to carry our father to a funeral home, one of them jerked a pillow from under him, allowing his head to thump heavily against the mattress. Our mother gasped.

Even now I can only imagine the weight Mother felt falling on her. Her whole world had collapsed, plunging our family into poverty. Other than our father, the family had few resources. The Social Security Act, passed in 1935, was not fully implemented. Our sister Alice, a recent graduate of Newell High, was working at a hosiery mill in uptown Charlotte. Earning twelve dollars a week, she was our only wage earner.

The outlook fed feelings of helplessness. Sad-eyed Jimmy was only three and just beginning to have memories. I was four and just learning to dress myself and tie my shoes. Our sister Anne was seven and in the second grade. Harold was twelve and in the sixth. Phyllis was fifteen and in the tenth. Our sister Alice was nineteen. Mother was thirty-seven, still pretty and vulnerable.

At the time Jimmy and I were unaware of it, but our father's death was the most debilitating event of our young lives. It left a hollow place in each of our inner beings. Without his sheltering presence, we never felt sure who we were or wanted to be. We were always busy making up for his loss, but we felt the difference in later years when teachers polled classmates about their fathers and Jimmy and I had to say our father was dead. It always felt like a stigma.

That afternoon as our older siblings returned from school, they began notifying neighbors and borrowing telephones to alert aunts, uncles, and cousins. That night a stream of visitors came, expressing shock, bringing platters of food and offers of help. We heard several suggest that Mother put "the boys" in Alexander Home, a Charlotte orphanage that our family had once supplied with milk and cream. Jimmy and I stood on wooden benches at the long kitchen table and ate what we liked from the large assortment of dishes: fried chicken, baked ham, sweet potatoes, rice pudding, and other staples of country cooking. I ate so much creamed corn that for years afterward I couldn't eat it without reviving the nausea of that woeful night.

The funeral was to be at a country church near Norlina, hard by the Virginia line where the Harton family owned a burial plot. It would be a long, cold ride for antsy children in Uncle Bill's four-door sedan. The Francis family that lived on an adjoining farm offered to keep any of Mother's children who were too young to make the trip. That turned out to be Anne, Jimmy, and me.

Before leaving for the funeral, Alice, Phyllis, and Harold went into the neighborhood borrowing suitable clothes to wear. None of them had winter coats appropriate for so solemn an occasion. It turned out they were needed. Several times along the way the car made prolonged stops while flat tires were fixed or an overheated radiator cooled.

Back at Newell, Anne, Jimmy, and I packed a few belongings in a pillowcase and headed to the neighboring Francis farm. We shivered against the raw wind and frozen ground. Our route took us across a small stream and past the shack of a Black couple that worked various fields in the village. We had passed that shack many times but had never been inside. As we approached it, the woman of the house stood at its doorway and called, "You chil'rin, come on in heah. Come in and warm yo'sels." She motioned us toward her and insisted that we go inside. The place smelled of wood smoke and lye soap, but it was warm. When we rushed to stand next to the red-hot stove in her tiny room, she led us aside to a sofa covered in quilts.

"You be too cold to stand by the stove now," she said. "Warm yo'sels while I make some cocoa."

As she cooked, she talked and seemed to know all about our father's death and where we were headed. Within minutes she served us steaming cups of hot chocolate and watched in satisfaction as we drank it. Then she let us stand closer to the stove, saying we should get our feet and hands good and warm before venturing out again.

Of all the compassion shown us during those doleful days, that woman's kindness stands out as the most welcome. Like many Southerners who have experienced similar instances of interracial empathy, our memory of her openhearted goodness and genuine concern did much to warm Jimmy's and my relations with Black people in a rigidly segregated South.

The Francis family received us graciously and treated us well, though it was obvious we were causing a bother. We slept on the floor on pallets close to the fireplace. Sensing the catastrophe caused by our father's death, Mrs. Francis spoke to us kindly, though we were not sure her children welcomed us. For Jimmy and me, two urchins, uncomfortable in strange surroundings and uncertain of our fate, the overnight wait until we could go home and sleep in our own beds seemed interminable.

The family shortly after our father's death

CHAPTER

5

Charlotte's Lure

The calamity of losing a husband and father—or a wife and mother—occurred often during the Depression. It was not always death that claimed them. Many men and women simply walked away in despair. Federal studies show that in the first five years of the Depression, North Carolina's farm population declined more than two hundred thousand—an average of forty thousand a year or three hundred a month—as families left the land and scattered. That was true across the country. By 1932 one of every eight American farms was up for auction.

As daunting as the future looked, our family worked to stay together, but even for someone as courageous and competent as our mother, carrying on was a daily challenge. She was not a complainer, but from time to time she let us know she was carrying a burden. She'd say, "Go day, come day, God, send Sunday."

Among her saddest responsibilities had been leading the family to our father's funeral. With her brother Bill Harton driving, she, accompanied our oldest sisters Alice and Phyllis, and our brother Harold on the trip up and back to the funeral site on the same day, a round trip of about five hundred miles. Before interstate highways, the roads were narrow, two-lane corridors with speed limits of thirty-five to forty-five miles per hour. They went first on

US 27 to Albemarle and Sanford, then on US 1 through Raleigh and north to Norlina. They left home in the gloom before dawn and returned in the biting cold of a black January night, where they were met by a desolate house without lights to guide them or fires to warm them.

Mother ignored suggestions that Jimmy and I be sent to an orphanage. My sister Phyllis said that on the journey from the funeral, Mother and our older siblings agreed the family should remain intact, and each pledged their support in keeping it that way. Though it was a brave compact, for years afterward whenever Jimmy or I exhausted Mother's patience she would vent by threatening to send us to the Alexander Home, a threat we never took seriously.

According to Phyllis, much of the trip home from the funeral was spent toting up the family's assets and liabilities. On the plus side was a crop of winter wheat ripening in the fields. Harvesting it would bring in a little money. There also was a fat hog that could be slaughtered and sold for cash. Mother was expert at that. Alice was working at an uptown hosiery mill, and after graduating from Newell School Phyllis would be eligible to work.

The negative side was bleak. Funeral expenses were coming due, as were payments on the tractor, the milk truck, Model-T, and other machinery essential to efficient farming. That equipment was likely to be repossessed, leaving us without the tools for maintaining a mechanized farm. That meant that instead of looking toward the future, the immediate need was to survive.

At the time, Charlotte, the largest urban place in the Carolinas, offered better opportunities. Led by Mayor Ben Douglas and City Manager Jim Marshall, Charlotte was fast recovering from the Depression. It was expanding its water, sewer, and street systems to support a larger population that Jim Marshall promised was coming. Under a WPA grant, it was converting four hundred acres of gullied land along the double-tracked Southern Railway southwest of town into a public airport to replace a private one that had gone bankrupt. Additional WPA grants were supporting the construction of American Legion Memorial Stadium and the reconstruction of the US Mint into the state's first public art museum.

For the Claibornes, however, even a move to Charlotte seemed a distant goal. On the journey home Mother asked twelve-year-old Harold if, without a tractor, he could harness the mule and do the plowing for spring planting. Always confident he could do anything he put his mind to, Harold said he could. It turned out he would need all that bravado and more. His boyhood was all but over. Ready or not, he had become the man of the house.

In blue denim overalls, dark brogans, and a loose-fitting jacket, Harold cut a handsome figure. He wore a rakish look that made him seem older than his years. He had a glint in his eye and a sprightly, "I know a secret" grin that apparently was irresistible to the Newell girls.

His boyish ebullience soon got a test. Shortly after the return home, Mother called him to her bedroom, pointed to a double-barreled shotgun hanging over the door, and, with Phyllis at her side, asked if Harold knew how to use it.

"Sure," Harold said.

"Show me," Mother said.

Harold took down the shotgun, cracked it open across his knee, inserted two shells in the breech, and clicked the gun shut. He raised the stock to his shoulder and, aiming upward at about forty-five degrees, pulled the trigger. BLAM! The blast blew a hole the size of a horse's hoof in the side of the house. Phyllis fainted as if she'd been shot.

After reviving Phyllis, Harold proved he also could replaster the inside wall and repair the splintered siding outside. Over the years the tale of Harold and the shotgun became one of the family's favorite stories, especially when told by Phyllis.

The day Mother killed the hog dawned steely gray with temperatures near freezing. Tom, the Negro man who shared the shack with the woman on the hill behind us, came to help. With a small pistol, Mother shot the long, black sow that was so ponderous she could barely waddle. Tom nailed its hind legs to a board and, with a rope and winch, hoisted it upside down with its spine against the trunk of a large tree. Mother slit its throat and let the blood gush into a tin tub. It was a startling sight.

With a fire under the black washpot, Mother heated water and, when the sow's bleeding stopped, used it to wash its carcass with a wire brush, then opened its belly and removed its entrails. From then on, the slaughtering was a family affair, requiring fast hands, sharp knives, and continuous work over the better part of several days. Mother, Alice, Phyllis, and Harold cut the carcass into hams, shoulders, tenderloin, chops, and ribs. Everything about the hog, even its ears and snout, was salted to be sold or saved. Even Jimmy and I were put to work, turning the crank of the sausage grinder. For us the whole grisly scene was an eye-popping look at the realities of farm life and the source of much of our meat.

Like all other members of the family, Jimmy and I had regular chores. Our mother believed that to encourage growth, she should ask her children to do things that were at the upper limits of their competence. Each week, under supervision by our oldest sisters, Jimmy and I used our small hands to wash soot from the glass chimneys of the kerosene lamps and trim the wicks so they would burn with a bright, white flame. We pumped water from the well, and on wash day added bluing in the rinse water. We gathered black walnuts that fell from a tree in the backyard and knocked off their hulls, an inky enterprise that dyed our hands a chartreuse green that wouldn't wash off easily. With bricks we tried cracking the rock-like nuts, but we crushed more walnut meats than we salvaged.

The limits of our capacity came when we tried digging sweet potatoes. We easily scuffed up the ground under the dying vines, but extracting whole potatoes was beyond our skills. Soon we were called off the job because our hoe blades were slashing grievous wounds in the pink-fleshed potatoes.

In early spring the threshers came to harvest the winter wheat. They brought with them a tractor with a big flywheel on one side and a wide belt that connected the flywheel to the threshing machine. Once the tractor and thresher were running in tandem, the high whine of the tractor, the clatter of the threshing machine. and the slap-slap-slap of the belt were deafening. At noon the ruckus ceased as Mother spread a long table with food and everybody paused to eat. Afterward the racket resumed. The threshers bagged the grain in burlap sacks and hauled it off to be sold, providing precious cash for the family and farm.

Later in the spring, part of that cash was invested in cotton seeds, which Harold and Phyllis planted. Working behind the mule, Harold barely weighed enough to keep the plow point in the ground. Every few steps he would leap to put his full weight on the plow handles and drive the plow point deeper into the soil. As his bare feet bobbed up and down in the freshly turned furrows, Phyllis came behind with a bucket under her arm, dropping seeds at regular intervals. After a summer of sun and rain and constant hoeing, those seeds produced rows of billowing cotton plants, flowering in white bolls that looked deceptively soft and pliable.

In the fall, rural schools like the one at Newell closed for a week to give students time to pick cotton. Like others in the family, Jimmy and I got a brief chance to experience that storied task. Wearing wide-brimmed hats, our sisters Alice and Phyllis knelt before each of us and fixed a burlap bag with a shoulder strap around our necks. Then they showed us how to reach deep into the prickly cotton pod, firmly seize the root of the boll, and pull hard. They warned that the sun-dried pods had sharp edges that would slit our fingers if we weren't careful. Then they left us to pick as best as we could and put our pickings in the burlap sacks. We were so small that even with our shoulder straps in place, the bags dragged on the ground. Once started, we had to pick as long as our mother and siblings because they couldn't stop to relieve us. We felt the sun beat down on our necks and arms. Our bare feet absorbed the heat of the parched earth. And the burlap bags weighed heavily on our shoulders. By the end of the day our gashed fingers were bloody.

The next day, the rest of the family went back to the cotton fields but left us at home to play in the harvested cotton stored on the cool, concrete-floored milk house until it could be ginned and baled. Jimmy and I rolled in it, threw handfuls of it at each other, marveled at the warmth it retained from the previous day's sun, and winced at the bloody stains we found on some of it. That whole experience—the sun, the stooping, the weight of the burlap sacks, the bloody fingers—convinced us that we didn't want to live on a cotton farm.

Fortunately for us, Franklin Roosevelt's earlier visit had resolved that issue. After cotton picking, our family, like many others across the land, moved to the city in hopes of finding better opportunities.

Harold at age twelve

CHAPTER

6

Becoming City Boys

In the fall of 1936 Charlotte was in the midst of an industrial transition. Redbrick spinning mills still dotted fringes of the central business district, but elsewhere newer, more sophisticated enterprises were rising to supply machinery, chemicals, dyes, warehousing, trucking, engineering, and financing to mills in surrounding counties. Charlotte was shifting from a cotton-mill town to a textile service center. A more entrepreneurial city was aborning.

Similar excitement was evident elsewhere. Tobacco markets were flourishing across North Carolina's Piedmont and Coastal Plain. Cigarette factories were sweetening the air over Durham and Winston-Salem. High Point and Hickory were making names for themselves as furniture markets. The Great Depression was losing its grip.

From our newly occupied, white-framed house at 1235 East Fifth Street, about a mile from the central business district, Jimmy and I could feel the pace quicken. City life offered exciting diversity. With a mother too busy to restrain us, we were free to roam the city and discover its urban delights.

Our house stood halfway down an idyllic, two-block street lined on each side by one-story homes, each fronted by shallow yards and paved sidewalks. The whole scene was like a Norman Rockwell painting in the *Saturday Evening Post,* with boys racing hoops down sidewalks and girls playing hopscotch on walkways. Unfortunately, that street no longer exists. It declined during the post-World War II expansion and was demolished in the 1970s to become the campus of Central Piedmont Community College, as did adjoining neighborhoods along Park Drive, Elizabeth Avenue, and East Fourth, East Seventh, and Cecil Streets. But in the late 1930s that area of East Fifth Street and its surrounding Elizabeth neighborhood was alive with pedestrians and the squeals of playing children.

The sights and sounds and, most importantly, the neighborhood people helped to shape our lives—and sharpened our competition with each other. Neighbors egged us on against each other. But mostly they looked out for us and kept us out of trouble.

Most neighbors were working people. One was a police radio dispatcher who drove a black squad car with a tall aerial whipping from its rear fender. Jimmy and I watched his hurried comings and goings and wondered, Was he headed to a crime scene? Another was a stout, graying fireman who often sat on his front porch in dress uniform, proud of himself and his honored position in the community. Still another was a slender, sinewy, power-company lineman bronzed by repeated exposure to the sun. He wore knee-high boots with metal spikes for use in shinnying up utility poles. Jimmy and I envied his long, tanned muscles and those sharp spikes.

Only a few neighbors had cars. Most rode streetcars to and from work. Jimmy and I loved the streetcars that seemed to glide majestically up and down Elizabeth Avenue, their wheels occasionally emitting a sharp squeal from the shiny steel rails. We once put a penny on the track to see it smashed flat and unrecognizable. On Halloween older boys greased the tracks to see the streetcars stall, their wheels spinning frantically on the Elizabeth Avenue hill.

All that changed in March 1938 when, ceremoniously, the streetcars were ridden to their South Boulevard barn and replaced by flat-faced buses with smelly exhausts. When fully loaded, the buses seemed to sag to the curbside, like a washerwoman shouldering a basket of clothes.

Even so, when Jimmy and I had nickels to spend, we rode the buses to the end of their line to see where they went and often got to scroll the directional sign over the windshield to show the return-trip destination.

The move to town added to the strain on our mother. Having sold the remaining farm implements and livestock to pay the bills at Newell, she needed money for city expenses. Perhaps on advice from Squire Newell, she applied to county officials for aid under the newly authorized public assistance program supported by Franklin Roosevelt. A woman from the county Welfare Department, wearing a dark gray suit with a jaunty matching hat, came to visit. She determined that Mother was eligible for help with moving expenses and child support. Later, when we were settled, she brought us canned foods and bags of powdered milk. She brightened our first Christmas in Charlotte with used toys, including a small, red fire truck, stockings filled with nuts and candy, and loose fruit that included raisins still clustered on the vine. Over the years I have heard many complaints about "welfare" programs but was always grateful to Mecklenburg County for that timely assistance.

Our oldest sister Alice continued to work at the hosiery mill. Our sister Phyllis entered all-White Central High and took an after-school and weekend job scooping ice cream at the Charles Store in the first block of West Trade Street. Later, with the help of Betty Ramsey, one of Mother's sisters who managed the Charles Store ladies wear department, Phyllis moved up to salesclerk. After completing typing and shorthand courses at Central High, she sought jobs as a secretary but was hired as a "looper"—one who stitched the toes of women's stockings—at a hosiery mill in suburban Oakhurst.

Thirteen-year-old Harold enrolled in the seventh grade at Piedmont Junior High eight blocks away, but with his skimpy Newell schooling, he found himself far behind academically, though like his father he excelled in woodworking. He brought home bowls and lamps he had turned on a lathe. He also learned to play street hockey on roller skates with neighborhood boys. Until the move to Charlotte, Harold had never seen roller skates, but he quickly learned to use them. With a tin can for a puck and a broom handle for a hockey stick, he became a deadly player with many a bruised shin to show for it.

Our only remnant of farm life was the flock of chickens Mother brought from Newell and stashed in sheds in our backyard. Jimmy and I fed the birds and gathered their eggs, but as Mother wrung the neck of one hen after another to feed the family, that responsibility waned and soon ended.

Best of all, Fifth Street provided playmates our age. When we moved in, we met Bobby Hoyle and his younger sister Joyce who lived across the alley. On their front porch was a wooden swing suspended from the ceiling by chains. Unlike children today whose fun usually comes in programmed packages, Jimmy and I and Bobby and Joyce invented all kinds of games to play on that swing. Often the four of us would sit sideways on the swing, straddling the seat, one behind the other. Instead of swinging to and fro in the usual arc, we would swing from side to side in a sawing motion that sent one end of the swing up and the other down. The tension strained the chain hooks at the ceiling, producing a crunchy, metallic sound. Jimmy, who was a good mimic, turned the sound into a chant that sounded something like "chooka-lacka, chooka-lacka, chooka-lacka," as if we were riding a bouncy train. For years afterward, whenever I wanted to put a smile on Jimmy's face, all I had to say was "chooka-lacka."

Among our other Fifth Street playmates were Charles and Walter Ross, who lived in a quadraplex two doors down. They taught us to play cops and robbers with extended forefingers as pistols and raised thumbs as firing pins. When it was time for them to come in, their mother would go to the front door and whistle a four-note melody that sounded like, "Charles and WAL-ter." They knew what that meant and would scoot home.

Farther down the street were the Harkeys, whose father owned a Hudson Terraplane sedan and on Sunday afternoons would take his children and Jimmy and me for cooling rides around the city. Sometimes we went as far as the new airport to see planes take off and land, a miracle of aeronautics we had never seen and didn't understand.

Beyond the Harkeys were the McKenzies, including Mrs. McKenzie, a grandmotherly type with her graying hair pulled back in a tight bun. She was a stickler for good order and discipline, but when we proved we could recite the Bible verses she had assigned us, she'd let us climb the cherry tree in her side yard and eat the plump red cherries.

Among the joys of Fifth Street were the vendors who came in profusion. Instead of shoppers going to the market, they brought the market to shoppers. Farmers came in mule-drawn wagons selling fresh corn, lima beans, summer squash, and other produce. Mother would go out to the curb in her apron, look over the wares, and ask where they were grown and when they were picked. She would squint at the dial on the scales that weighed them and haggle over the price. Pennies, nickels, and dimes were significant sums in the 1930s.

The coffee man arrived in a sleek, brown, panel truck polished to a high gloss. It had a rear hatch that when opened flavored the air with the smell of fresh coffee, like walking into one of today's Starbucks bars. It made Jimmy and me wish we were old enough to drink coffee.

There were others, men selling magazines or Fuller brushes or offering to sharpen scissors or knives. The vendor who most excited Jimmy and me was the iceman, who came two or three times a week. His big, horse-drawn wagon—painted green with red piping and topped by a black leather roof—rolled along on big, wooden-spoked wheels with iron rims that gave off a gritty thrum as they ground slowly down the street. Sitting high up front, the driver, one of the few Black men among the vendors, would call in a tenor voice, "ICEman." If they hadn't done so, neighbors would run to hang a sign on their doorpost, indicating their order for a twenty-five-, fifty-, seventy-five-, or hundred-pound block of ice to be delivered to the icebox in their kitchens. It was a rare home that had an electric refrigerator.

In response to a sign, the iceman would stop, go to the back of his wagon, and with a pick chip the requested order from a large block of glistening ice. Then, throwing a leather pad over his shoulder, he would take his tongs and heave the smaller block onto the pad. Bowing under the weight, he'd climb the steps to the house, deliver the block to the owner's ice chest, and collect the payment. In retrospect, the sight of White people allowing a Black man to walk through their homes despite 1930s segregation was something of a marvel.

While we enjoyed freedom on the street, our three-bedroom, one-bath house was more confining. It sheltered nine people—our mother, her six children, and my mother's sister Betty Ramsey and her husband Wade. Harold, Jimmy, and I slept on pallets on an enclosed porch so cold in winter that we wrapped ourselves in newspapers to keep warm. Without closets or chests of drawers, we learned to organize our possessions, pick up our clothes, and be neat, habits that have lasted a lifetime.

In the snug little household we were admonished to play quietly. That instruction was reinforced one spring morning as Jimmy and I were bouncing a small ball in the room where Mother was sewing. "Boys," she said in her most patient tone, "you know better than to play ball in the house."

Indeed we did, but just as those words were out of her mouth, our ball broke the bottom pane in the French doors leading to the next room. Knowing we were in trouble, we split—through the house, past the kitchen and out the rear door. Plump little Jimmy hid under the back stoop. I crossed the yard and squeezed into a narrow space between our garage and the one next door.

From my hideaway I saw Mother come out the back door, select a switch from a shrub, and spy the pudgy Jimmy squatting under the back steps. She pulled him out and whacked him several times across the legs. I could hear his cries and, vicariously, feel his pain, but I stayed hidden. Mother looked around briefly, then returned to the house. I saw Jimmy play in the backyard, then heard him play in the street. I heard the shouts of children cavorting with him, but I stayed hidden—through lunchtime, through the early afternoon, through the shouts of older children returning from school. Finally, I realized I wasn't hidden. I was trapped. I decided to come out and take my punishment.

When I walked into the room where Mother was sewing, she looked up in mild surprise and, staring over her rimless glasses, asked, "Where on earth have you been?"

"Out back, between the garages," I said.

She looked troubled. "You mean you've been there all morning and all afternoon?"

"Yes, ma'am," I said.

Her face clouded. She looked down at the floor as if weighing the offense and considering punishment options. As she looked up, a smile slowly slid across her face. She said softly, "Then the joke's on you, son. You've been punished enough."

I felt relieved but not redeemed. Having seen Jimmy take his whipping, I thought I was getting off easy. In later years as a Sunday school teacher, I told that story often as an example of how sin leaves us between the garages, isolated, disconnected, and hiding shameful parts of ourselves. The easier options are confession and, as in my case, forgiveness.

To supplement the family income, Mother took in sewing, which she stitched on a treadle-powered sewing machine. She also made curtains to order, slipcovers for chairs and sofas, and sometimes quilts. When not in use, her sewing machine became a toy for Jimmy and me. When she wasn't looking, we would slip the thin leather belt off the flywheel and see who could pump the treadle faster.

Jimmy and I were Mother's errand boys. If she needed needles or thread, we ran to get them—five blocks to the ten-cent store at Elizabeth Avenue and Hawthorne Lane. If she needed a last-minute item to cook for dinner, we went one block up the street to Patterson's grocery, the place with the awning that sheltered us during President Roosevelt's visit. The store's owner, John Patterson, was slim, gray-haired, and balding, a taciturn man of formal bearing. He spent most of his time sitting with his wife Sammie next to a pot-bellied stove in a tiny room at the rear of the gray, unpainted grocery. Like dozens of other neighborhood groceries dotting the city, his was people-centered. He extended Mother a line of credit—no contracts to sign, no credit ratings to check, simply neighborly trust.

When Mother had a longer grocery list, we pulled a borrowed red wagon four blocks east to a small A&P at East Fourth and Torrence Streets where we had to pay cash. At each store you didn't go up and down aisles to find what you wanted. You gave a clerk your order and he got each item from tall shelves behind him. Once the order was filled, the clerk bagged the goods and gave you the bill.

One day as we passed Patterson's store on our return from the A&P, Mr. Patterson came out in his gray suit and tan grocer's apron. He looked at the brown-paper sacks lining the bed of our wagon and said, "Uh huh. When you need credit you come to me, but when you've got cash you go to the A&P."

It was a fair complaint, but eight-year-old Jimmy was equal to the moment. With an innocent grin and a tone laced with humor, he drew on conversations he had heard around the dinner table to say something like, "We went where the choices were wider and prices lower. If you were us, what would you do?"

The response visibly shocked Mr. Patterson, who seemed stunned by so telling a retort from so young a patron. The grocer scowled, shook his head, and silently re-entered his store.

In truth, we liked Mr. Patterson and he seemed to like us. We were in and out of his store often, buying last-minute items for Mother or stopping on our way to and from school. If we had a dime in our pockets, we would buy a brick-like slab of chocolate cake with thick white icing and argue over how to split it between us. Occasionally, Mr. Patterson would reach into his glass showcase and reward us with a piece of penny candy.

Jimmy and Jack at the armory

CHAPTER

7

Going to School

Charlotte's street life helped to shape our boyhood, but the city's greatest gift came from its public schools, then under the auspices of the city government. In the 1930s and '40s Charlotte's segregated schools were among the most admired in North Carolina, thanks to the enlightened leadership of superintendents Alexander Graham, Harry Harding, and Elmer Garinger. They hired excellent teachers and paid them a hefty supplement to their state salaries.

At the time, women had few career options. Those who later might have become doctors, lawyers, engineers, or journalists went into teaching in public schools, which were attended by almost every kid, rich or poor. Back then Charlotte had no comparable private schools.

It was from the schools that Jimmy and I learned not only to read, write, and cipher but also to befriend classmates, be team players, and occasionally be leaders.

In September 1938 I left Jimmy behind and entered the first grade (public kindergartens were not available until the early 1970s) in all-White Elizabeth School, only five blocks from our home. My encounter with arithmetic had begun earlier. With a birthday eighteen days past the school system's first-of-October deadline for becoming six years old, I couldn't qualify for enrollment until I was almost seven. Jimmy suffered the same penalty. We didn't know it at the time, but that extra year of maturity gave both of us an advantage over many of our classmates.

From our house on East Fifth Street, my sister Anne, who was entering the fourth grade, walked me to the school. She left me in the auditorium, telling me to sit until my name was called. Wearing my best clothes and on Sunday school behavior, I looked around at other kids my age, trying to determine who they were and what they were like. Their heads bobbed up and down over the auditorium's curved seat backs. The girls wore crisp dresses and bow ribbons in their hair. The boys looked scrubbed in white shirts and short pants.

On the advice of older siblings, some classmates hoped to get assigned to the lenient Miss Gray's or Miss Hart's first grade. My older siblings knew nothing about the first grade at Elizabeth School, so I sat and waited, resigned to accept whatever came. When the roll was called for Miss Lucille Agnew's class, I was summoned to take my place in the line behind her. I had never heard of Miss Agnew, a tall, willowy woman with carefully coifed brown hair and a brown print dress, but she led us majestically down the hall to her first-floor classroom. In that line of jittery boys and girls, all anxious and wide-eyed, I felt comfortable and looked forward to learning to read. It was the beginning of a lifelong adventure. I immediately loved school and the chance to learn new things.

Our classroom was big and bright and clean with big windows overlooking Park Drive. After several days its clean smell of floor wax and sweeping compound was replaced with the scent of sour watercolor paints and the aroma of apples and bananas ripening in lunch bags that classmates shelved under their desks.

Each day's instruction began with prayer, a Bible reading, and the pledge of allegiance to the flag. Like other children, I was often asked to learn and recite Bible verses. As we got older, especially in our teens, the familiarity of that practice bred contempt, and many of us made fun of it. In the early 1960s the US Supreme Court declared group prayer and Bible reading in schools a violation of the constitutional prohibitions against establishing a state religion, a decision still resented by many people. As a thirty-year-old adult, I applauded the decision and its constitutional foundation. Even though Bible readings breach the wall between church and state, hearing passages read from the King James Version of the Bible impressed on me the beauty and majesty of the English language. Who can forget such passages as "The earth is the Lord's and the fullness thereof and all that dwells therein"?

Like most others at Elizabeth School, Miss Agnew's class included between thirty-five and forty students, equally divided between boys and girls. She had no teaching assistant but was always fully in command. There were few disciplinary problems.

Apparently I was one of them. Miss Agnew seemed to like me and called on me often in class but couldn't overlook my loquacity. Each of my quarterly report cards was filled with *S*'s for "satisfactory" on all subjects except "refrains from unnecessary talking." On that I was always graded "unsatisfactory."

Early in the year Miss Agnew asked us to bring an apron to wear when we painted with watercolors in front of easels. My mother didn't have money to buy an apron but made one by shortening the legs of old bib overalls and folding them up to create front pockets. At first I felt abashed at wearing it, but my confidence grew when classmates wanted one like it.

Among the things I liked about school was singing. We had a music teacher, aptly named Miss Sharp, who came once a week with a pitch pipe and led us in singing. She drew on the blackboard and began teaching us to read music and later divided the class into thirds and introduced us to singing rounds—"My Grandfather's clock was too old for the shelf, so it stood ninety years on the floor..." The rounds taught us to ignore the voices singing next to us in preparation for later learning to sing in harmony.

Best of all, when the school day ended at 1 p.m. and I arrived home, Jimmy was waiting to ask what I had learned. No matter how much I told him, he seemed to want more. He was envious and didn't like being left behind. Of course, I loved being his mentor.

The next fall as I entered the second grade, I walked him through the same auditorium routine with the same happy result. He was assigned to Miss Ophelia Hart's first grade, and he loved it. Before and after school I saw signs of his budding charisma as he drew classmates around him and charmed them with his engaging manner and bubbling humor. He also got a painting apron made from cutoff overalls, but at the end of each day when I asked what *he* had learned, he didn't talk about phonics or reading but about playing dodge ball and how good he was at it.

Throughout our years at Elizabeth School we had teachers who liked us and often went out of their way to show it. My second-grade teacher, an imaginative young woman named Alice Reid, brought a hand-cranked turntable to class and expanded our curriculum by teaching us to dance the minuet. When her husband got tickets to the annual Golden Gloves boxing tournament at the Charlotte Armory, they found the first night's bouts too brutal for their tastes. She gave tickets for the remaining tournament to Jimmy and me. The next night there we were, at ages eight and seven, sitting on the stage in pricey front row seats at eye level with the ring, watching the three-round matches and marveling at the boxers' footwork that amounted to a kind of athletic minuet.

My third-grade teacher, an earnest but disheveled woman named Caroline Constable, "perfumed" the hallway in her end of the school by boiling suet into a pudding and teaching us to stuff it into pine cones hung outside the windows as bird feeders. Then she encouraged us to identify the birds that came to eat. Miss Constable also maintained a rock garden in a corner of the schoolyard and encouraged her students to help maintain it. I volunteered to stay after school to help plant, weed, or transplant. Through the rock garden, Miss Constable taught us how plants needed water and sun and that they took in carbon dioxide and gave off oxygen—just the opposite of humans, who take in oxygen and give off carbon dioxide. Every school should have a teacher like Miss Constable and a garden in which to teach children about the interdependencies of life.

Of more immediate concern was who would carry our class flag in a parade the local American Legion post was organizing to show that it had raised enough money to buy an American flag for every classroom in the city. Miss Constable asked me to carry our flag, an assignment that hardly thrilled me. I knew the parade would be long and the flag heavy. But one of my classmates, red-haired John Brock, told Miss Constable that because my new shoes had worn a blister on my heel, it would be a kindness if he carried the flag instead. Without examining my heel, Miss Constable let John carry the flag, which he did, proudly dressed in a new white suit and matching shoes. But just as the long parade of fluttering Old Glories was nearing its destination on North Tryon Street, a bird, perhaps one that had feasted on Miss Constable's pinecones, flew over and relieved itself on John's curly red hair, bright new clothes and fancy footwear. Nothing was said about the incident at the time, but John privately interpreted it as divine retribution for having cheated me of the flag-waving honor. In our adult years, after John had become an official at Gardner-Webb College near Shelby, he confessed his guilt, allowing us both to laugh at the memory of it.

In the fourth grade my teacher, Mrs. Virginia Lawrence, asked what we wanted to be when we grew up. With Franklin Roosevelt leading us into World War II, I said I wanted to be president of the United States. The class gasped and Mrs. Lawrence chuckled. "I appreciate your gumption," she said, "but that's a chancy, one-of-a-kind goal. I suggest you select an alternate, just in case."

I didn't know what good advice that was until years later when I saw dozens of governors, congressmen, and senators futilely aspire for that office. Even so, Mrs. Lawrence continued to watch my career. Fifteen years later, during the reception after my wedding, I looked down the receiving line and saw among the well-wishers a grinning Mrs. Lawrence, ready to give me a big hug. She said she was proud of me and wished me happiness and continued success. She didn't mention my hopes of becoming president.

"Unlike today, when uptown buildings are massive and storefronts few, the town's tight little central business district hummed with pedestrian traffic around narrow, street-level shops."

CHAPTER

8

Walking the City

As Jimmy and I entered school, our shaggy locks needed professional shearing. The barbering Mother had done with comb and scissors was no longer sufficient. Fortunately, Charlotte had a barber college across West Trade Street from the post office, about three blocks west of the town square. Priced to match the expertise of the student barbers, haircuts there were cheaper—and riskier—than those in regular barbershops. About every eight or ten weeks our brother Harold would walk us uptown, Jimmy holding one hand and I the other, to the barber college, more than a mile from our house.

Everything about the barber college was fascinating. Housed in a narrow, high-ceilinged room, it was lined on one side with polished green barber chairs. Behind each chair was a wide mirror framed in dazzling lights. On shelves below were bottles of mysterious tonics, lotions, and conditioners, all adorned with women's faces, as if using them would make men more appealing. From every barber's chair hung a white pinstriped bib to shield customers from falling hair. On the opposite arm from the bib hung a tan leather strop for honing straight razors. Protruding from the floor behind each chair was a long lever used to raise, tilt, or lower the seat as needed. Jimmy and I always had to be cranked up to the barber's eye level.

The barber college attracted all kinds of customers, some well dressed, some in tatters. Some needed haircuts, some needed shaves. For two country boys, watching a barber shave a man was a study in concentration. It was all done with surgical precision, something rarely witnessed in today's tonsorial parlors. The barber began by reclining the chair until the patron was almost lying down. Then he washed the man's face, dried it, and wrapped all but his nose in a warm white towel, making him look like a mummy. While the towel softened the man's stubble, the barber stropped a straight razor and, with a mug and brush, whipped up a thick lather in a small cup. Removing the towel, he lathered the man's beard and with the razor slowly shaved him in long, deliberate strokes, finishing with quick, short nicks around his nose, mouth, and chin. Once the shaving was done, the man's face was lotioned and patted dry. Then his chair was returned to a sitting position, bolting him upright like a corpse rising from the dead.

Haircuts were priced at fifteen cents, twenty-five cents, and fifty cents. After a barber completed a haircut and collected his pay, he would loudly pop his empty bib to shed the fallen hair and call, "Next fifteen," or, "Next twenty-five." One of us in the waiting area would look around and, if no one had been there longer, go to the empty chair.

As soon as seven-year-old Jimmy was seated he would engage the barber in lively banter. He'd say something like, "I really need a shave but only have money enough for a haircut." The barber would chortle and they would chatter and laugh throughout the barbering. Unable to think of anything clever to say, I usually sat in silence as my hair was trimmed. Harold, Jimmy, and I always got fifteen-cent haircuts—and for the next couple of weeks looked as if we had been skinned.

In time the experience of walking to town with Harold qualified me to run another of Mother's errands. Occasionally, she would give me a white envelope filled with dollar bills and loose change and tell me to deliver it to Mr. Spearman at Home Realty and Management Company on the ground floor of the ten-story Wilder Building at Third and Tryon Streets, two blocks from the town square and about a mile from our house. Mother emphasized that I was delivering the monthly rent money and was not to surrender that envelope to anyone but Mr. Spearman. It was a mission of great trust that made me feel mature—and, for the moment at least, superior to Jimmy. I made the trip several times, always alone and at my own pace.

That was my real introduction to center-city Charlotte, known as "uptown" rather than downtown because no matter from which direction you came you went uphill to get there. In the late 1930s Charlotte was still an overgrown country town. Its stores closed on Wednesday afternoons, and farmers came in mule-drawn wagons to shop on Saturdays. Nothing was open on Sundays except churches—for both morning and evening services. Sunday observance was so commanding that Ivey's department store shrouded its storefronts on Sundays to discourage window-shopping.

Unlike today, when uptown buildings are massive and storefronts few, the town's tight little central business district hummed with pedestrian traffic around narrow, street-level shops. Most storefront facades dated from the 1880s and 1910s. Often next to the storefronts were scuffed stairs leading to second-floor businesses, some with signs in their windows. One said, "Alterations While You Wait." Another said, "Chiropodist." Interspersed among the street-level shops were arcades and narrow alleys that offered additional services.

After my delivery to Mr. Spearman, I could leisurely peek into the shop windows. I liked looking into The Rex, a beer hall, bowling alley, and poolroom where you could hear the clack of cue sticks hitting billiard balls. I was too young to go in but could stand on tiptoe to see the green felt tables and watch players pivot into position for their next shot. The place smelled of beer and cigarettes, which I equated with vice.

A few doors north was the Tryon Theater, which played B-grade movies and flavored the air with the fragrance of freshly popped corn. Its "Coming Attractions" placards often featured scantily clad women. Just beyond the Tryon was Tanners, an orange juice outlet where with every cup of orange drink you got a packet of salty redskin peanuts that made you thirst for even more orange drink. Tanners had no seats but served all comers, White or Black, standing up. In the 1950s it inspired Jewish satirist Harry Golden's mocking "Golden Vertical Integration Plan." Noting that Southerners willingly stood before bank tellers or Tanners' drink counters unbothered by the racial mixing around them, Golden said the obvious solution to integrating the schools was to remove the seats and let students learn standing up.

Next to Tanners was the century-old Central Hotel, a four-story, yellow-brick structure that was showing its age. Once acclaimed as the best hotel between Washington and Atlanta, it had a fireplace in every room. At the end of World War II, it gave way to a shiny new S. H. Kress five-and-dime store that stood twenty-five years until the early 1970s when it was razed as part of an urban renewal project. On its site rose a glass-curtained trapezoidal tower that for awhile was headquarters for NCNB, one of the many forerunners of what is now Bank of America. On a plaza outside, the bank erected a Grande Disco sculpture celebrating an urban center in a rural setting, a portrayal of Charlotte's ambitions.

Around the corner, in the first block of East Trade, was the State Theater, then famed for ten-cent "kiddie shows" on Saturday mornings. Each show featured a cowboy movie, many of them starring Charlotte's own Randolph Scott, who was said to have made more cowboy movies than any actor except John Wayne. On weekdays the State showed adult movies. I saw the classic "Ox Bow Incident" there and never got over the injustice of a mob-induced lynching.

Farther down East Trade were numerous pawnshops. One, Uncle Sam's Loan Co., featured three golden globes hanging over the sidewalk. In its show windows were banjos, accordions, and guitars, reminders of the Depression's pitiless bite. Added evidence of the Depression were the used clothing and furniture stores, one of which had a sign saying, "Yes, We Undersell." To an eight-year-old who had seen his mother sell the family's livestock and farm equipment at distressed prices, that sign evoked a pang.

An inveterate reader of plaques and historic markers, I was fascinated by a cast-iron plaque on the wall beside a black trestle (later replaced by concrete) carrying a railroad over East Trade Street. Under a pair of crossed anchors, lettering on the plaque said the Confederate Navy Yard once stood on that site. I wondered why the Confederacy would build ships more than two hundred miles from the sea. Years later I learned that the navy yard was really a shell-loading plant moved to Charlotte from Norfolk, Virginia, early in the Civil

War. After the war many of the navy yard's skilled workers stayed to become part of Charlotte's industry-attracting labor force.

My favorite storefront was at the Charlotte Fish & Oyster Company, under the eastern shoulder of that black Trade Street trestle. It smelled of the sea, and its show windows were filled with beds of ice displaying all kinds of colorful fish with their heads on and their eyes open, not the kind of thing a farm boy would have been exposed to. I was mystified by the dark gray flounders, which had two eyes on one side of the head and none on the other. And who could not admire the muscular red snappers or be unnerved by the bewhiskered catfish?

Farther east were big Victorian houses, relics of a glorious past. From the 1870s to the mid-1920s, that stretch of Trade Street, then known as East Avenue, was lined with impressive homes of the wealthy, including William R. Myers, said to be the richest man in town. When the development of Dilworth began in the 1890s and of Myers Park in 1911, East Avenue lost prestige. In the mid-1920s Charlotte bought the entire block between Davidson and Alexander Streets as the site for a new city hall. A year later the county acquired the adjoining block as the site for a new courthouse. With those developments, that part of Trade Street became increasingly commercial.

Over time, I got so familiar with the uptown route that I could recite from memory the names of the establishments along the way as if I were reading from a city directory. The whole experience gave me a deep appreciation of the town and was great preparation for a boy who later would become a city editor and an urban historian.

"On that night, amid the discarded programs, peanut hulls, popcorn boxes, and candy wrappers, we found a crumpled two-dollar bill. Neither of us had ever seen such a prize, but we added it to our earnings and raced home to hand it to Mother."

CHAPTER
9

Cultural Crossroads

In the fall of 1938 we moved two blocks away into a different world, a larger house at 1200 Park Drive. Perched high on a corner lot, it was the only two-story house in the neighborhood and overlooked the armory auditorium, Memorial Stadium, and Central High, all once part of a lake that was the city's water supply. Each offered cultural or sporting events that attracted streams of people. For two boys eager to survey the environs around them, it was like living in a three-ring circus.

The house had a distinctive look, with green shingled siding trimmed in white with a weeping willow sheltering the west side of a wide front porch. But it had been abused and needed scouring. It was also infested with large rats, which Mother zapped with traps or Harold shot with a .22-caliber rifle. With a large living room, dining room, and kitchen downstairs and three bedrooms and a sleeping porch above, the house enabled Mother to put aside her sewing and open a rooming and boarding house.

As her first roomers she invited her youngest brother, eighteen-year-old Jimmy Harton, a recent graduate of the Junior Order Home, an orphanage in Tiffin, Ohio. Jimmy brought along a classmate, Irby Todd, who had no other home. Both immediately found jobs in Charlotte, Jimmy as a plate maker at Lassiter Press, a printing house three blocks away, and Irby as an advertising salesman for the *Charlotte News,* an afternoon daily. Both were good talkers with Midwestern twangs and lively imaginations to enrich conversation at our dinner table. Over time they also exerted an intellectual influence on Jimmy and me.

The move to a larger house also enabled Mother to let her oldest daughters marry. Alice wed H.A. Barnhardt, a handsome Arkansan who kept books for a Charlotte motorcycle dealer. After the wedding they moved to a house across town. Phyllis married Jack Stuart, a promotion and advertising man she had met at Charles Store. After their wedding they took the largest room upstairs and began paying room and board. Jimmy Harton and Irby Todd took the next largest room and also paid room and board. That left Mother and our sister Anne to share the smallest bedroom, one leading to a screened porch where Harold, Jimmy, and I slept. The porch allowed Mother to monitor the comings and goings of the teenage Harold.

The screened porch also contained an unexpected menace. One night as I slept, I dreamed my head was caught in the meat-slicing machine at Patterson's store and cried out in pain. Harold, who had just come to bed, picked up his .22 rifle and shot a big rat that was nibbling on the rim of my left ear. I awoke to find my pillow soaked in blood and the rat's remains splattered on the wall behind me. I didn't think anything of it, but for days afterward as Mother treated the ragged edge of my ear she harangued Harold about taking such a risk with my life.

Directly across the street stood the brooding, dark-brick armory, hastily built in 1929 to host a national reunion of Confederate veterans. It rose like a giant box from a deep ravine. The cavernous building had a stage and a balcony but no permanent seats on the main floor. Its portable wooden seats could be configured in a variety of ways, enabling the armory to serve as a combination auditorium, coliseum, convention center, merchandise mart, exhibition hall, dance floor, concert palace, or National Guard post. The armory, later renamed Grady Cole Center, was the city's main venue for indoor entertainment until the aluminum-domed Charlotte Coliseum opened in 1955.

At the time, Charlotte's ongoing fascination was professional wrestling. From our front porch we could look through the armory's open windows and watch the Monday night wrestling matches, often pairing the snarling Ray Vilmer against "Cowboy" Luttrell. The famous Jack Dempsey, once the heavyweight boxing champion of the world, sometimes refereed a match, affording Jimmy and me the thrill of meeting him and shaking his huge hand.

Boxing matches were also a big draw at the armory, as were lectures, sales promotions, political rallies, high school commencements, and all kinds of music events, including operas and symphony concerts. When the Tommy Dorsey orchestra came to town, Jimmy and I were there to watch it unload and rehearse. It included a famous drummer named Buddy Rich and a yet-to-be-discovered crooner named Frank Sinatra.

One afternoon when guitar-strumming Gene Autry, America's beloved "singing cowboy," was in town to perform, Jimmy talked us into the backstage area where we met the Stetson-hatted Autry and his famous horse Champion. Autry could not have been kinder. He knelt in his gray gabardine jeans to talk with us and ask for our names and the kind of songs we liked. He made us feel important.

In the armory's basement were dressing rooms for teams playing in the stadium, conference rooms for National Guard and Army Reserve units, and a boxing ring for Central High pugilists. Boxing was then an interscholastic sport. Jimmy and I often watched high school boxers spar under the tutelage of Vince Bradford, their otherwise kind and mild-mannered coach. Looking up from the edges of the ring, Bradford would shout instructions like an old-time corner man: "Drop your shoulder!" "Lean in!" "Move your feet!" "Use the jab! Use the jab!" We were impressed at the way the boxers strengthened their feet and legs by jumping rope and honed their hand-eye coordination by hitting a speed bag, "ratta-tat-tatta, ratta-tat-tatta, ratta-tat-tatta."

One year the armory hosted a lavish food show by Charlotte wholesalers. Jimmy talked us through the gate and made friends with a woman who staffed the booth for Lance Packing Company, a maker of peanut butter crackers and cookies. She provided us a steady supply of Big Town cakes, a cinnamony moon pie glazed with white icing. I made friends with the Dr. Pepper bottler, who for several years thereafter was our host at elegant banquets for fatherless boys. Organized by civic-minded business leaders, the banquets were a product of the religiosity of the period—Charlotte then billed itself as "the city of churches." The banquets were another example of the helping hands available in that era. Held in Hotel Charlotte's grand ballroom, the banquets featured rows of white-clothed tables sparkling below Palladian windows and served by tuxedoed waiters. The multi-course dinners began with grapefruit halves dotted with green cherries, a new treat for us.

Behind the armory auditorium sprawled the American Legion Memorial Stadium. In the 1940s and '50s, the stadium was home to fifty or more football games a year. Each fall it welcomed the season with a lush green gridiron that by late October was worn to light brown and by Thanksgiving had become a mud pit. In addition to games by the six local high schools, the stadium hosted home games for Davidson College and Johnson C. Smith University. Each year NC State played Clemson there, and each Thanksgiving Wake Forest played South Carolina, pairing two colorful coaches, Rex Enright of South Carolina and the wisecracking Clarence "Peahead" Walker of Wake Forest, who once famously said that playing to a tie game was "like kissing your sister."

Later the stadium welcomed games by a variety of semi-pro and professional teams. All those events offered Jimmy and me opportunities to earn money.

Beyond the stadium was the seemingly endless Independence Park, a turn-of-the-century gift from William R. Myers, then the leading landowner in town who also gave the land for Johnson C. Smith University and whose legacy includes Myers Park. During our boyhood, Independence Park was the most popular playground in the city.

Our favorite of its five distinctive play areas was a wide, flat greensward large enough for two back-to-back baseball fields and space between for schoolboy football. Beyond the larger of the two baseball diamonds was a terraced, tree-shrouded picnic area that doubled as a playground for Elizabeth School, where Jimmy and I played at recess and organized after-school games of baseball.

The park often sheltered homeless men, victims perhaps of the Great Depression. They slept on benches or in the concrete dugouts at each side of the baseball diamond. One afternoon Jimmy led us in following one of them "home," which we discovered was a cave on the banks of Briar Creek behind the newly established Mint Museum. Afterward, we saw him in other parts of town, always wearing a thick mustache and a stained and fraying three-piece suit as if trying to put his best foot forward. Jimmy and I wondered who he was, what loss he might have suffered, and why he chose to live in such meager circumstances.

Across from Elizabeth School was Caldwell Memorial Presbyterian Church, with a congregation that included many Charlotte business leaders. The seven members of the Belk family that ran the town's biggest department store arrived en masse each Sunday. Led by the imposing patriarch William Henry Belk, they sat in birth order in the same pew. When at age seven I recited the Child's Catechism (Q: "What is the chief end of man?" A: "Man's chief end is to glorify God and enjoy him forever."), I received an 1881 silver dollar from William Henry Belk himself, who presented it with his thick gray mustache twitching over his lip.

Caldwell Church supported a vigorous Sunday school whose devoted women teachers taught Jimmy and me the Bible, the Golden Rule, and other Christian principles. More impressive were the teachers' preparation, patience, and persistence, which set examples for each of us. As adults we each became Sunday school teachers ourselves.

Until our voices changed, Jimmy and I sang in Caldwell's youth choir, which occasionally provided music for the Sunday morning worship service. Seated high above the pulpit, we could survey the sanctuary. But we were hardly choirboys. During preaching we folded the church bulletins into paper airplanes and after monthly communion sneaked into the sanctuary and drank the leftover grape juice.

Beyond Caldwell Church were Presbyterian and Mercy Hospitals, where careening ambulances came roaring up with sirens wailing. Jimmy and I got our first look inside a hospital when our brother Harold required an emergency appendectomy and was recovering in a white-framed bed in Mercy Hospital's charity ward. Undaunted, the ever-sunny Harold pulled back the sheets to show us his incision, closed not with sutures but with a large metal clamp. Etched in our memories for years, the sight of that clamp led Jimmy and me to quake at the slightest abdominal twinge for fear it might be appendicitis.

On the west side of our Park Drive house stood the Central High athletic field that was clearly visible from our dining room. On fall mornings the school's national championship marching band rehearsed. We could hear Lonnie Sides, their cigar-chomping director, shouting instructions to keep their lines straight and their stride even as they marched from one end of the playing field to the other. We often ate our breakfast oatmeal to the strains of the "Washington and Lee Swing," the fight song of Central High athletic teams.

Central High soon became the object of our attraction. The school's proximity allowed us to attend classes there even before we were old enough to enroll. After our elementary school classes ended at one o'clock, Jimmy and I would mosey over to the high school, where athletes would take us to their classes. As an eight- and nine-year-old, I sat through several sessions of plane geometry taught by Miss Bertha Donnelly, the grand dame of the school's faculty. With a hooked nose, tangled hair, and an icy stare, she terrified many of the athletes who thought that bringing along a small boy might insulate them against one of Miss Bertha's chilling reproofs. And it did. Years later, after Miss Bertha had retired but still tutored Central High students struggling to learn math, I occasionally walked her up Elizabeth Avenue to her rooming house. Along the way she confided that she liked teaching boys best.

Incredibly, Central High, built in 1922-23, still stands as part of Central Piedmont Community College. It has survived Charlotte's rush to obliterate much of its past, despite the school's precarious site. Built on a boggy marsh next to Sugar Creek, it was often flooded during summer storms that left a scum of mud on the ground floor. Jimmy discovered we could squeeze through a ground-floor classroom window, get into one of the long, terrazzo-floored halls, and with a running start slide on our bellies through the mud past most of the classroom doors. It was great fun until one afternoon Dr. Elmer Garinger, the school's gentle, soft-spoken principal, caught us.

Admired for his innovations in education, Dr. Garinger was clearly provoked. He glowered while informing us we were breaking the law by entering the school. Further, he said, we were putting the school at risk. If anything happened to us, the school would be liable. Finally, he warned that we were endangering our health. We had no idea what filth was in that slime and where it had come from. Then he paused.

Jimmy and I squirmed under his gaze. He knew who we were and where we lived. We knew he could be tough. We had seen him wade into crowds to break up fights and pull smokers by the collar from hedges behind the school and haul them to his office. But in this instance, he didn't call the police or notify our mother. Looking grim, he said, "Boys, let this be a lesson to you. What you are doing is both against the law and dangerous. Don't do it again." Then he ushered us out the school's rear door.

The Central High side of our Park Drive house also offered a long driveway leading to a stone garage. We hadn't lived there long before Jimmy and I discovered that when an event at the armory or stadium drew large crowds, we could earn money by allowing people to park in that driveway and garage. We would stand at the driveway's entrance, facing oncoming traffic, and yell "Parking! Parking!" and point to the garage and driveway. On a good night we might bring home a dollar or two, welcome contributions to family upkeep.

One chilly night before college freshmen were eligible to play varsity football, the frosh from UNC Chapel Hill played their rivals from Duke University in Charlotte's Memorial Stadium. Their clash drew a large and rowdy crowd. Jimmy and I parked cars and after the game joined others in combing the stadium grandstands for soft-drink bottles. For each twenty-four-bottle crate we filled, we earned a dime. Often in the search for bottles we came across a bonus of dropped coins. On that night, amid the discarded programs, peanut hulls, popcorn boxes, and candy wrappers, we found a crumpled two-dollar bill. Neither of us had ever seen such a prize, but we added it to our earnings and raced home to hand it to Mother. She rejoiced as if it were a godsend. For years afterward the event was remembered in the family as "the night the boys found a two-dollar bill."

ALL-AMERICAN BATBOY

THE youngster below is Jimmy (Slug) Claiborne, bat-boy for the Central High baseball team during the past season and its most enthusiastic backer. Jimmy never misses a football, basketball or baseball practice at Central; he knows all the players and talks sports terms in his sleep.—(Observer Staff Photo.)

Slug as Central High batboy

CHAPTER

10

Jimmy Becomes Slug

After our move to Park Drive, Mother let neighbors know she was serving meals family style. She equipped the dining room with a long table and enough chairs to seat twelve. Her meals were composed of the staples of Southern cooking: fried chicken, baked ham, roast beef, and baked pork chops so tender they fell off the bone. My favorite was chicken and dumplings, a savory dish that Jimmy spurned as "wet dough."

At least once a week Mother's menus included seafood. She served mackerel or flounder or catfish and urged us to eat it as "brain food." All Mother's meals included biscuits, hot, thin, and crispy.

Like the rest of the family, Jimmy and I became kitchen helpers, learning to peel, chop, and grate, as well as wash dishes and empty garbage. We also learned to set the table with the sharp side of the knife blade toward the plate and the water glass at the tip of the knife.

Occasionally, Jimmy and I got in the way. One afternoon after Mother had baked two lemon meringue pies, our sister Phyllis, lean, quick, and sharp-tongued, was carrying them palms up to cool on a side porch. Just as she crossed the threshold from the dining room, Jimmy and I came romping past. Plop! Plop! went the pies, face down on the hardwood floor.

Phyllis was furious. "All right, get down and *lick it up*!" she said in her most stentorian voice. I stood frozen in fear, but Jimmy was instantly on his knees, his back bent and his head bobbing up and down as he gobbled up the mess. Looking on in horror, Phyl's anger gradually faded and she saw humor in the situation. At length, she chuckled, reached down to pull the meringue-smeared Jimmy to his feet and apologized. Jimmy looked disappointed.

Among the regulars at our mother's table were two women from up the street, Mrs. Whitlock and Miss Fannie. In the fall and winter Mrs. Whitlock, who clerked at Belk's, hired Jimmy and me to bring in scuttles of coal for the stove that heated her house and to carry out the ashes. Jimmy would fill the assignment one morning and I the next. Mrs. Whitlock was persnickety about where we dumped the ashes, often asking us to move them from one spot to another. For that she paid us a dime a day.

Jimmy and I had plenty of places to spend those dimes. Among the most memorable were summer swimming outings. The dimes would take us by bus to the west side of town, past the city incinerator and up the hill to the Municipal Swimming Pool, built in 1938 with a $120,000 WPA grant. Dimes paid our admission to the pool and the rent for black woolen bathing suits with the initials MSP stenciled in white on the right leg. Few people today would dare rent a bathing suit at a public swimming pool, but in the post-Depression years doing so was as routine as renting bowling shoes today.

Our Park Drive neighborhood offered many diversions, but the most captivating was our discovery of baseball, something we had not been exposed to on the farm or Fifth Street. The discovery occurred in the spring of 1939 when Central High baseball players came walking past our house in flannel uniforms and spiked shoes en route to batting and fielding practice at Independence Park. Intrigued by the clatter of their spikes on the sidewalks, we followed them. The players were teenagers—sixteen, seventeen, eighteen years old—but to boys seven and eight, they looked like grown men.

On the practice field they engaged in constant chatter: "Come on babe." "Way to go babe." "Atta boy babe." We made ourselves useful by picking up bats and chasing down foul balls. We also listened as coaches taught fundamentals—how to hit, how to bunt, how to make the double play, how to slide into bases. We learned that baseball was a game of grace and speed, skill and guile, and required constant attention to small details.

It was during Central High's baseball practices that my six-year-old brother became "Slug." Almost all Central High players had nicknames. The big, tenor-voiced catcher was "Truck." The fleet shortstop was "Skeeter." The diminutive second baseman, clearly the team leader, was "Dynamite." I would like to say Jimmy acquired his nickname after some heroics in a noble cause, but that was not the case. Jimmy was more a mediator than a gladiator.

The real story is that the afternoon newspaper, the *Charlotte News*, had begun carrying a daily comic strip named "Nancy," about a little girl whose nemesis was a short, rotund, crew-cut boy named Sluggo, who resembled my brother in size, shape, and especially temerity. It was Bill "Dynamite" Starnes who began calling Jimmy "Sluggo," and almost overnight everyone else referred to him as Sluggo and later simply Slug. Just watching him race down the left field foul line in pursuit of a foul ball, his stubby legs pumping and his fat hands flapping at each stride, was a picture of perseverance. The name Slug stuck to him like skin. We didn't know it at the time, but that nickname was the greatest gift he ever got—and one he didn't seek.

Our enthusiasm for baseball was magnified when Central High played a game across town at enclosed Hayman Park. Hidden behind a lumberyard on narrow little Winona Street in Charlotte's Third Ward, the park was home to the professional Charlotte Hornets, a minor league baseball team whose games Slug and I had heard on the radio but had never seen.

We rode to Central High games there in an A-Model Ford driven by Al Hayes, the school's Hollywood-handsome left fielder. With the sheikh-like look of Rudolph Valetino, he drew jeers from opposing left field fans who called him "our pretty boy" and hooted, "Don't let any of those mean ol' fly balls hit your pretty head." Al took the razzing in stride and with a strong arm regularly threw out runners trying to stretch a base hit into a double.

Like something from a Bonnie and Clyde getaway, Al's A-Model Ford had a rumble seat that could accommodate two teammates with two batboys sitting on their laps. I can still hear the tinny ching-ching of that A-Model as it throttled through uptown traffic. We waved and cheered at pedestrians, letting everyone know we were from Central High.

The Slugger and I found Hayman Park more accommodating than Independence Park. It had a cavernous wooden grandstand painted dark green, with rows and rows of seats curving from third base around to first base, all covered by a slanted roof and protected by a batting screen. It smelled of pine tar, popcorn, and stale cigarettes. Its outfield fences were lined by brightly colored advertising. It was a cacophonous site where ballpark sounds were often drowned out by a loud horn from the lumberyard next door, signaling work hours and startling everyone in the ballpark. To Slug and me, it was a marvelous place where we once saw a Central High lefthander pitch a no-hit game, a rarity in any league.

Later that summer, as Slug and I were roller-skating on the smooth concrete in front of Central High, newsboys appeared selling extras with big black headlines about war in Europe. It was September 1, 1939. Germany had attacked Poland, and the rest of Europe was choosing up sides for another world war. That enlivened talk at our dinner table. People argued over whether the United States should get involved. Before the distraction of television or radio, stories in the two daily newspapers set the agenda for public discourse. Jimmy Harton and Irby Todd, both avid newspaper readers, were full of condemnation of Hitler, Neville Chamberlain, and Germany's brutal "blitzkrieg" tactics.

A few months later, such talk faded as Jimmy and Irby read of Charlotte leaders' boast that the city's population would exceed one hundred thousand in the upcoming US census. They responded to the boosterism with jeers. At the time, Charlotte and Winston-Salem were vying for the honor of being North Carolina's largest city. Charlotte had won that distinction in 1910 by eclipsing Wilmington, only to lose it in 1912 when Winston and Salem merged into one municipality. Spurred by a 1920s building boom, Charlotte reclaimed the title in 1930 and hoped to expand its lead in 1940.

When the 1940 census fell barely short of one hundred thousand, Jimmy Harton and Irby Todd hooted. Chastened, city leaders urged canvassers to count again and mounted a campaign to make sure everyone, Black and

White, was included. Jimmy and Irby continued to scoff until the recount showed that indeed Charlotte's population was 100,899, surpassing Winston by more than 21,000 residents.

Slug and I were delighted. We both wanted to live in a "big city." That one-hundred-thousand-plus tally brought Charlotte to the attention of national companies looking to increase sales by including Charlotte in their advertising and marketing. It also made Charlotte more attractive as an industrial site.

Yet baseball at all levels remained important in Slug's and my lives. As in cities and towns across the country, Charlotte industries sponsored baseball teams to raise worker morale and offset low wages and working conditions. Teams representing the city's largest manufacturers—Lance Packing, Highland Park Mills, Hudson Hosiery, Larkwood Hosiery, Southern Bell, Cramerton Mills, Leaksville Mills, and others played games in the Twilight League at Independence Park. The league reflected remnants of the city's cotton-mill economy. Many of their semi-pro players had once played professionally, so the play was polished, the competition was keen, and the fan support loud. The games were played in late afternoons before crowds of co-workers, many wearing bib overalls.

The teams brought their own batboys, relegating Slug and me to picking up soft-drink bottles in the gray-stone grandstand that still arcs behind home plate. An incident during our bottle-pickup routine left a deep wound in our fraternal relations. Our goal was to fill twenty-four-bottle crates as fast as possible and earn a dime a crate. When a crate we were filling was nearly full, I tried to carry it several rows down to where Slug had gathered a handful of empties. On the way there the crate tipped, spilling about half the bottles onto the gray stones. The sound of breaking glass turned heads throughout the grandstand. The Slugger looked at me in disgust and shouted, "You don't carry the crate to the bottles! You carry the bottles to the crate, dummy!"

His words cut deeply. I was publicly shamed. As I gathered the broken glass, I could sense the eyes in the grandstand watching and felt the full sting of Slug's reproach. Though I had long thought I was inferior to Slug in personality and athleticism, I had always considered myself his superior in intellect and reliability. His rebuke caused me to doubt even that slim advantage.

Several days later came a compensating opportunity. I noticed that Ken Gilliland, a one-armed man who submitted reports of Twilight League games to local newspapers, needed someone to post inning-by-inning totals on a big scoreboard visible to the crowd. Abandoning bottle pickups, I volunteered to sit beside him at a desk atop the third base dugout where he kept a play-by-play score sheet. From him I not only earned dimes for putting up scores but also learned the mysteries of baseball scoring, that all the defensive positions were numbered from one through nine—the pitcher was one, catcher two, first base three, second base four, and so forth. A ground out from third to first was scored 5-3, a strikeout was a K, a home run was HR. I didn't know it at the time, but I was preparing to become not a baseball player but a sportswriter.

"We saw the gritty side of
segregation that was beyond
the power of pre-teen boys
to rectify, but the time would
come when we could help
do something about it, and
we did."

CHAPTER

11

Observing Injustices

The Park Drive neighborhood exposed Slug and me to some of the seamier sides of Charlotte. We often saw drunks passed out in the stadium grandstands or on one of the surrounding embankments. We saw scalpers selling tickets outside the armory at inflated prices. We saw people play tricks on demented men who lacked the skills to be vendors at the stadium. Worst of all, we saw the impact of racial segregation.

There were also good influences within our Park Drive environment. Among the best were the Moseley brothers, Bob and Hubert, who were five and three years older than we were and lived two houses up the street. Occasionally, Slug and I would "camp out" with Bob and Hubert in the Moseley backyard and bake potatoes in the ashes of a campfire. The potato skins came out black, but their insides were hot and, when flooded with butter, memorably delicious.

While they were still teenagers, the Moseley boys acquired a concession stand at Memorial Stadium and out of neighborliness hired the Slugger and me as vendors. I began selling chewing gum and candy up and down stadium aisles, and in the next year I looked up to see Slug selling right behind me. We quickly learned the arithmetic of making change. A year later, when we were stronger, we hauled buckets of iced drinks and shouted, "Cold drinks here!" "Aye, get a Coke!" During football season we worked several nights and usually ended the weekends froggy-voiced but with coins in our pockets.

Beyond the Moseleys lived the Lineberry brothers, Stanhope and Charles, whose father was the county police chief, allowing them to get away with more daring mischief. Once, in demonstrating the mysteries of a Molotov cocktail, Stan Lineberry struck a match to a rag hanging out of a bottle of gasoline. When it burst into flames, he flung it aside but accidentally hit Bob Moseley in the face, setting his hair and clothes afire. Bob began to run, but Stan tackled him and rolled him over to extinguish the flames. Bob was hospitalized, looking like a mummy in his facial bandages but mercifully came out unscarred. His straight hair grew out curly.

The pranks of even more daring boys made Halloween an ominous night in the neighborhood and across the city. Before World War II, no children dressed in costume and went trick-or-treating on Halloween. Few under twelve were allowed out after dark. Teenage boys roamed yards and alleyways looking for "tricks" to perform—overturning porch and lawn furniture, spilling garbage cans, suspending rocking chairs from tree limbs. It was a policing nightmare and probably the stimulus for the more innocent "trick or treat" tradition that has succeeded it.

Offsetting such mischief was Slug's discovery of a rusting golf club in a muddy splotch of Independence Park. It was a wooden-shaft two-iron usually used to fly a ball from the fairway to the green. We used it for everything—driving, pitching, and putting. We found golf balls in the park and converted the Central High athletic field into a golf course. I could rarely hit the ball where I wanted it to go, but Slug developed a smooth swing and soon was driving for distance and accuracy. It was the beginning of his love of a sport that would give him a lifetime of pleasure, enabling him to pal with famous golfers and ultimately take him to Scotland.

At the time, however, golf could not compete with our interest in football. Slug and I attended Central High football practices and absorbed lessons as coaches shouted instructions about blocking and tackling and the fine points of passing and punting. We sat in on "skull sessions" as coaches stood before blackboards and with X's and O's diagrammed plays and defenses.

When it was time for games, our focus was on Memorial Stadium. At least two and sometimes three of the city's six high school teams—Central, Harding, and Tech for White students; and Second Ward, West Charlotte, and Plato Price for Blacks—played there every weekend. It was a happy place. Before each game, recorded music—including Sousa marches and old favorites like the "Beer Barrel Polka"—blared from the public address system. Often people entered the stadium singing along.

Before we were old enough to be vendors, Slug and I earned money by hanging scores on the stadium's hand-operated scoreboard atop a field house at the open end of the horseshoe-shaped arena. We climbed a two-story ladder to get to our perch, which was exposed to the elements. On breezy October and November nights we kept our hands and feet warm by burning cans of Sterno, a jellied fuel used for heating steam tables. The cost of the Sterno often ate up our earnings as scorekeepers.

From our post we couldn't help but notice the disparities in uniforms and equipment for White schools and Black. Often Black teams had headgear for only their starting eleven. Any substitute had to wear the sweaty helmet of the player he replaced. Sometimes that exchange also included shoulder pads and uniform jerseys. Aware of the abundance of athletic equipment at Central High, we winced at the Black exchanges. In growing up we noticed the institutional segregation around us—in housing, education, and employment—but that was simply the way things were. In those helmet exchanges we saw the gritty side of segregation that was beyond the power of pre-teen boys to rectify, but the time would come when we could help do something about it, and we did.

Frequently Memorial Stadium hosted college games. Davidson College and Johnson C. Smith University played home games there. When NC State played Clemson there, the halftime shows featured not marching bands but uniformed cadets from each school's Reserve Officers Training Corps, their rifles twirling as they executed close-order drills. Then there was the annual Thanksgiving clash between South Carolina and Wake Forest. Those games didn't get to Charlotte by accident. Local business leaders negotiated to attract them as entertainment for Charlotte residents.

It was fun to watch the college crowds stream toward the stadium. In those days people dressed up for football games, men in coats and ties and women in skirts and jackets. On their coats women frequently wore bright yellow chrysanthemums, festooned with ribbons in their favorite team's colors. Often a lettermen group from Johnson C. Smith came to the stadium singing, the harmony of their male voices echoing through the night as they approached the arena.

The 1940 repeal of the city's blue laws brought not only Sunday movies but also sports events, whetting Charlotte-area appetites for professional football. That hunger was initially fed by the semi-pro Charlotte Clippers, composed of stars from past college teams. Organized by real estate developer Floyd Simmons, the Clippers held their practices in Independence Park, where Slug and I could watch. Before World War II, the Clippers were led by Jim Lalanne, once a star at UNC Chapel Hill. After World War II they were led by burly Butch Butler, formerly of Clemson. He shed tacklers like a tugboat splashing through choppy waters. Butler's running mate was a slim triple threat (runner, passer, punter) named James "Casey" Jones, who as a senior at Union College in Tennessee made the Little All-American team. Jones threw passes to an elastic-armed end named Rocky Spadaccini as the Clippers won games by lopsided scores.

In succeeding years, Charlotte's pro football hunger was fed by several teams, one called the Charlotte Stars and another, the Charlotte Hornets. Then in 1994 that hunger was assuaged with great rejoicing when the business and sports community persuaded the National Football League (NFL) to accept the Carolina Panthers as a new franchise, giving Charlotte an enduring image on the national sports map.

For most of those football games, whether high school, college, or professional, Slug and I were trying to earn money selling candy, Cokes, or simply picking up bottles. Our greatest bonanza came by accident one December after a Shrine Bowl football game between North Carolina high school stars and similar all-stars from South Carolina. Sponsored by Shrine temples across the two states, the game was always a sell-out benefiting the Crippled Children's Hospital in Greenville, South Carolina. At the end of one 1940 game, Slug and I were at the back of a grandstand, waiting for the crowd to clear so we could pick up bottles. To pass the time, we were playing a little football ourselves, using a round oatmeal carton as our ball. Happy, red-fezzed Shriners were coming and going all around us, congratulating each other on another successful fundraiser. As Slug bent over to snap the oatmeal box to me, a half-drunken Shriner reached down to lift him by the seat of his corduroy knickers. Unfortunately, those britches and the underwear beneath had been washed and worn so often they were threadbare. Rather than lifting Slug, the Shriner came up with a fistful of rotting cloth, leaving the Slugger's bare behind exposed.

The Shriner was mortified. He squatted, scooped up Slug, hugged him close and apologized profusely. After putting Slug down, he reached in his pocket and pulled out a twenty-dollar bill. "Here, this ought to cover the damages," he said, and beat a hasty exit from the stadium. Slug and I forgot all about picking up bottles and hurried home to show Mother the twenty-dollar bill. She used it to buy not only new knickers for Slug but also a pair for me and matching corduroy jackets for each of us.

"while he [Slugger] could charm with personality, I could shine with words."

CHAPTER

12

War and Food Service

After football season the next major event for Slug and me was Christmas. Our family's celebrations on Fifth Street had been spartan, but at Park Drive the festivities were joyous. Mother painted holly and ligustrum leaves gold and silver and bunched them around candles on the mantel and in windowsills. She baked extravagant coconut cakes that looked like giant snowballs and a multi-layered caramel cake that glistened with copper-colored icing.

Best of all was the Christmas Eve merriment. For supper Mother always served steaming oyster stew, dappled with little round crackers. Afterward, Slug and I were sent to bed upstairs to await Santa Claus. Meanwhile, Mother's brother Bill Harton and two of Mother's sisters and their spouses arrived. With Alice and H.A., Phyllis and Jack Stuart, and Jimmy Harton and Irby Todd, they began to party. They drew names and gave gag gifts that provoked whoops of laughter. Slug and I would steal away from our bed and sit in the shadows atop the stairs to listen to their jokes.

Santa Claus never was much of a mystery. Slug and I knew Mother and her elves were behind it all. The gifts we got were usually socks, stocking caps, gloves, and winter clothes. One Christmas Uncle Bill brought us boxing gloves and insisted that we demonstrate them. So there I was, under the colored lights and sparkling tinsel of a tall cedar tree, having to duke it out with my battling brother. With pillow-sized gloves on each of our hands we couldn't do much damage, but we fought until we could no longer lift our arms, then called it a draw. Later I confided to Slug that I didn't like having to fight him in front of an audience. He said he didn't like it either. "With Mother watching, I had to go easy on you."

Jimmy Harton and Irby Todd often gave us books and impressed on Slug and me the importance of reading. He gave me *The Wizard of Oz,* which I devoured. Jimmy Harton also got a kick out of teaching me to spell and pronounce big words, such as "gastronomical" and "sagacity." Slugger was not interested in such foolishness, but it showed me that while he could charm with personality, I could shine with words.

After the Christmas of 1940 the weather turned severe and brought ice storms that made streets and sidewalks treacherous. Our walks to and from Elizabeth School in thin shoes and light coats were punishingly cold. Each of us caught colds that descended into our chests, resulting in pneumonia, which before the availability of antibiotics was life threatening. Mother relied on country remedies. She set up a bed downstairs and moved us into it, then kept vigil through the nights. She'd awaken us periodically to dispense spoonfuls of sugar soaked in something that smelled and tasted like kerosene. At intervals she covered our chests with mustard plasters to help us sweat out the illness.

As we got better, fearing constipation, Mother added castor oil to our regimen. Having taken cod liver oil as a tyke, I could tolerate castor oil, but Slug refused to accept it. Late one Saturday afternoon my sister's husband Jack Stuart volunteered to help. He knelt next to the Slugger's side of the bed and in soothing tones explained that castor oil was a good thing. Slug told him it was nasty and he wasn't going to take it. When Jack Stuart continued to press it on him, the Slugger challenged, "I'll take it if you will." Accordingly, Jack Stuart poured himself a big spoonful, swallowed it, and then poured another for the Slugger, who obediently gulped it down. That solved the problem but cancelled any plans Jack Stuart and our sister Phyllis might have had for the evening.

During our confinement my second-grade teacher, a young woman named Alice Reid, came to call and left us a book, Robert Louis Stevenson's *A Child's*

Garden of Verses. It was a treasure. Lying side by side, Slug and I turned through it often, admiring the black-and-white drawings and memorizing some of the poems. I especially liked, "I have a little shadow that goes in and out with me and what can be the use of him is more than I can see..."

Though I was often offended by Slug's show-off antics, I had to admire his empathy. A good example came on Easter Sunday after our recovery from pneumonia. The day had brought us several tiny yellow chicks that were cheeping across the kitchen floor on spidery little feet. In one corner Mother had set out jar lids of food and water. Having raised chickens on the farm, she welcomed the little biddies. That evening when the house was quiet and Mother, Slug, and I were in the dining room listening to the radio, Mother asked Slug to turn out the light in the kitchen. Doing so required him to stand on a stool and pull a cord dangling from the ceiling. As he did and jumped down, his foot landed full force on one of the baby chicks. The sight of the tiny animal lying on the floor with its legs smashed, its innards seeping out, and its tiny beak cheeping death throes was more than Slug could stand. He dashed headlong to his mother pleading forgiveness with tears flooding his fat cheeks. Mother gathered him up, held him close, and comforted him. With a nod she bade me to remove the injured chick. I did so, but it took Slug the rest of the night to recover.

In those weeks, morning and evening newspapers bore black headlines about Germany extending its grip on Europe. Closer to home German U-boats were sinking merchant ships, some of them daringly close to the coast of the Carolinas, leaving bodies of English sailors to wash up on beaches. In time North Carolina ceded a plot on its Outer Banks to Great Britain as a burial ground for its seamen.

As the rationing of gasoline and tires was being implemented, Slug and I sneaked into a rally at the armory, where angry traveling salesmen—representing a large segment of the city's wholesaling, warehousing, and distributing economy—gathered to protest. They carried placards saying, "Grass will grow on the highways." That prediction seemed so preposterous Slug and I had to laugh.

Throughout 1940, the United States had an army of fewer than one hundred eighty thousand men equipped with World War I weapons, prompting the nation to begin preparations for national defense. Congress approved the nation's first peacetime conscription. In 1941 the War Department ordered Army Reserve and National Guard units to hold war games in the Carolinas, where the goal was to capture Charlotte.

Overnight, public spaces across the city were clotted with pup tents as soldiers bivouacked as if they were on a battlefield. Independence Park, Memorial Stadium, and the grounds around the armory were littered with tents and field equipment. Slug and I ran barefoot among them, peering in to see what was going on and standing in line with borrowed mess kits to sample field-kitchen food, which we learned was "chow."

On Saturday night when their "war" duties were done, soldiers in starched khakis and shined shoes strolled past our house on their way to town for a night of fun. Sitting on a stone wall in front of our house, Slug and I watched them pass. One of them called out, "Hey, boy. Where's a good place to eat around here?"

Without hesitating, the Slugger crooked a thumb over his shoulder and said, "Right here."

"How much is it?" the soldier asked.

Again without hesitance, Slug shot back, "Twenty-five cents."

I was astonished. I would never have given such answers to those questions, but there was my younger brother responding with a confidence bordering on audacity.

The soldier looked at his buddy and asked, "You want to try it?"

The buddy said, "Sure."

Within minutes the Slugger had our living room lined two deep in soldiers waiting to get to our mother's table. Mother called me into the kitchen and said, "Quick, run into the neighborhood and borrow chicken."

Throughout each meal Mother made sure the biscuit platter was sumptuous. When it looked lean she went to the kitchen and returned with a full plate of "hot 'uns." The evening went so well that within days a wooden sign went up in our front yard saying, "Meals 25 Cents." The Slugger's first venture into food service had been a success.

My food-service experience was more mundane. Through the intercession of Jimmy Harton, our brother Harold, then in the tenth grade at Central

High, got a job at Lassiter Press as a helper on a large lithographic press. After school he worked from three until midnight, earning money to support the family. Every evening Mother fixed him a plate of hot food, wrapped it in waxed paper, and wrapped it again in newspapers. Then she laid on top a separate packet of hot, buttered biscuits and handed me the whole bundle, instructing, "Take this to Harold and be careful. Hold it level and don't tarry. I want him to eat it while it's hot."

I walked straight to Lassiter Press at the corner of East Fourth and Cecil Streets, entered a side door to the deserted plant and was greeted by intoxicating odors of inks, oils, gums, and cleaning agents. In the twilight gloom I threaded my way through large machines to a freight elevator and pushed the button to the second floor, where I could hear a powerful press running full tilt. From the elevator I could see Harold standing over the delivery end of the press as three-foot sheets of freshly printed hosiery labels slid across drying flames of natural gas and settled on a wooden pallet. Harold was always glad to see me and sat down immediately to eat while I roamed the pressroom looking at the many dials and levers and gadgets, wondering what each of them did and enjoying a special pride in knowing that my brother *knew* what they did. In time the smell of Harold's dinner so impressed his pressman boss that he asked if he could sign up for such meals, and Mother added his plate to my nightly deliveries.

I enjoyed those dinner errands and felt honored in running them. They were further evidence of Mother's trust in me. They were also evidence of our family's reliance on the otherwise fun-loving Harold. Unfortunately, after the tenth grade, he was so far behind in his studies that he dropped out of school. He went on to make a career out of running lithographic presses and with that skill supported his wife and their ten children.

By the fall of 1941, as Slug and I approached ages nine and ten, we moved up to the more profitable privilege of selling soft drinks at the stadium. That required us to carry a bucket of ten bottles—Coca-Cola, Pepsi, Royal Crown, Nehi Orange, Dr Pepper—submerged in chipped ice. For every bucketful we sold the Moseley brothers paid us a quarter.

Each of us was selling cold drinks in the stadium on a pleasant Sunday afternoon as the Charlotte Clippers hosted the Norfolk Shamrocks. The game was well underway when the public address announcer interrupted the action to say something like, "Attention, all military personnel. You are to return to your posts immediately." A buzz rose from the crowd, and uniformed soldiers, sailors, and marines began climbing stairs leading to the exits. About an hour later the public address announcer again broke into the play-by-play to say, "Ladies and gentlemen, we are authorized to report that the Japanese have bombed American naval and air bases at Pearl Harbor. All military personnel and defense workers are to report to their duty stations."

An audible gasp rose from the crowd and many people got up to go. As they exited the stadium, they encountered newsboys selling extras proclaiming the United States was at war with Japan. Slug and I had no idea what that meant, but at the game's end we cashed in our soft drinks and ran home to consult a map that would help us locate Pearl Harbor.

The next morning, December 8, having read newspaper accounts of the toll on American lives and property, Irby Todd went down to the post office and, like scores of other North Carolinians who volunteered for service in the Army, Navy, or Marines that morning, joined the Navy, which turned him into an intelligence officer.

Jimmy Harton was not far behind. After weeks of newspaper maps showing the extent of Japan's aggression in the Pacific and Germany's expanding onslaught in Europe, he joined the Army. It was not a war Americans wanted and for more than a year looked like one we might lose.

Mother in the yard at 1217 Elizabeth Avenue

CHAPTER

13

Adjusting to War

The war made an immediate impact on Charlotte and communities large and small across the country. It also disrupted the routine at Mother's boarding house. As the nation geared up for the fight of its life, she responded by moving us to a larger house three blocks away at 1217 Elizabeth Avenue. In addition to four bedrooms, it had two baths and would allow her to rent more rooms and serve more meals.

For boys nine and ten years old, it was another step up in opportunity and excitement with new people to meet and more chances to earn money. Most of our neighbors were professionals. One was an architect, another an auditor, another a film distributor. Across the street lived a chemist, a painting contractor, and the county sheriff. We got to know them all, cut their grass, and frequently ran their errands.

Among the other benefits of living on Elizabeth Avenue was the Hazelton family that moved into a large Queen Anne house across the street. The family included a frisky, freckled boy known as "Buddy," who attended Elizabeth School with us and joined us in pickup football, basketball, and baseball games. The Hazelton house had more rooms than the family could occupy. It also had numerous porches, turrets, galleries, and arched balconies that overlooked the surrounding grounds. Buddy, Slug, and I took down curtain rods from empty rooms, pulled them apart, and used the halves as fencing swords. As we "fought" on the battlements of the big old house, we pretended to be the "Three Musketeers," Athos, Porthos, and Aramis, right out of the novels of Alexandre Dumas.

News from the battlefields described barbaric fighting, but the exotic place names were mind-expanding: Odessa, Rangoon, Corregidor, Sumatra, Tobruk. Occasionally, Slug and I went uptown to the Carnegie library to consult maps and widen our knowledge of geography. We also learned to endure blackouts and mock air raids. Each block had its own helmeted air raid warden. In addition to occasional fire drills at school, we practiced rushing into hallways, sitting with our knees under our chins, and bowing our heads as if bombs were falling. All of that made the war seem real and near.

When the rationing of gasoline and rubber was extended to sugar, meat, butter, shortening, and shoes, an elaborate coupon system was devised. One Saturday morning Slug and I wandered into the Central High gymnasium and found teachers working at tables scattered across the basketball court. They were collating sheets of ration stamps, some red, some blue, some green. We volunteered to help and soon were stapling assembled sheets into booklets.

Like other Americans, we learned to substitute honey and saccharine for sugar and to use margarine as a substitute for butter. In those days margarine came in white one-pound bricks with a cellophane packet of yellow coloring. Slug and I kneaded the yellow powder into the white brick and shaped it into what looked like a mound of butter.

People were encouraged to plant "victory gardens." Mother sent Slug and me into the backyard with mattocks to dig up the red clay and break down stubborn clods. She came behind with a hoe, creating furrows and planting corn, okra, lima beans, sweet peas, tomatoes, and other vegetables. The garden flourished, and so did Mother's menus.

As on Park Drive, neighbors who lived in Elizabeth Avenue's rooming houses soon came to eat at our table. Soon after our move, Mother rented the large front room upstairs and converted the downstairs living room into a rental bedroom. Renters and boarders were mostly women in town to be near husbands stationed at nearby training camps. Military bases were established all around the Carolinas.

At the city's invitation, the Army Air Corps turned Charlotte's three-year-old Douglas Airport into Morris Field, a base for training bombardiers. To accommodate more men and bigger planes, the Air Corps more than doubled the size of the airport, laying the foundation for an aviation hub that later would make Charlotte one of the nation's busiest travel centers. At Fayetteville the Army turned Fort Bragg into headquarters for the Eighty-Second Airborne Division. On the western edge of Monroe, it established Camp Sutton for infantry training. Later a glider and paratroop base sprung up at Camp Mackall near Laurinburg, and an infantry replacement center named Camp Croft sprawled near Spartanburg, South Carolina. Each of those installations and others across the South changed the culture of their host communities. Menus at my mother's boarding house were a good example. To suit the tastes of people from other parts of the country, Mother had to vary her menus to include what for us were exotic foods (spaghetti, stuffed bell peppers, and Spanish pork chops).

Having rescinded its blue laws to permit Sunday entertainment, the city welcomed throngs of uniformed service men on weekends, some from as far as Cherry Point and Camp Lejeune Marine bases in eastern North Carolina. Slug and I watched as workmen turned the basement of the armory into a United Service Organizations (USO) canteen.

Adding to the local excitement was a glamorous new football team representing the Third Air Force at Morris Field. Nicknamed the Gremlins, the team practiced on the Central High athletic field and played its games in Memorial Stadium. Slug and I were always there to watch and learn. The team included many college stars we had read about, including Charlie Trippi, a wiry, bandy-legged all-American running back at Georgia. A study in contrasts, with a large upper body and spindly legs, he ran light-footed like a hummingbird gathering nectar in quick darts, dashes, twists, and turns that made him as elusive as lightning. When he carried the ball, the public address announcer at Memorial Stadium would say simply, "Trippi.... running..." After the war, he became a leading rusher in the NFL and a member of pro football's Hall of Fame.

In addition to military bases, the war brought new investment to the South. Charlotte offered land and facilities to secure several wartime industries that changed the face and feel of the surrounding region. The largest was a huge shell-loading plant employing ten thousand workers off York Road southwest of town. Slug and I rode the bus there to see what it was like. It was a community all unto itself and left a lasting mark on the city. After the war it was bought by a consortium of young businessmen, led by textile-machinery merchant Pat Hall. Together they turned it into Arrowood Industrial Park, which attracted many big industries, including a huge General Electric turbine plant, and brought many new people into the city. Today the whole area hums with activity.

We also rode a bus to Thrift Road west of town, where the National Carbon Company operated a radio-battery plant employing eight hundred workers, most of them women. We were disappointed to find it looked much like a cotton mill. On Statesville Road, where the Ford Motor Company once assembled streams of A-Models, the Army converted the seventy-five-acre complex into a Quartermaster Depot employing more than two thousand workers. They warehoused everything from toothpicks to battle gear and distributed it to military bases across the Carolinas and Virginia. After the war, the depot became a plant for assembling Douglas anti-aircraft missiles, which helped Charlotte upgrade its image from a textile center to something sleek and high-tech.

The shell plant, the battery plant, the quartermaster depot, and other war industries attracted workers from around the Carolinas and endowed them with skills beyond those required in cotton mills. After the war, many of those workers stayed to swell Charlotte's labor pool and enable the city to attract sophisticated manufacturing.

Under federal rules, the war plants hired without regard to race or gender, laying the groundwork for a future push toward equal employment. Having worked side by side with men and Whites in defense plants or in the armed services, women and Blacks resisted going back to post-war segregation. Their voices helped ignite the racial and gender revolutions of the 1950s and '60s.

Unlike our previous homes, the Elizabeth Avenue house had central heating, produced by a rusting hulk in the basement with octopus-like pipes extending into every room. Among Slug's and my chores was tending the furnace. We learned to feed it coal, bank the fire at night, revive it in the morning, and carry out the ashes. Each time a ton of new coal was delivered to the backyard, we had to shovel it into the basement coal bin.

We also were charged with washing dishes and cleaning the kitchen after boarding-house meals. I would scrape and wash one night, and Slug would dry and put away. The next night we'd swap roles. What we did jointly was mop the kitchen floor. After splashing it with water, we sprinkled it with Rinso, a popular laundry powder. We whipped that into lather and began diving and sliding across the floor, as if we were stealing second base. In time we rinsed away the suds and mopped the floor dry. It was great fun and left the place squeaky clean—until Mother caught on and made us stop.

After chores, our interests always returned to Central High, less than a block away. Every day after school we watched football, basketball, or baseball practice, soaking up the fundamentals. When we weren't hobnobbing with the athletes, we were in the tiny office of Bob Allen, a gap-toothed ex-football coach who oversaw athletic programs at all Charlotte schools. Catalogues of sports equipment choked the shelves in Allen's cubby overlooking the Central High gymnasium. We studied those catalogues, looking at shoulder pads and punching bags, baseball bats and catcher's masks, tennis racquets and football shoes, and imagined the thrill of owning them. But with baseball as our first love, we mostly coveted catcher's and first-base mitts. Slugger wanted to be a catcher; I wanted to be a first baseman. Coach Allen chuckled over our debates about which mitts were best. One day he promised that if we'd come up with a down payment, he'd arrange to get each of us a mitt at wholesale prices.

Immediately we began saving our nickels and dimes. We made money selling programs at the armory during each winter's weeklong Carolinas Golden Gloves boxing tournament, a regional event that drew raucous crowds and reinforced Charlotte's allure as an entertainment center. The tournament brought to Charlotte fighters from Fort Bragg and Camp Lejeune, as well as from boxing clubs in Kannapolis, Florence, Shelby, and other towns in the Carolinas. The winners went on to fight at Madison Square Garden in New York. Jim McMillan, later to win fame as a Charlotte lawyer and federal judge, fought in the Charlotte Golden Gloves tournament as a member of a boxing team from Laurinburg.

We also earned money selling peanuts, popcorn, and cups of soft drinks at the countywide basketball tournament held annually in the Central High gym. The tournament matched men's and women's teams from the county's sixteen all-White rural schools and drew crowds from communities like Steele Creek, Oakhurst, Bain, Berryhill, Long Creek, and other suburban places, some of whose names have since faded as Charlotte has sprawled into a metropolis. The rural schools anchored their villages and preserved their identities. For that reason, each school's basketball team attracted loud and loyal followings.

We also earned money cutting neighbors' grass, an extension of our home responsibilities. We had an old-fashioned push lawn mower with a rotating reel in front that forced grass against a sharp blade. The mower worked well when grass was short, but in tall grass it was like pushing a lead sled. One of my lawn customers was a widow who let her grass grow ankle deep before offering me a quarter to cut it. It was sweaty work. I had to go over the lawn two or three times to get it looking trim. One day when I was about halfway through the job, she called me in for some "refreshment." I was looking forward to a Coke or perhaps a glass of lemonade. Instead, she served me a tumbler of powdered milk. Somehow I managed to drink it.

One spring the ever-enterprising Slug fell into a novel way of earning money. When the graduating class at Central High staged a fundraising carnival, he volunteered to sit atop a dunking booth over a small pool behind the gym. Slug was perched over a trap door about six feet up while barkers below invited patrons to throw balls at a target that when properly hit would send the Slugger plunging into the pool. It was just the job for Slug's personality and showmanship. Clad in bathing trunks and a T-shirt, he razzed those who stopped by, daring them to try dunking him. When they missed, he jeered. When they hit, he plummeted into the pool with a great splash. He would surface and say as he clambered back to his post, "Betcha' can't do it again." He earned two dollars that night and probably had more fun than any of those who paid to dunk him.

For the Slugger and me, the good news was the completion of Charlotte's new baseball stadium. As old Hayman Park was being demolished, the

American League's Washington Senators built Clark Griffith Park on Dilworth's Magnolia Avenue, then on the southern edge of town. The new park was to be home for the Charlotte Hornets, the Senators' class B farm team. While the Hornets were completing spring training in Florida, Central High took the opportunity to play the park's first game. Slugger and I were on duty as batboys that afternoon when John Muse, the Central High first baseman, hit a prodigious drive that barely cleared the left field fence twenty feet high and 340 feet away. As Muse trotted around the bases to the cheers of teammates, Slug and I lit out for the groundskeeper's gate and the weeds beyond. Our goal was to retrieve that home run ball, not as a souvenir for John Muse but to be put back in play. In 1942 baseballs were scarce.

So were professional baseball players. The war's manpower demands forced the Charlotte Hornets to disband after the 1942 season, but Griffith Park remained something of a summer home for Slug and me. In the days before Little League baseball, we bat-boyed for various high school, American Legion Junior, and all-star baseball teams. All were coached by the gentle, soft-spoken Joe Moody, a Charlotte fireman who for more than a decade was the arbiter of Charlotte's boyhood baseball and later a talent scout for the Cincinnati Reds and the St. Louis Cardinals. We were bat-boying at Griffith Park on the night a Moody-coached North Carolina high school all-star team played a similar team from South Carolina. Hamp Coleman, a tall, lean right-hander from Whiteville with an arm like a leather strap, struck out batters from a South Carolina all-star team with one whistling fastball after another.

We were also at Griffith Park the night a rag-tag bunting and base-running team from Shelby defeated a team from Oak Park, Illinois, to win the national championship of American Legion Junior Baseball. The Shelby victory extended the record of a Carolinas team winning the championship every five years, Greenville, South Carolina, in 1935; Albemarle, North Carolina, in 1940; and Shelby in 1945.

The American Legion Junior tournament matched teams from eight regions across the country, from Washington State to Arizona, from New Jersey to Florida, in a win-or-go-home series. People came from all over to fill the four-thousand-seat Griffith Park grandstand, overflowing temporary bleachers along the left and right field foul lines, and standing two and three deep at the base of the outfield fences, cordoned off by ropes. At the time, it was probably the biggest baseball event in Charlotte history, even though every year as major league teams worked their way north from spring training in Florida they stopped to play exhibition games in Charlotte.

When Shelby won, Slug and I rode the boisterous Shelby team bus uptown to the team's headquarters in the Selwyn Hotel, where a jubilant crowd filled the hotel lobby and spilled across Trade and Church Streets, singing in celebration, "Shelby will shine tonight, Shelby will shine..."

Over time we made friends with Griffith Park's grizzled Black-American groundskeeper Buster Sloan, who, according to Hornets general manager Phil Howser, could "grow grass on a battleship." Buster Sloan often let us in the field gate to watch Negro league games. His favorite player was Cool Poppa Bell, said to be a master at beating out bunts and stealing bases. According to Sloan, Poppa Bell was so fast he could turn out the light in his hotel room and be in the bed before the room was dark. After the war, Jackie Robinson came out of the Negro leagues to desegregate Major League Baseball (MLB), paving the way for dozens of other Black stars. Slug and I probably saw a lot of famous Black players who later made it to the major leagues, but we were unaware of them at the time.

As schoolboys we also had fun becoming Junior Commandos, a youth organization meant to mirror military teams operating behind enemy lines. By bringing to school wastepaper, used rubber, flattened tin cans, and other scrap metal, we could gain rank in the Commandos as sergeants or even lieutenants. Slug and I went door to door collecting salvage but made little progress until the Slugger mined a treasure.

When the water heater at our Elizabeth Avenue house was replaced, the old tank was left in the backyard. Long, round, and rusting, it weighed more than 150 pounds and, if we could get it to Elizabeth School, would greatly increase our standing in the Commandos. We tried lifting it but decided it was too heavy. Even so, one morning I looked out and there was Slug in the backyard, dressed for school and, with his foot, rolling that tank, one push at a time across the yard and toward the rear alley. When I offered help, he declined it, saying the idea was his and he intended to get full credit for it, ignoring the fact that technically the water tank was partly mine. I could have been angry but had to admire Slug's ingenuity and persistence. Slowly, painstakingly, with his feet he rolled the tank through the alley to Fox Street, down Fox to Park Drive, and up the hill to Elizabeth School, a distance of about five blocks. It took extraordinary effort and showed me, as if I needed further evidence, that my brother would use any means to outshine me. The rumble of his approach alerted classmates standing outside the school. They watched as he rolled that tank uphill toward the building where scrap metal was stored. He won a coveted Junior Commandos sweatshirt with a captain's rank and, like the competitor he was, wore it with pride.

"Not only had Slug and I grown, but so had Charlotte and the rest of the country— in ways that at that moment nobody quite understood."

CHAPTER

14

The Paths to Peace

As the war intensified, Slug and I watched other members of our household enter the military. Like millions of families across the country, we hung blue-star pennants in our front windows in tribute to their service. When our men entered combat zones, we lived in dread of receiving a War Department telegram saying, "We regret to inform you that..."

In 1942 Jack Stuart, our sister Phyllis's husband, entered the Navy, which taught him to catapult planes off ships and into flight. Uncle Bill Harton, Mother's reliable brother, joined the Army Air Corps as an airplane mechanic. Assigned to Sebring, Florida, he wrote urging Mother to let Harold sign up for the same program, saying it was safe, stateside duty. Otherwise, he warned, Harold might be drafted as cannon fodder.

Harold was eager to volunteer. As one after another of his neighborhood buddies entered the military, he pestered Mother to let him go too. He saw aircraft mechanics as a potential career, but Mother was not ready to give him up. Since our father's death, Harold had been her go-to guy and in recent years the family's principal breadwinner.

Over time, however, acknowledging that sooner or later he would be drafted, Mother relented. At age nineteen, Harold applied for the Air Corps mechanics' school at Sebring, Florida. The assignment turned out to be less safe than advertised. By 1943 the Air Corps was intensifying air raids over Germany and needed more mechanics, who doubled on bomber crews as gunners. Harold was assigned to a gunnery school and afterward joined a crew flying a four-engine bomber called a B-17. In addition to being a mechanic, he was a ball turret gunner, a perilous post with a high mortality rate. We made sure Mother did not know that or she would never have slept a wink.

His crew was assigned to Foggia, Italy, just north of Naples, to join the Eighth Air Force in bombing the Ploeste oil fields in Romania. As the main source of fuel for German tanks and planes, Ploeste was heavily fortified with anti-aircraft guns and swarming Messerschmidt fighter planes. Many US bomber crews didn't survive raids there.

After completing ten bombing missions, Harold's buddies warned him to consider himself dead, that his number would come up soon. That might have deterred others, but not the happy Harold. He wrote of scrambling through unheated B-17 fuselages awash in hydraulic fluids to get to his turret. Despite the dangers, he continued to have a portion of his monthly salary, including flight pay, sent home to Mother as his "military allotment."

Slug and I wondered what flying was like and how it felt to fire a .50-caliber machine gun. At the public library, we studied profiles of American planes and learned to distinguish B-17s from B-24s and B-25s. We vowed that when it came our turn to serve, we would join the Air Corps. We learned its theme song, "Off we go into the wild blue yonder, climbing high into the sun..."

As soon as Jack Stuart finished boot camp and was assigned to catapult training at Navy Pier in Chicago, our sister Phyllis, only twenty-three but encouraged by Mother, hurried to be with him. She got a secretarial job, learned to push and shove her way on and off elevated trains, and learned to endure Chicago's arctic winters. In chatty letters that Mother read aloud to us, she told of wearing a scarf over her mouth and cheeks "like a bank robber" to keep her face from freezing. Even so, she said, she often arrived at work with icicles in her eyebrows. Slug and I laughed at the image of our ninety-pound sister looking like a bank robber.

Much of the war news of 1942-43 was bad as the Germans and Japanese pressed their offensives. That was a source of worry for many of Mother's roomers whose husbands might soon be in combat areas. It was a scary time, but Mother tried to console them.

With roomers and boarders coming and going, Mother was making ends meet until health inspectors arrived. After looking over the kitchen and dining room, they said Mother needed to turn up the gas to produce hotter water and to install a double sink for washing dishes, pots, and pans. That would cost money Mother didn't have.

She wrote for help. Our sister Alice and her husband H.A. were in Wilmington, North Carolina, where H.A. worked in a shipyard. They sent twenty dollars. Phyllis and Jack Stuart also sent money, as did Bill Harton and Harold. Somehow Mother came up with the price and a double sink was installed. Slug and I regarded the whole affair as absurd, vowing that no double sink would improve the sanitation of *our* dish washing. For the Slugger, who later would run seventeen restaurants and cafeterias, it was his first brush with health inspectors.

It turned out those sanitation measures were not entirely foolish. All that winter and spring, Slug and I had been dogged by recurring sore throats and earaches. Mother took us to a doctor, who recommended that we have our tonsils removed. That was another expense Mother could not afford. Working through the city health department and county welfare agents, she arranged to have the surgeries done in the charity ward at Charlotte's three-year-old Memorial Hospital (later Carolinas Medical Center and now Atrium), where many of its four hundred beds were going unused.

My memory of our hospitalization is hazy, but both Slug and I underwent the procedure on the same morning. I remember having a mask placed over my face in preparation for an anesthetic. I didn't wake up until late in the afternoon when a nurse was feeding me ice and Mother was there to greet me. Slug was in the next bed. The two of us discovered that during the tonsillectomy we also had been circumcised. Our penises were bandaged and sore.

Everything went well until the middle of the night when I awoke gagging and coughing up blood. Two nurses appeared and began swabbing my throat and feeding me ice. Awakened by the commotion, other children in the ward sat up and stared, much to my unease. Soon a man in a white gown joined the nurses, and the three of them lifted me half naked onto a gurney and rolled me to a brightly lit room where they bathed my throat, sprayed it with foul medicine, and transfused me with a pint of blood. When they returned me to the ward, I slept the rest of the night. The hardy Slugger never woke up, leading him to brag that he was the more invincible.

When we were discharged the next morning, my mother was unable to pay for the pint of blood given me, so she gave the hospital a pint of her own.

In the spring of 1944 Harold completed his thirtieth bombing mission, enough to earn a trip home. He wrote Mother that he was coming but didn't say when—until he walked in on us one afternoon as Mother, Slug, and I were in the kitchen doing laundry. Suddenly, he appeared out of nowhere, dropped his olive-drab flight bag with a thud, and hugged each of us long and lovingly. Mother was immediately in tears. Looking at Slug and me, he asked, "What have you been feeding those two? When I left they were boys. Now they've grown up."

It was a relief to see him looking so vital, grinning and handsome, his garrison cap tilted on the back of his head and a spiffy Eisenhower jacket fastened snugly at his waist. His return reinforced our feeling that the war had turned in our favor. In Europe the Allies were preparing to invade France on D-Day, and in the Pacific the Marines were island-hopping toward Japan. After ten days he was gone, this time to Chanute Field, Illinois, to train on B-29s that might soon bomb Japan.

That fall I left Slugger behind and moved up to Piedmont Junior High eight blocks away. Its seventh grade included students from four other elementary schools, meaning I would know only a few of my classmates. I walked alone each morning and afternoon, deeply aware of Slug's absence. Each of us began building separate circles of friends, though at home we still shared chores, clothes, and sleeping arrangements.

I immediately discovered that junior high was more isolating than elementary school. At Elizabeth we spent the entire day as a unit—in the same room with the same teacher and classmates. In junior high we changed classes every hour, each of us moving separately from teacher to teacher. The old community was gone.

Meanwhile, vending at the armory and stadium was still profitable, but Slug and I wanted steadier incomes. We looked into carrying the morning *Observer* but found we had to be fourteen. Yet when the route for nearby East Fourth Street, from Hawthorne Lane to Thompson Orphanage, came open, I got it, though I was slightly underage. It meant getting up at a quarter to four in the morning to pick up the papers at four o'clock under the shelter of a service station three blocks away. With pliers I cut the wires that bound the bundles of paper and with a flashlight spent a few minutes scanning the front page for war news and the sports section for the latest scores.

The silence of the city at that eerie hour and shadows from streetlights created a sinister atmosphere. I often caught myself turning quickly to make sure nothing was moving in the darkness around me. As I entered the second half of my route, the sun rose and I felt safer. Walking along in daylight, throwing papers on porches, I read poems from a little book I carried. I skipped the serious stuff in favor of "Casey at the Bat," "The Shooting of Dan McGrew," and "The Cremation of Sam McGee," all of which contained marvelous words and memorable rhymes. What boy would not be enthralled by the lines, "… when out of the night which was sixty below and into the din and glare there stumbled a miner fresh from the creeks, dog dirty and loaded for bear"?

My subscribers included a number of notable Charlotteans. One had been my music teacher at Elizabeth School. Another was Neil Griffin, later a victim of polio who, from a wheelchair taught generations of Charlotte youngsters how to play all manner of musical instruments. Another became the city attorney. Still another was Harvard-educated Sydnor Thompson, later a partner in the Parker Poe law firm and an influential member of the city's power structure.

In walking my route, I met Jim Babb, a boy my age who lived in Dilworth and rode a dairy truck owned by the father of evangelist-to-be Billy Graham. Grasping a handle over his head and with his knees folded under his chin, Jim sat on a ledge at the back of the truck until it stopped to make deliveries. Then he'd run bottles of milk to customers' front doors and bring back the empties. On many mornings he traded me a half-pint of chocolate milk for a copy of the *Observer*. That turned into a lifelong friendship as both of us pursued careers in communications, Jim in broadcasting and I in newspapers.

About a year later Slug again one-upped me. He got the *Observer* route for Elizabeth Avenue with a tonier clientele. The route stretched six blocks downhill from Presbyterian Hospital to just past Central High. Every morning he picked up his papers under an awning at Douglas and Sing Mortuary, about halfway down Elizabeth Avenue. Frequently, as the *Observer* truck dropped off the bundled newspapers, its open rear door would knock the mortuary's awning askew, leaving the Slugger to console the aggrieved mortuary owner, former mayor Ben Douglas. They had many confrontations, but Slug, being Slug, managed to keep their relations cordial. The ex-mayor became one of Slug's fans, and in time I became an admirer of him as one of Charlotte's best mayors.

Slug's route included many wealthy subscribers—bankers, lawyers, doctors, architects—who gave him generous tips at Christmas. His route provided one memorable experience for us in introducing us to the Charles Candy Company, a tiny little store snuggled under the rear corner of a big white house near the western end of Slug's route. Despite sugar rationing, Mr. Charles often had Hershey bars, Milky Ways, and Juicy Fruit gum when other outlets didn't. If we were anywhere near that big white house, Slug and I stopped to check the Charles candy counter. We dropped by there on April 12, 1945, and heard a radio news bulletin that President Roosevelt had died of a brain hemorrhage in Warm Springs, Georgia. We were stunned. It was hard to believe. He had just been sworn in for a fourth term as president. We asked ourselves, How could the man who had lifted the nation from the Great Depression and led it through a terrible war be dead? Slug and I had never known any other president. We rushed home to share the news with Mother and found her and the rest of the family already in tears.

A day later, when the train bearing Roosevelt's body was scheduled to pass through Charlotte, we joined thousands of others lining the Southern Railway tracks serving the passenger terminal on West Trade Street. We got there at dusk, but a large crowd had already gathered, and more people were arriving by the minute. Police and National Guardsmen were spaced along the tracks to keep the crowd in order, but they were hardly needed. The throng was quiet and respectful. People talked in low murmurs. Farther south, lining an embankment beyond the terminal, we could hear the faint voices of a cluster of Blacks softly singing "Swing Low, Sweet Chariot."

It was dark and muggy when far down the tracks to the south the headlight of a locomotive swung around a curve and beamed over the gathering. Suddenly, stillness fell over everything. You could hear the National Guard commander order his troops, "Present arms!" and the sharp slap of leather as soldiers swung their rifles to an upright position chest high. As the train slowly passed, not a sound was heard except the squeak of steel wheels and the groan of wooden ties as the heavy cars rolled over them. When the lighted coach bearing the president's flag-draped bier passed, we could see uniformed servicemen standing at each corner of the casket. The whole scene was deeply moving and inexpressibly sad.

Three weeks later, on May 7, 1945, that sadness was replaced by joy. All students at my junior high were summoned to the auditorium. The principal, a young man with the Germanic name Otto Dahlem, announced that Germany had surrendered, ending the war in Europe. The huge room erupted in squeals and applause. A decade of fear and barbarism had ended in Europe. Now the United States could pour its full might into defeating Japan.

Late that summer Americans were reading astonishing war news. The United States had dropped a secret weapon—an atomic bomb, whatever that was—that had destroyed the entire city of Hiroshima. Three days later the United States dropped a similar bomb that obliterated Nagasaki. Unless Japan surrendered, the United States threatened to drop more. Newspapers carried stories suggesting that Japanese warlords were suing for peace. The whole world waited in wonder: would the outcome be an armistice or Armageddon?

I was attending a movie uptown when news of the Japanese surrender came. From the back of the theater somebody shouted, "The WAR's over!" Instantly people from all over town rushed into the streets, climbed light poles, clambered atop buses, hoisted flags, danced, cheered, blew horns, hugged, and gave thanks. It had been a long, frightening four years since December 7, 1941. Not only had Slug and I grown, but so had Charlotte and the rest of the country—in ways that at that moment nobody quite understood.

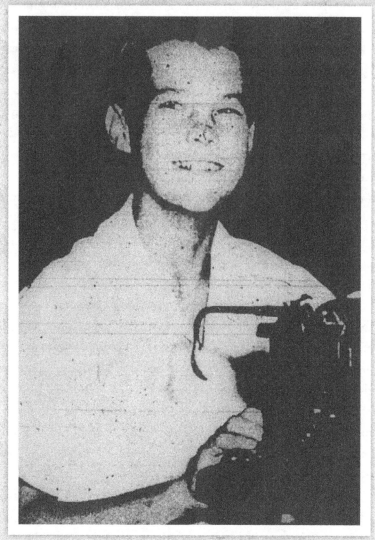

Jack at fourteen, the sportswriting winner

CHAPTER

15

Unexpected Prizes

The end of World War II brought optimism and accelerating activity to every corner of the country and especially to Charlotte. Almost overnight the city's pace quickened. Newspapers trumpeted plans for new subdivisions, new industries, new business ventures. Slug and I watched in boyish wonder as the city rushed to become something bigger, more celebrated, more sophisticated. Along the way also came surprising, life-changing opportunities.

The wealthiest subscriber on my *Observer* route was Robert Lassiter, a lawyer who lived in a big white house with grounds covering an entire block of East Fourth Street from Baldwin to Lillington Avenues. Lassiter paid his *Observer* subscription by mail, so I had never seen him or seen anyone around his houses. But I had seen the swimming pool nestled among the hedges lining his backyard. One warm spring morning, after delivering the heavy Sunday papers, Slug suggested that we climb the fence behind the Lassiter house, slip out of our clothes, and play in the swimming pool.

As we paddled about, a pair of brown shoes suddenly appeared at the pool's edge. They were worn by a tall man with an aggrieved look. He gathered our clothes into a pile in front of him and ordered us out of the water. As we stood dripping before him, he told us we were trespassing, which was not only an invasion of his privacy but also against the law. He lectured us on the dangers of swimming without a lifeguard. If anything had happened to us, he said, *he* would have been liable, and he didn't like that. He took our names and addresses and said he would consider our punishment. Then he let us reclaim our clothes and sent us away.

For the next few weeks Slug and I worried over what might happen. We dared not say anything to Mother. Nor could we say anything to Harold, whose job at Lassiter Press, we feared, might be in jeopardy. Lassiter Press was owned by Hanes Lassiter, a brother to Robert. We kept an eye out for police cars, hoping none would stop in front of our house. Finally, the mail brought an envelope containing two YMCA memberships and a note that said, "Here's a place to swim safely in all kinds of weather." It was signed "Robert Lassiter."

Years later, as a reporter and editor at the *Observer*, I learned more about Robert Lassiter. He had been educated at Woodberry Forest, then at Yale, where he was captain of the football team. After graduation he studied at Cambridge University in England, then returned to enter the Harvard Law School and also learned to fly airplanes, often for commercial airlines. After law school he returned to Charlotte to practice law with Claude Cochrane and Frank McClenighan. When World War II broke out, he joined the Navy as a flight instructor at the Pensacola Naval Air Station. After the war he again returned to Charlotte to join Harvard classmate William Van Allen in forming Lassiter, Moore, and Van Allen, one of Charlotte's premier law firms.

As an outspoken advocate for the airport and later for UNC Charlotte, Robert Lassiter was among a cadre of young men who came after the war to help Charlotte fulfill its ambitions. Others included John Belk, who ran the Belk department store empire and served six years as mayor; Pat Hall, the textile machinery merchant who helped to found Arrowood Industrial Park and a theme park named Carowinds that made Charlotte a tourist destination; Bill Lee, the grandson of a Duke Power founder, who engineered the Cowans Ford Dam that created Lake Norman as a residential and recreational playground that ignited growth in the towns of Huntersville, Cornelius, and Davidson in the northern corner of Mecklenburg County; and Cliff Cameron, a real estate developer who came from Raleigh to take over First Union National

Bank and turn it into a financial powerhouse. Cameron was succeeded in that expansionist zeal by Ed Crutchfield.

After the war, several new enterprises sprang up in our neighborhood. A bottling plant for TruAde soda, a lawn-care shop featuring Toro gasoline-powered mowers, and a Lay's potato chip kitchen were established within two blocks of our house. Slug and I discovered that when trucks dumped raw potatoes down a chute into the Lay's basement, we could gather those that spilled over the chute's edge and take them to the family larder. Also new to the neighborhood were an ice cream parlor, a grocery store, a launderette, a fur storage house, and a variety of medical offices, including a veterinary clinic that offered us after-school and weekend employment. We washed and curried dogs, held cats during spaying, cleaned cages, and even witnessed the autopsy of a large German shepherd.

Best of all, the rush of World War II veterans seeking education under the GI Bill of Rights forced the creation of after-hours junior colleges—the Charlotte Center of the University of North Carolina (CCUNC) for Whites with night classes in Central High buildings and Carver College for Blacks with night classes in Second Ward High School. Slug and I met the CCUNC director, Charles Bernard, a soft-spoken, red-haired graduate student from Chapel Hill. He was busy hiring part-time faculty—Harry Golden to teach Shakespeare; *Charlotte News* editor C.A. "Pete" McKnight to teach Spanish, and Bonnie Cone, an indomitable Central High teacher to teach all levels of mathematics. Three years later, as the enrollment crunch eased and Charles Bernard returned to Chapel Hill, Charlotte wouldn't let the fledgling CCUNC die. A determined Bonnie Cone succeeded Bernard as the school's director and persuaded Charlotteans to tax themselves to support both CCUNC and Carver College. The CCUNC became Charlotte College, a doorway to higher education for students who couldn't afford to go away to school. Carver College was later melded into Central Piedmont Community College.

The CCUNC fulfilled an old Charlotte ambition—to host a public college. In the 1880s Charlotte had offered an attractive site on undeveloped land off what is now the Plaza for what became NC State, but Raleigh won that bid. In the 1930s Charlotte tried mightily to attract the second two years of the UNC medical school, but that plumb went to Chapel Hill instead.

Though Slug and I had watched Central High athletes win scholarships to major universities and hoped we might do the same, we looked on Charlotte College as a fallback option. We got to know Bonnie Cone and cheered the school's early athletic teams, known as the Owls because they went to school at night. Who could forget the football team's star running back named "Goat" Davis, who never learned the designated plays but still ran with abandon.

Elsewhere in town the end of rationing fueled a frenzy of buying and selling as Charlotteans rushed to relieve five years of pent-up demand for clothes, shoes, cars, appliances, and especially housing. Men and women coming home from the armed forces or work in defense plants looked for a place to live in a city that had built few houses since 1940. Our family typified the housing crunch. Our brother Harold, our sister Phyllis, her husband Jack Stuart, and our uncle Jimmy Harton returned from the war looking to Mother for lodging. Somehow she squeezed all of us into the Elizabeth Avenue house with four bedrooms and two baths, though Phyllis and Jack had a new baby and Jimmy Harton had a wife. Elsewhere people were converting all kinds of structures into makeshift shelters.

In response to the upsurge, city officials began expanding and modernizing public services. Charlotte established its first Planning Commission and Zoning Board. The Chamber of Commerce hired its first economic development officer. Business leaders organized the Charlotte City Club that turned the upper floors of what had been the Buford Hotel, an 1880s show place at Fourth and Tryon Streets, into a sanctum in which to dine, discuss business, and privately hatch plans for civic and political ventures. It was at that moment, Ben Douglas later said, that Charlotteans realized they had a chance to build a significant city.

Amid the bustle, comedy often accompanied the progressive spirit. The Junior Chamber of Commerce, comprised of go-getter young men anxious to do good works in the community, began staging an annual fundraising minstrel show before packed houses in the armory. Called the Jaycee Jollies, the show featured end men Jimmy Shoemaker and Henry Swanzey, both of whom led important businesses in the city. Shoemaker was head of the shoe department at Belk's and Swanzey ran a regional dental laboratory. They danced and sang risqué songs and often made fun of local politicians. Slug and I didn't always understand the jokes, but we enjoyed the laughter and never missed a performance.

Some of the comedy occurred at our front door. One night shortly after Harold's return from the Air Corps, he and a group of neighborhood buddies went on a toot that lasted into the wee hours. It was nearly three in the morning when a car pulled up at the curb to let Harold out. As he exited the car's street-side rear door, there was a gasp followed by an unmistakable thud as a brown paper bag containing a bottle of whiskey hit the pavement and shattered. Harold uttered an oath as the liquor spread like ink over the black asphalt. At the time, whiskey was hard to get in Charlotte. The nearest liquor stores were in South Carolina. (Charlotte didn't get legal liquor stores until September 1947.)

Mother, who was always semi-awake until Harold was safely under her roof, heard the commotion, scrambled into a bathrobe, and flew to the front door. From the porch she called, "Is that you, Harold?"

"Yes, Mom," Harold said.

"Harold, are you drunk?" she asked.

"Yes, Mom," he said.

"Well, come in as soon as you can," she said.

Still mourning the loss of the precious whiskey, the teetering Harold didn't move fast enough. A police car pulled up beside him. A patrolman got out and shined his flashlight on Harold and his companions. Mother ran to the hall stairwell and called for Jack Stuart to come quickly, lest Harold be hauled off to jail. Jack threw on some clothes and, sensing the need for a delicate intervention, came down wearing his most diplomatic manner and most soothing voice. He scurried to the street.

"Good morning, officer. Is there anything I can do to help?" he asked.

He explained that Harold was his brother-in-law, just back from bombing Germans in Europe and training to bomb the Japanese. Harold and his fellow returning GIs, he said, had been enjoying a welcome-home party that was just breaking up. "If you'll let me, I'll take him inside to get him off the street and out of danger," he said.

The officer hesitated, looked appraisingly at Jack Stuart, considered the situation, and grudgingly assented. Harold was led inside, safe from an arrest and an expensive court appearance.

Sleeping on a rollaway cot in the same room as our mother, Slug and I watched from a window and heard most of that. Though the incident was funny, it was also serious. We shared the feeling of relief when Harold was safely inside. To us, he was more than a war hero; he was a family treasure—as he would soon again demonstrate.

The housing shortage spurred sudden spikes in Charlotte real estate values. The woman who owned our Elizabeth Avenue house offered Mother a chance to buy it at an inflated price or pay an exorbitant rent. Mother could afford neither. As he had in other crises, the twenty-two-year-old Harold stepped up with a solution. A smaller house around the corner was for sale at a price he could afford on the GI Bill, a post-war government program for veterans. Its loans required no down payment and low interest. In buying the house Harold could lift the Claibornes up another rung on the socio-economic ladder. For the first time in fifteen years, we would again be buying instead of renting. The smaller house would put Mother out of the boarding-house business, but that was one of Harold's goals. He wanted to lighten her load, he said.

The brown, one-story house at 214 North Cecil Street stood directly across from the Central High gymnasium, a plus for the Slugger and me. Central High had just hired a new, promotion-minded football coach whom the Slugger and I were eager to meet. Further, the Cecil Street house was heated by an oil furnace, which meant we could at last put aside our coal shovels and ash cans. The move also meant our family could enjoy a measure of intimacy without the intrusion of roomers and boarders.

Shortly after our move to Cecil Street, Mother asked Harold to make sure Slug and I, approaching ages fourteen and thirteen, knew the facts of life. Harold called us aside and asked, a little sheepishly, if we knew about "the birds and the bees."

Slug frowned. "You mean sex?" he asked.

Harold laughed and said, "Yes."

With a you've-got-to-be-kidding look, Slug said, "After all we've seen in cars around the USO Club and in the bushes behind Central High, we'd be pretty dumb if we didn't."

A relieved Harold nodded, lowered his voice, and said, conspiratorially, "In that case, my word to you is keep it in your pants. Do you hear me?"

Slug and I answered affirmatively, and Harold went away. Having seen Harold woo various women in the neighborhood, Slug said with a chuckle, "*He's* the one who needs to keep it in his pants."

At the time, sex was of minor importance to us. We were more interested in Central High's new, high-energy football coach. He was from Albuquerque, New Mexico, and symbolized the post-war mobility of Americans in moving to distant parts of the country. His name was Bill Brannin, a big, bluff redhead with a gap-toothed grin and an air of great confidence. He had played college football, trained as an Olympic boxer, and served in the Army as a physical fitness officer. For the next six years he became an important influence on our lives. Slug and I met him on his first visit to the school gymnasium. He was still wearing his Army dress uniform with silver captain's bars on his shoulders. We quickly became his errand boys and from him learned not only about football but also about ginning up excitement.

One of his first promotional moves was to have painted on a ten-square-foot canvas in vibrant yellow, brown, and black colors the face of a snarling wildcat, the Central High mascot. On game nights, that canvas was suspended from a wooden frame at the open end of Memorial Stadium. Each time Central High players took the field, its players came plunging out of that wildcat's mouth, a menacing sight for the opposition and an exciting experience for Charlotte-area football fans. It was but a sample of the verve that Bill Brannin brought to the Charlotte sports scene. No matter whether his teams won or lost, they did so with swagger and style.

When Central High's pre-season football practice began in August, Slug and I attended the fitness drills at seven in the morning, the skull sessions in the gym at eleven, and the scrimmages on the practice field at four in the afternoon. We learned to make ourselves useful—wrapping players' ankles to prevent injury, applying Benzoin to toughen players' skin before applying adhesive tape, dispensing salt pills before scrimmages, and snapping open ammonia capsules to revive those left woozy from hard contact.

In those days, high school football was a big attraction in town, and for Charlotte boosters, Bill Brannin was their kind of coach. To boost attendance—and enhance Charlotte's standing as a rising city—he scheduled games against big-name schools in Louisville, Atlanta, and Miami. He even brought in an opponent from Mexico City for a Saturday afternoon game preceded by a noisy, Latino-themed parade through the city. Under his leadership, Central High teams that had been drawing about five thousand fans for home games began playing before crowds of ten thousand or more.

That fall the Slugger entered junior high and joined me in walking to and from school, but that didn't close the gap in our relations. He quickly became a favorite among his new classmates and a leader on the playground. As I struggled to diagram sentences and solve math problems, I felt obscured by his popularity.

With the assistance of our sister Anne, we both learned to dance. The wartime USO center in the armory's basement had become a teenage canteen where Slug and I began showing an interest in girls. Anne showed us how to ask them to dance, how to escort them to the dance floor, how to hold and talk to them, and how to escort them back to their seats.

In 1946 new cars, which had not been produced during the war, again began rolling off assembly lines. Billboards, newspapers, and magazines bore photos of sparkling new models trimmed in dazzling chrome, creating a car culture that brought dramatic change to the country. Charlotte and state officials hurried to draft plans for new and wider roads to accommodate increased traffic. Charlotte hired its first traffic engineer, a grinning, fast-talking Hoosier named Herman Hoose. At high-traffic intersections he put in traffic circles known as roundabouts and turn-lane barriers that won him the nickname "Thousand Island" Hoose.

During the war, a new corridor known as Kings Drive had been slashed through the woods along the eastern bank of Sugar Creek, creating a link between East Morehead and Queens Road West. Now lined with towering willow oaks and two-story houses, it was then a barren concrete ribbon that invited racing among high school boys testing their fathers' fast new cars. With the increase in cars came a profusion of drive-ins—drive-in movies, drive-in banks, drive-in restaurants, drive-in lodgings such as Holiday Inns, popularly called motels.

When I learned that a drive-in ice cream shop was opening at the corner of Kings Drive and East Morehead, I borrowed a bicycle and rode over to apply for a job as a curb hop. The work was from four in the afternoon until midnight and would pay a dollar a day plus tips. At age fourteen, I got one of the jobs. Wedged between Sugar Creek and Kings Drive, the ice cream shop enjoyed a steady flow of traffic. I learned the curb-service routine, memorized the flavors of ice cream available, and when my sale was ended would say, "Come back and call for Jack."

Among my repeat customers was Hugh Ashcraft, a Charlotte native who became famous as a World War II pilot by limping his damaged bomber over the English Channel and warning air traffic controllers he was "coming in on a wing and a prayer." The phrase became the title for a popular song. In his stops at the ice cream shop, he drove a sturdier vehicle, a green Studebaker sedan that looked the same from behind as it did from the front.

Soon I was bringing home fifteen to twenty dollars a week, good pay even for an adult in the mid-1940s when the federal minimum wage was forty cents an hour. I quickly gave up my *Observer* route and stopped getting up at a quarter to four in the morning. Later that summer when a new drive-in ice cream shop called Charlotte Maid opened within a block of our house, Slug and I both got curb-hop jobs there. Soon each of us was bringing home about twenty dollars a week. I opened a savings account at American Trust Company, later to become a cornerstone of Bank of America.

I soon needed those savings. That summer the *Charlotte News* renewed its "My Favorite Hornet" sportswriting contest, offering the teenage winner a ten-day road trip with the Charlotte Hornets baseball team and the chance to write a daily story for the *News*. The Hornets had disbanded during the war, but when they resumed play in 1946, Slug and I and Uncle Jimmy Harton often went to Griffith Pak to see them play. Uncle Jimmy, who earlier had encouraged me to read books and use big words, insisted that I enter the sportswriting contest.

Entering required my writing a three-hundred-word essay about my favorite Hornet, first baseman Carl Miller, who, like most of his teammates, was a war veteran taking a last longing look at restoring the skills that had melted away during the war and testing his chances of making it to the big leagues. In joining the team late in the spring, Miller was heralded as a home-run threat but proved instead to be a team player hitting about .250 but driving in runs with timely singles and doubles, a point my essay emphasized. I signed my piece "Jack E. Claiborne."

I wasn't especially proud of my entry and had entered only to end Jimmy Harton's needling about it. I was startled a week or so later when Furman Bisher, then a writer for the *Charlotte News* and later a renowned columnist for the *Atlanta Constitution,* phoned to say I had won. Bisher invited me to the *News* offices to be interviewed and photographed. He referred to me as "Jackie Claiborne."

In gathering information for a story about the contest, Bisher told me the boy who finished second was a thirteen-year-old named Charles Kuralt, whose father was director of the Mecklenburg County Welfare Department. Charles was an especially gifted boy destined for fame as a writer and broadcaster but was snakebit in the *News* sportswriting contest. He entered the competition again the next year and again finished second. I got to know Charles when we both attended Central High and he won a national "I Speak for Democracy" contest. He was always approachable and not at all impressed by his talent. He inherited his bottom-of-the-rainbarrel voice and a mine of incidental information from his influential father.

A good example of his father's impact occurred one Sunday afternoon during our high school days when a group of us were at the Kuralts' Sharon Road home, eating grapes under a scuppernong arbor. Charles's mustachioed father came out in shirtsleeves to quiz us. "You guys are so smart," he said. "Do you know what keeps an airplane up?"

Our guesses flew fast and furious: "The propeller." "The engines." "The tail." "The wind under the wings." At each answer, Mr. Kuralt shook his head in the negative.

Finally, he told us: "It's the wind going *over* the wings." The wings are curved downward, he said, gesturing with his hands. The wind passing over them creates a vacuum on their upper surface. Because nature abhors a vacuum, the wings rise to fill the void, and that keeps the airplane up. That explained the aeronautics I had wondered about since those Sunday afternoon trips to Douglas Airport in Mr. Harkey's Terraplane. For years afterward, whenever a plane I was aboard hit bumpy air, I would remind myself, "Nature abhors a vacuum," and feel secure.

Charles and I continued our friendship at the university at Chapel Hill, where he edited the campus newspaper, the *Daily Tar Heel*. Afterward, he won prizes as a reporter and features writer for the *Charlotte News* and went on to national fame as a broadcaster at CBS.

My winning the *Charlotte News* sportswriting contest upset my mother, who frowned at the idea of my not working for ten days and having to dip into savings to buy summer clothes for the ten-day road trip. She thought I should wait until fall to buy clothes I could wear during the school year. She also disparaged my desire to write for newspapers. Like many people, she had the motion-picture image of newspapermen as drunks, ne'er-do-wells, and skirt chasers.

On the night the *News* announced the contest results, I was invited to a Hornets game at Griffith Park and took the Slugger with me. Photographers took a picture of me with first baseman Miller and another with the Slugger. During the game, J. B. Clark, the WAYS radio announcer who called the play-by-play of Hornets games, invited me to his broadcast booth and asked me to describe the action for an inning or two. I had heard many radio broadcasts of baseball games but hardly knew how to begin. With time I gained confidence and soon was uttering every baseball cliché I'd ever heard.

That evening was one of the few times the Slugger regarded me with anything approaching awe. I loved it. That feeling was magnified the next day when a photo of us appeared in the *News* and the caption identified him as "Slub."

The Hornets' ten-day road trip began at Griffith Park, where I joined the team on a chartered bus bound for a four-game series in Spartanburg, South Carolina, and another four-game series at Asheville, North Carolina. Phil Howser, the Hornets' florid-faced general manager who talked breathlessly, as if he had just run up a flight of stairs, gave me an envelope containing the same amount of meal money he gave each Hornet player. He asked whether I wanted to watch the games from the press box or the players' dugout. When I chose to be with the players, he said that would require my wearing a uniform. The bus's departure was delayed until Howser could find a uniform small enough to fit me.

My seatmate on the team bus was always Carl Miller, but my caretaker was Chappie Johnson, the team's Black trainer, a distinguished man with graying hair and impeccable manners. For part of the trip Chappie and I shared a hotel room. At the time, that didn't seem strange, but in retrospect I thought it remarkable that in the days of strict segregation, White hotels in the Carolinas would accommodate a Black trainer traveling with an all-White baseball team. That was a tribute to Chappie Johnson, who was also an athletic trainer at what was then Clemson College. In manner he was patient, kind, and philosophical. Though we shared a hotel room, he was not allowed to eat with us in restaurants. Even as a fourteen-year-old, that bothered me. Having grown up in a segregated society, I hadn't thought much about the racial barriers, but Chappie's exclusion from our meals seemed unfair and impolite, like a slap in his face.

In Spartanburg, one of the players' favorite stops for meals was an Italian diner that served something called "pizza pie," which I had never heard of. Pizza might be as old as Homer's *Odyssey*, but it was not widely available in the South until after World War II, when service men encountered it in other parts of the country. At the urging of Carl Miller, I tried it and, like millions of other Americans, became a pizza fan.

During the ten-day road trip, I was too busy adjusting to hotel living, talking to players, and going to games to be homesick. But on a Sunday in Asheville, where blue laws prohibited Sunday movies, sports events, or anything else to compete with church services, most of the players, including Carl Miller and Chappie Johnson, left for a day off. I felt lonely and amused myself by buying plump peaches from a street vendor and eating them at the railroad depot as I watched passenger trains come and go. In the mid-'40s, long before the coming of interstate highways, most intercity travel was by bus or passenger train. Many of the trains were still pulled by steam engines.

I had no trouble finding material for my daily stories. They appeared in the *News* under the heading "Jackie's Junket." I wrote them in longhand and took them to the Western Union office. I had never sent a telegram before, but I loved plunking down my copy and saying, "Send this night press rate collect, please." I knew then that I wanted to be a newspaper writer, no matter what Mother said.

Two years later, Slug entered the same sportswriting contest. He told *News* sportswriters that he entered because I had "talked so much about the trip" he wanted to see if it was true. He vowed that I hadn't given him any help in writing his entry, which was true. His favorite Hornet was an outfielder recently graduated from UNC at Chapel Hill, but his essay finished second to that of a girl. She had signed her entry "Lee Simmons," and *News* sportswriters didn't know until she answered the telephone that "Lee" was a female. *News* editors decided they couldn't send a teenage girl on a road trip with randy baseball players, so they awarded her a season pass to all Hornets games and sent the Slugger instead. His daily dispatches appeared in the *News* under the heading "Slug at Bat" but by then the Hornets were a different team. Seeing his words in print did little for the Slugger, who preferred being a performer rather than a reporter, though I always thought with his gift for making people talk he would have made an excellent newsman.

Jack with J. B. Clark

CHAPTER

16

Finding Jobs

After winning the sportswriting contest, I entered the ninth grade as something of a celebrity but couldn't take advantage of it. On the first day of classes, my homeroom teacher, a young woman fresh out of UNC Chapel Hill, asked me to stand and talk about traveling with a baseball team and writing a newspaper story every day.

It was an impromptu opportunity that Slug, who never saw a stage he didn't like, could have exploited with charm and humor. For me it was torture. My hands shook, my tongue thickened, and I couldn't find the wanted words. I stumbled through a painful two-minute talk and sat down, assured that any distinction I had earned in winning the sportswriting competition had just been squandered.

At the same time, the Slugger was making a name for himself. He entered the eighth grade as a starter on three sports teams and built a wide following. Our relations, once easy and candid, were increasingly guarded. We still wore each other's clothes but quarreled frequently over who was going to wear which shirt or sweater on what day.

My sportswriting plaudits won me a prominent place in the school newspaper and probably contributed to my appointment as captain of the school's basketball team. While I looked good in pregame drills, I proved to be a weak defender and poor scorer and was relegated to a seat on the bench.

Beyond athletics, I enjoyed the ninth grade and pursued a college-preparatory course. That required me to take an introduction to algebra under Miss Julia McCrae, a tough teacher who compared doing math to laying bricks—every step had to be firmly in place before moving to the next. I also took a course in typing, which prepared me for a career in front of keyboards.

As teenagers, Slug and I began paying attention to girls. Without a car available, we walked or bused our dates to movies or putt-putt golf courses or the corner for a Tasty Freeze ice cream. Often we escorted our favorite dance partners home from the teenage canteen in the old USO center under the armory. One night, to impress my dance partner, I walked her more than a mile from the armory to the Wilder Building at Third and Tryon Streets, two blocks from midtown. There we took an elevator to the tenth-floor studios of WBT radio where disc jockey Kurt Webster, Charlotte's self-proclaimed "night mayor," was playing records. We danced, spoke briefly with Kurt Webster, heard our names spoken over the air, and then walked home. It was something few teenagers dared, but my dance partner seemed unimpressed. She denied me a good-night kiss.

Slug's first dates were with JoAnn Bailey, a pretty brunette and a popular eighth-grade classmate. Like Slug, she was a good dancer. She lived on The Plaza, within walking distance of our house. Slug called at her home so often that her mother began inviting him to Sunday dinner. JoAnn's parents were stoic and formal and not sure what to make of her loquacious boyfriend. Instinctively, JoAnn knew he was special. She admired his vitality, warmth, and optimism. Theirs was a budding romance.

A more serious romance was blossoming at home. Our brother Harold was engaged to marry Maria Therese Flynt, known as Tere (pronounced "Terry"). She was a glamorous blonde he had met when both attended Central High. After Harold's Air Corps discharge, they met on an uptown street corner. Harold got her phone number and began seeing her. Within a year they were making plans to marry.

Slug and I endorsed Harold's choice, but our mother had doubts. Tere was Catholic and came from a worldly, well-to-do Myers Park family. Her great grandfather, Dr. Manuel Amador, was the first president of Panama. Her grandfather, Felix Ehrman, was the US vice-consul to Panama at the time of the Panamanian Revolution. Her father, a New Englander, had soldiered in World War I and after the 1918 armistice met Tere's mother while visiting Paris.

Coming from a deprived rural culture, our mother worried that Harold might be marrying "above his raisings." After meeting Tere and experiencing her generous spirit, Mother changed her mind. Workmen soon were adding a kitchen, bath, and bedroom to the rear of the house as an apartment for Harold and his bride.

Attending their wedding required Slug and me to wear coats and ties. Together we went uptown and with our own money shopped in men's stores rather than boys' departments. We selected matching outfits—white, oxford-cloth shirts, brown trousers, and tan blazers. Each of us bought brown ties with gold stripes and brown penny-loafers. Never had we felt so grown up.

The wedding, a happy, inclusive celebration, became the grandest social event in our family's memory. Alice and Phyllis were there with their husbands. Our sister Anne served as a bridesmaid. After the ceremony in St. Patrick's Cathedral, we attended a relaxed reception in the Flynt home on Westfield Road. Our mother took her place in the receiving line with Harold and Tere, Mr. and Mrs. Flynt, and other members of the wedding party. At first, she seemed a little self-conscious in a cobalt blue suit she had made herself, a matching, broad-brimmed, straw hat that she wore slanted across her head, and chunky blue shoes. But the woman who had entertained more than a hundred people in celebrating her twelfth wedding anniversary, who had welcomed dozens of boarders and comforted streams of roomers, seemed to be equally adept in greeting that cheerful crowd.

Harold made mortgage payments on the Cecil Street house but stopped contributing to our household expenses. That required Mother, our sister Anne, and Slug and me to earn more money. Mother went to work as a fitter of women's foundation garments. Our sister Anne, a senior at Central High, became a receptionist in a dental office. I got a job at a dairy bar and came home nightly with sticky elbows from dipping deeply into tubs of ice cream.

Slug got a Friday-Saturday job providing curb service for a nearby dry cleaner owned by the restless, cigar-chomping Zeke Stinson. Slug and Zeke were like twins. Each had crew-cut hair and a magnetic personality. Slug met cars at the curb, took in dirty clothes, and delivered clean ones. As each car rolled up, Zeke would chomp on his cigar and say, "Go get 'em, Slugger."

In seeking a more promising job than dipping ice cream, I learned that Curtis Johnson, publisher of the *Charlotte Observer*, often hired boys with initiative and encouraged them to work their way up in his organization. Since buying the *Observer* in 1916, Johnson had built it into the largest newspaper in the Carolinas, one that made Charlotte the marketplace for much of the two states. Going to ask him for a job was a daring move. Summoning my courage, I dressed in the clothes I had worn to Harold's wedding and went to the newspaper offices, then in a slim, three-story structure wedged against the sidewalk at Stonewall and Tryon Streets, six blocks from midtown. I climbed the stairs to Johnson's office and met his secretary, a lovely woman with a kind face, a warm smile, and a melodious Southern accent. Later I learned she was Eudora Garrison, wife of the *Observer* sports editor. She asked for my name and the purpose of my visit. I said I had heard there was an opening for a boy with initiative, perhaps running copy or filing engravings.

She smiled, went into Mr. Johnson's office, and returned saying he would see me in a few minutes. I took a seat, nervously rehearsed what I would say, and soon was shown into Mr. Johnson's sanctum, a long sliver of an office, with Mr. Johnson's desk at the far end, giving him plenty of time to look me over as I approached.

He was a short, stout man with a large, bald head and a perpetual frown. He wore a three-piece suit with a dusting of cigarette ash on the vest. When I finally stood in front of him, he didn't wait for me to recite my spiel but asked, "How old are you, son?"

When I told him I was fifteen, he rose from his chair, came around the desk and, with an arm on my shoulder, began walking me back to the door. "I'm sorry," he said in a rich baritone, "but in the eyes of the law, this is a manufacturing establishment, and child-labor restrictions won't let me hire anyone who is not sixteen. Come back in a year or so and maybe I'll have something for you."

I left more relieved than disappointed. Confronting Curtis Johnson had been intimidating. After meeting him, I wasn't sure I wanted to work within his purview. I told myself there had to be easier ways to get into the newspaper business.

That spring Slug and I went up and down Elizabeth Avenue looking for summer employment. Each of us inquired at the newly opened Mercury Sandwich Shop, one of many new businesses in the neighborhood. The Mercury was a small diner run by the Anderson brothers, Bill, Jimmy, and Pete, Greeks newly discharged from the Army. That was long before fast-food chains like McDonald's or Burger King, but the name Mercury implied fast service. It was the launching of what would become a Charlotte landmark.

The Anderson brothers told me they didn't need help but suggested that when business improved, they might. At the end of the school year, Slug hitchhiked to Myrtle Beach and got a job washing dishes (he called it "pearl diving"). I went back to the Mercury Sandwich Shop and was hired as a waiter and soda jerk. To get the job at age fifteen, I had to survive separate interviews with each of the Anderson brothers and get a work permit and a Social Security card. My hours would be from three in the afternoon until eleven at night.

Working with the Andersons proved to be fun as well as a learning experience. Each of the brothers had a different personality and a separate slant on how to run the diner. Curly-haired Jimmy looked like the boxer Rocky Graziano but was friendly, even-tempered, and all business. Bulky, broad-shouldered Pete was laid back, talkative, and funny. He conjured up new items for the menu, only to have his brothers reject most of them. Bill, the oldest, was quick, explosive, and ambitious. During breaks in business he would sit at the counter, drink coffee, and on paper napkins draw logos for a chain of Mercury Sandwich Shops he envisioned opening across the country.

I learned to make coffee by the urn, iced tea by the gallon, and simple syrup by the quart. In time I also mastered the secrets of grilling hamburgers, scrambling eggs, and making pots of creamy grits. I also picked up cooking tips—add a pinch of salt to the grounds to give coffee a robust flavor, start grits in cold, salted water and stir constantly to make them soft and creamy, and add a dab of horseradish to tuna salad to give it extra zip.

When Slug came home from the beach and found I had taken the diner job, he went across the street to the Hawthorne Barbershop where he once had delivered papers and began shining shoes. The shop was the last tonsorial parlor between uptown and the mansions of Myers Park and Eastover. Though it served many of the city's corporate sachems, they didn't faze the Slugger. His quick wit and lively banter brought in customers and increased tips. Barbers lunching at the Mercury often would report, "Your brother's rolling 'em in the aisles across the street."

The Mercury Sandwich Shop was a tightly configured place with ten stools at the counter and four booths along the window front. Customers were so close they could see every move I made, and I could see their response to the food and service. I earned sixteen dollars a week, plus an occasional tip. I gave Mother ten.

I also learned to speak a little Greek. The Andersons' mother spoke no English but came to the diner once a week after having her hair done. To welcome her, I learned to say something like "*Tah mal yah sue fehr noon day arraya*," which was supposed to mean, "Your hair looks lovely." That always made her smile, whether at my pidgin Greek or at the compliment about her hair I was never sure.

Occasionally during the winter, in the slack hours between the busy breakfast and frantic lunch rushes, the old tramp, the man Slug and I had once followed to his cave-like home behind the Mint Museum, would come in for a cup of coffee. Wearing the same mustache and ragged three-piece suit, he would sit alone at the end of the counter, slowly sip his hot coffee and get warm, then leave a dime under the saucer and quietly take his leave. I wanted to talk with him and ask questions but didn't dare.

He was one of a dozen or so street people that interested Slug and me, but we didn't question. Another was a Black man in a crisp black suit who stood on the northeast corner of Independence Square wearing a sheaf of fresh flowers on his lapels. He spoke to almost everyone he encountered in front of what was then Liggett's drug store. Then there was the man who stood on the southwest corner of Tryon and Fourth Streets, selling the *Charlotte News* by shouting headlines in a bullhorn voice that echoed down the Tryon Street canyon. There was also the sad-faced man who meekly sat at the mouth of an alley halfway down the south side of East Trade's first block. Beside him stood a small felt-draped table bearing color portraits of people. I never saw anyone stop to talk with him or respond to his obvious offer to photograph them.

In the fall of 1947 I again left the Slugger behind and entered the tenth grade at Central High. I continued to work at the Mercury—from three till eleven Wednesdays through Sundays. On Saturdays and Sundays I sometimes switched hours to help open the place, working from six in the morning until three in the afternoon. Whether working nights or days, I lived in dread that some of my high school classmates might come through the doors, requiring me to wait on them. Fortunately, that rarely happened.

After busy nights I found it hard to decompress and was often awake into the wee hours. I slept late, was often tardy at school, and sometimes dozed in class. Jim Suber, my world history teacher, once asked, "Will someone please wake Jack Claiborne before he sleeps through the eighteenth century?"

While I worked, Slug played football at junior high. With an instinct for exploiting defenses, he was the team's blocking back and signal caller. He stopped shining shoes in favor of working at a neighboring veterinary clinic, where mostly he washed and groomed dogs. He also worked as an after-hours janitor for a neighborhood architectural firm, emptying trashcans and sweeping out the place. Later he began running the concession stand at the armory during weekend events.

At the armory he became friends with Jim Crockett, an elephantine boxing, wrestling, and dance-band promoter who also ran popular Charlotte restaurants. Leaning against the counter at the concession stand, Crockett oversaw events on the armory floor and talked with Slug about promoting and running restaurants. Slug absorbed it all.

My work schedule shut me out of Friday night football games and most weekend social events, leaving me isolated from classmates. Growing increasingly surly, I complained to Mother about having to work. She calmly advised that my sisters Alice and Phyllis, my brother Harold, and my sister Anne had sacrificed in behalf of the family. Now it was my turn, she said. When I argued that Slug was playing sports while I was working, she said Slug was working part time as I had done in the ninth grade. Besides, she added, "You've got a good job. You are learning skills that will help you all your life. Stick with it."

The Andersons treated me like a member of their family. They trusted me to run the cash register as routinely as they did. I grew to admire their work ethic and social values. One Saturday when I was working mornings, a woman with an infant came in just before the noon rush and asked if she could nurse her baby in one of the front booths. Jimmy Anderson said, "Sure," and gestured to the last booth in the line. The woman was discreet, but when the lunch crowd began barging in, one of the regulars, a guy known for frequent complaint, yelled to Jimmy, "Why are you letting that woman expose herself in a public place?"

From his station in front of the grill and with his back to the crowd, Jimmy paused a moment, then half turned and with a shrug said, "Hey, everybody's got to eat." The place erupted in laughter, followed by applause. The complainant left. Shortly afterward, the nursing mother buttoned her blouse, gathered up her baby, and took her leave, silently mouthing thanks to Jimmy. The incident taught me a lesson in compassion and grace.

That winter I did better in school. My grades improved, but without a social life, my attitude didn't. My clashes with Mother continued largely over work schedules and my inability to attend sports events. A break came in the spring of 1948 when the Andersons announced they were closing the sandwich shop for a few weeks while creating a restaurant in the larger building next door.

Jack at the Mercury Sandwich Shop

CHAPTER

17

Opening Important Doors

During the Mercury Sandwich Shop's closing in the summer of 1948, a polio epidemic struck hard in the Carolinas, especially in Hickory, North Carolina, and neighboring Gastonia, where tent hospitals were erected to house an overflow of victims. All of that spread fear of paralysis or death, especially among young people. Photos of stricken children wearing leg braces or breathing with the help of barrel-like iron lungs persuaded Slug and me to obey a regional quarantine. We avoided movies, swimming pools, playgrounds, and any place there were crowds. We stayed home, played cards, popped popcorn, made lemonade, and waited for the quarantine to be lifted, which it was later that summer. Among the events we missed was the formal opening of mammoth Freedom Park. For months after World War II, Charlotte newspapers had run streamer headlines over their mastheads urging readers to contribute to a park honoring World War II veterans, in the same way that American Legion Memorial Stadium honored veterans of World War I. Slug and I had looked forward to the new park's opening, sensing that it would eclipse Independence Park as Charlotte's most popular gathering place. The site of the new park had once been the city's polo grounds, if you can imagine polo being played in Charlotte in the 1910s and '20s. Those same grounds also served as a landing strip for dual-winged, crop-duster-type airplanes offering Charlotteans Sunday afternoon flights over the city.

When equipment from the Mercury Sandwich Shop was moved into the building next door, the diner was demolished to make room for a parking lot. I walked up Elizabeth Avenue to see how renovations were going and peek at my station in a new restaurant, to be called the Anderson's.

The restaurant's opening night in late August remains a blur in my memory. Studded with ferns and flowers from well-wishers, it buzzed with the talk and laughter of happy patrons old and new who streamed through the front door. Never had I worked so hard or so fast. In addition to waiting on people seated at the long counter, I filled bread and drink orders for waitresses serving the big dining room. Among the many well wishers that night was my mother. She sat at the counter where I could serve her and was impressed by the attention she got from the Anderson brothers. As busy as they were, each came over separately to speak with her. That strengthened her resolve that I should stick with the restaurant business.

The Anderson's restaurant instantly became one of Charlotte's favorite dining spots, a haven for families visiting Presbyterian Hospital or for business and political leaders to discuss pending issues. It remained a civic asset until its closing in 2006, after the Anderson brothers had died or moved elsewhere.

My hours were from three in the afternoon until eleven at night, five nights a week, with Mondays and Tuesdays off. The Anderson brothers assured me that with advance notice I could get off on a Friday or Saturday night in exchange for working a Saturday or Sunday from six in the morning until three in the afternoon.

One Saturday morning when I was helping Jimmy Anderson open the place, we had hardly made coffee and warmed the grill before nurses leaving the night shift at Presbyterian Hospital came bounding through the door. One sang out to Jimmy, "I feel like having a waffle this morning. Can you make one this early?"

Jimmy said, "Sure," and poured a splotch of batter on the hot waffle iron. As the aroma of that baking waffle floated across the dining room, it inspired orders for more. Jimmy beckoned me and whispered, "Run to the kitchen and make more waffle batter. Just remember eight—eight scoops of flour, eight eggs, eight tablespoons of sugar, eight half-pints of milk, but only three tablespoons of soda. Got it?"

I rushed to the kitchen, found the ingredients, and began stirring them into a sticky glob, which I poured into a pitcher and presented to Jimmy. He immediately scooped some onto the waffle baker. It wasn't long before the batter came bubbling out on all sides. Jimmy called me over and asked, "What did you do?"

"I did as you said. I put in eight of everything," I said.

"Did you put in eight tablespoons of soda?" he asked.

"Yes, sir," I said.

He shook his head, laughed, and pointed to the overflowing waffle baker. "That won't do," he said, and trotted to the kitchen. In a few minutes he was back carrying three pitchers of waffle batter. "It's all right," he said. "I compensated for your overdose of soda. Now we've got enough batter to last a while."

I was grateful for Jimmy's good humor. He might have blown me away, but he didn't, and I learned a valuable lesson about baking soda. More important, I learned a lesson in tolerance.

While I was helping to open the new restaurant, the Slugger was vying for a spot on Central High's varsity football team. He got up early to attend morning conditioning drills and stayed late to join sweaty afternoon scrimmages. As high school players went, he was small—about five nine and weighed maybe 150 pounds—but he was what football followers call "a hitter," meaning he liked contact. Coach Brannin admired Slug's sense of the game. When time came to issue game uniforms to those who made the varsity, Slug received the smallest jersey the equipment manager had, one bearing the number forty-one, a numeral previously worn by several Central High stars.

For Slug, who had been following Central High football since he was six, it was the fulfillment of a dream.

I was still working on my dream of becoming a sportswriter. Knowing that Bill White, the Central High student who had previously covered high school sports for the *Observer*, was going off to college, I went to the newspaper in hopes of replacing him. Rather than face the daunting publisher, I chose to talk with Wilton Garrison, the sports editor, whom I had met a number of times at either the armory or stadium. Again, I dressed carefully and instead of using the front door entered the newspaper's side entrance. I climbed the stairs leading to a green metal door marked "Sports Department." On a landing between floors, I paused to steady my nerves and rehearse my opening spiel. A man behind me walked past and entered the green door. I gave him a few minutes to complete his business before I went in.

The big door was heavy and closed with a loud bang, alerting everyone that I had entered. I felt five pairs of eyes looking at me. The place smelled of stale tobacco and sour paste. I recognized the pipe-smoking Garrison and directed my little speech at him. I said I lived across the street from Central High, knew a lot about its sports teams past and present, and wondered if the *Observer* needed someone to replace Bill White in covering high school sports.

Garrison looked pained. He removed his pipe, knocked its hot ashes into a mesh trash basket beside his desk, and turned away as if thinking how to respond. Four other men watched and waited. At length Garrison said in a soft, South Carolina accent, "Uh, ah, I'm sorry but we've just hired a man to cover high school sports. He's Dick Pierce, sitting right there." He nodded toward an adjacent desk. Then he added, "He's new in town, though, just out of Appalachian State, and might need some help. You should talk with him."

I turned to face the crew-cut Dick Pierce and recognized him as the man who walked past me on the stairway landing. He smiled, offered me a chair, and asked what sportswriting experience I had had. While we talked, he took down my phone number, then introduced me to others on the sports staff: Eddie Allen, the department star who got most of the good assignments; Herman Helms from neighboring Monroe, who covered athletics at small colleges in the region, and desk man Sam Miller, so bald he wore a felt hat even when editing copy and writing headlines. He was the son of the late Julian S. Miller, who for years had been the newspaper's editor and chairman of the North Carolina Board of Education.

Their sports office was a male sanctum, its walls covered with large black-and-white photos of famous athletes: Babe Ruth, Joe Louis, Bobby Jones, Duke football Coach Wallace Wade, North Carolina running back Charlie Justice, and action pictures of boxing matches, baseball games, and golf tournaments. There was even a photo of Bill Gallon, a Charlotte horse that once won the Hambletonian, the trotting horse equivalent of the Kentucky Derby.

I went away disappointed but not discouraged. I felt good about the reception I received. I liked Dick Pierce and Herman Helms and thought they liked me. I walked home impressed that Eddie Allen, now the ace of the sports staff, had started as a Central High sports reporter, at the same level I was reaching for.

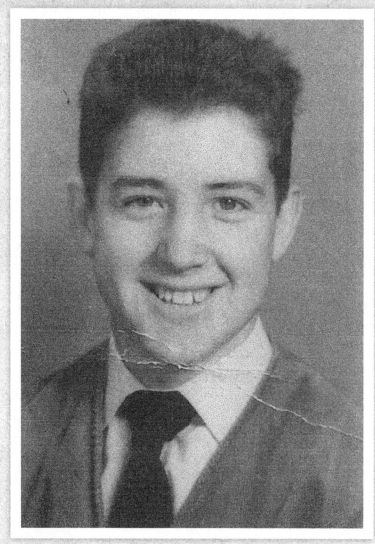

Slug as shoeshine boy

CHAPTER

18

Angst and Darkness

When school opened in the fall of 1948, Slug entered Central High on a wave of popularity. His nickname gave him instant recognition, even among kids from rival junior highs. In addition, he had formed a friendship with an extraordinary athlete named Larry Parker, a strong, raw-boned boy with a shock of curly hair and an "aw shucks" manner. Larry was not only an exceptional running back in football but also the kind of kid who could beat you at any other athletic endeavor, be it marbles, mumbly peg, billiards, darts, you name it, but he couldn't meet people and make small talk as easily as Slug. I understood their relationship, but it hurt to know my place at Slug's side had been usurped.

Slug was immediately elected vice president of the tenth-grade class and the next year was nominated to be treasurer of the student body. Having to make a campaign speech before several student assemblies, he sought my advice on what to say—one of the few times he ever came to me for oratorical assistance. I wrote brief remarks emphasizing that he had held many jobs and knew not only how to make money but also how to spend it wisely. The clincher said, "There'll be no slugs in your treasury with Slug as your treasurer," which drew a big laugh. He was elected in a landslide.

When football season began, Dick Pierce invited me to sit with him in the press box, identify players involved in the action, and keep statistics—first downs, yards gained or lost, etc. Eagerly I made arrangements with the Andersons to have Friday nights off. Twice I traveled with the Central team to out-of-town games and phoned the *Observer* with post-game notes but never got a byline on the next day's stories. At the end of every month, however, I got a twelve-dollar or fifteen-dollar Observer Company check for "correspondence." I used the money to buy a trenchcoat, thinking it would make me look like a real correspondent.

Those were the good times. Interspersed were the bad. Throughout the fall of 1948 and the spring of 1949, our household—reduced to Mother, our sister Anne, the Slugger, and me—suffered some of the most distressing moments of our lives. It was also an unsettling time for Charlotte, where the wartime spirit of patience and collaboration had given way to self-interest. People were at dagger points about the snake-like route for a proposed cross-town boulevard that threatened neighborhoods from the east side to the west. They were also bickering over whether to issue bonds for a proposed auditorium and coliseum to replace the Charlotte Armory. It took three separate referenda to finance that transformative complex.

I continued to complain to Mother about having to work at the Anderson's when I wanted to be writing for the *Observer* and taking part in high school activities. She insisted that I was only doing what my older brother and three sisters had done. My fear was becoming less than a full student and dropping out of school as my brother Harold had done.

It was not a happy time for Slug either. The thrill of making the varsity football team was offset by his limited playing time on a team that was wallowing through a dismal season. That year, Central High won only four games, lost four, and tied four. Slug complained that when he did get into a game, the outcome was already decided. After hours he was working at the concession stand in the armory.

It was also a distressing time for my sister Anne, who wanted to marry a man Mother disapproved of. He was four years older than Anne, a veteran of World War II, and a student going to college on the GI Bill. Mother thought he was too old, had a dubious future, and that at nineteen Anne was too young to marry, though at age fifteen Mother had married a man twenty-one years older.

Adding to the unhappiness was Mother's outlook. She hated her job, resented her supervisors, and often came home with a chip on her shoulder. Not running a boarding house and not being in charge left her feeling diminished. She also was lonely. Her oldest daughters, with whom she was closest, had married and moved on. That left her with a trio of restless teenagers more concerned with their futures than with hers.

As night fell on Valentine's Day, an event seldom observed in our family, she was feeling unloved until Slug came in from the armory and brought her a candy bar. It was a thoughtful gesture that touched something deep within her. When she told me about it the next morning, I felt guilty—and a little jealous of Slug, though secretly I dismissed it as another instance of his grandstanding to make the rest of us look bad.

Throughout the winter and early spring, the *Observer* asked me to cover high school events that Dick Pierce couldn't get to—basketball games, golf matches, track meets, spring football workouts. I had to decline because of my work at Anderson's. That worsened my relations with Mother.

In early March, my outlook got a lift. The Central High boys' basketball team qualified for the 1949 state tournament in Durham, and Jack Baugh, one of my wealthy classmates (later a state senator and a Duke University trustee), planned to go and asked if I wanted to accompany him. He had a four-seat airplane that could fly us up and back, allowing us to miss only one day of classes. He also offered to arrange lodging for us at the home of a Duke faculty member. I leaped at the opportunity and called the *Observer* to ask if I could cover the tournament for the paper. Thinking the tournament too large an assignment for so green a reporter, sports editor Wilton Garrison said the paper would rely on coverage by the Associated Press.

Still, I made arrangements with the Andersons to miss work. We left school after classes on a Thursday, boarded Baugh's yellow plane at the airport, and took off. It was my first flight and proved to be reassuringly smooth. It was also surprisingly short. We were in Durham in less than an hour and visited the Central High team at the Washington Duke Hotel before its first game.

Central was immediately eliminated by a team from Durham. At the game's opening tip-off, Central's stringy "Jippy" Carter faced Durham's taller, stronger Roger Craig and, like the rest of the Central team, was overmatched. "Jippy" Carter went on to play basketball at UNC and became a Charlotte lawyer. Roger Craig went on to NC State and became an MLB pitcher and later manager of the world champion San Francisco Giants.

Despite Central's loss, Jack Baugh and I spent the night and the next day toured Duke University. The tour included a stop at a lab where med students were dissecting a cadaver. It was my first look at a major college campus, and to my innocent eyes Duke's Gothic quadrangles, though not quite twenty-five years old, had the look of antiquity and erudition.

After our return to Charlotte, I told my mother that after high school I wanted to go to Duke. She didn't argue, but she wrote my sister Phyllis that my ambitions were running far ahead of reasonable expectations. She feared I was headed for a great disappointment. A year later, as I filled out applications for college admission, I put Duke at the top of my list but also applied to Davidson and UNC at Chapel Hill. I indicated I would need a campus job and financial aid. Thanks to the low birth rates of the early 1930s, I was accepted by all three schools, though my chances of actually enrolling anywhere seemed remote.

About three weeks after my Duke trip, as I was entering the journalism room for my last class of the day, Slug appeared out of the crowd surging through the hallway and pulled me aside. He looked stricken. "Harold just called," he said. "Mother suffered a cerebral hemorrhage at work this morning. They've taken her to Presbyterian Hospital. I'm going there now."

I felt myself tremble. "A cerebral hemorrhage?" I said. "That's what President Roosevelt died of. Did Harold say how Mother was?"

Slug said, "No. He just said she was at Presbyterian. I'm going there now."

"You go on," I said. "I'll be along shortly."

I went into the classroom and took my regular seat behind the girl who edited the school newspaper. "What's happened?" she asked. "You look as if you've seen a ghost."

"I may have," I said but didn't elaborate. My hands shook so wildly I knew I couldn't write or edit anything. I sat and thought about the impact of a cerebral hemorrhage. People who survived were usually paralyzed, wheelchair-bound, or unable to speak. I tried to imagine our mother, active, forceful, competent, always in command, being confined to a wheelchair. "Good God," I thought. "That would be awful—for her as well as for us."

After about ten minutes I went to Miss Jessie Henderson, the wispy little woman who advised the school newspaper staff, and whispered that I had a family emergency and needed to be excused. She nodded her approval and I left. I stopped by the house and found my sister Anne hurriedly clearing tables and picking up clothes.

"No matter what happens," she said, "we're going to have a flood of people in here tonight, and this place looks just like we left it this morning. Help me make beds and straighten rooms."

We spent about twenty minutes clearing the house before walking toward Presbyterian Hospital six blocks away. The household chores and the brisk walk helped to calm both of us. That was a blessing because when we got to the hospital's front entrance we met Harold, our sister Alice, her husband H.A., and Slug coming out with long faces.

"She's gone," Alice said. "There was nothing they could do. The hemorrhage was too massive."

No one was crying. All looked stunned. We avoided eye contact.

Harold told how Mother had called him from her office saying she was sick and needed him to "come quickly." When he got there, he found her slumped face down at her desk, saying, "I'm so mad. I'm so mad." He wondered what she was mad about until he noticed that she had soiled her clothes. Her office mates had called an ambulance, and he rode with her to Presbyterian Hospital. By then Mother was unconscious. At the hospital Harold phoned Alice, Phyllis, and Anne, then called Central High asking to speak to either Slug or me. The school receptionist found Slug first.

In the afternoon sun we stood on the hospital grounds, shuffling our feet, not daring to look at each other or ask questions. We were trying to take in the enormity of the moment. Mother had always been the adhesive that held the home and family together. What would life be like without her?

Only when Harold and Alice began talking of arrangements to be made did the rest of us begin to talk, though Slug and I had little to say. At length all of us crowded into H.A.'s car for a short ride back to the house. As we pulled up, two men from a funeral home arrived to hang a white wreath on the front door, a sign that there had been a death in the family. That's when everyone began to weep—except me.

Hours later, long after darkness had fallen, our sister Phyllis and her husband Jack arrived after driving non-stop from their home in Savannah. The wreath on the lighted front door was the first signal Phyllis had that Mother had died. She was inconsolable. Again, everyone cried but me. For some reason I couldn't shed tears.

I felt the immensity of the moment as much as anyone and was certain I loved Mother as much as my siblings, but I couldn't bring myself to weep. I knew she had relied on me, but she rarely showed me the warm affection she lavished on Slug. For years Mother had warned that the day would come when we'd have to fend for ourselves. She had taught us to cook, to clean, to sew, to iron, to make beds, and manage money. I looked around at the family and told myself, "She got us ready for this. Now it's up to us." If she had lived a few years longer, she would have found she had done a better job than any of us at that moment realized.

Though we had quarreled often, I had tender memories of her. I remembered how she bit her lower lip when she was trying to concentrate, how she squinted to thread a needle, how she held the end of a pillow in her teeth when putting on a pillow slip, how she adjusted the hearing-aid receiver inside her blouse when the sound was too loud, how her puffy hands kneaded the dough she then shaped into biscuits, how when she laughed the sound burbled up from deep within and shook the rest of her body, how she could be both angry and amused at the same moment—as when Slug and I were in the backyard sailing old seventy-eight-rpm phonograph records like Frisbees and I failed to leap high enough to avoid one that hit me in the ankle, leaving a deep gash filled with black chips from the shattered record. When Mother stopped what she was doing to clean and dress the wound, she said she didn't know whether to laugh or cry at our foolishness.

Mother was smart, resourceful, and steadfast and in another era might have been anything she wanted to be. But in the struggle to raise six of us—without a husband for the last thirteen years—she had spent her last ounce of energy. The old tenderness, patience, and tenacity were exhausted. After all she had been through, she was entitled to rest, though she was only fifty years old.

Earlier I had called the Andersons to tell them my mother had died and I wouldn't be coming to work. Shortly after Phyllis's arrival, there was a knock at the front door. When we answered, no one was there, but on the porch was an orange crate filled with all kinds of food—a baked ham, roasted chicken, fresh fruit, vegetables, crackers, and cheese. Tucked among them was a note that said, "We share your sorrow. The Andersons." That moved me to tears.

That night and for the next two nights, the house was full of people. Neighbors, relatives, people from Caldwell church, friends from work, classmates from school, even John Otts, the Central High principal, came to express condolences. Jimmy Harton and his wife came. We couldn't reach Irby Todd, who was still serving in naval intelligence.

After the funeral, attended by most of Mother's brothers and sisters, we came home to a quiet house and a moment of peace. Anne, Slug, and I were sprawled in the living room, silently pondering our futures when Harold came in and said he wanted to speak to Slug and me—alone.

"Boys," he said, "I want you to quit your jobs and concentrate on school. I don't want what happened to me to happen to you. I want you to graduate from high school and, if you can, go on to college. You've got a better chance than any of us. Tere and I have talked. We are going to move into this house, rent the rear apartment, and we want you to live with us as long as you need to. Anne is going to live with Phyllis in Savannah. Jack, Mother has often told us about your wish to quit work at the restaurant. You can call them now and tell them to hire somebody else."

Then I understood why I couldn't cry. I felt liberated to do the all the things I had longed to do. I didn't phone the Andersons. I walked up there and told them in person. They were understanding and supportive. If I ever needed a job, they said, I could always have one there. Then I went home, phoned Dick Pierce at the *Observer,* and told him the next time he had assignments I was available.

Harold the family protector

CHAPTER

19

Startling Awards

If the days leading to our mother's death were dark and dismal, the following fifteen months were among the brightest and most exhilarating of Slug's and my boyhood. We took leadership roles in school, Slug as a three-sport athlete and I as co-editor of the school newspaper and a bylined sportswriter for the *Observer*.

Dick Pierce welcomed my call and asked for help in covering high school baseball at Richardson Field off Irwin Avenue, behind what was then Harding High School. He warned that I would have to submit my stories before *Observer* deadlines. I told him that would be no problem. Richardson Field was fifteen blocks from the newspaper office. I could easily walk.

I soon learned why he welcomed my help. Until then I had experienced only the glamour of sportswriting. At Richardson Field I suffered its discomforts. When warm spring afternoons became chilly nights, Richardson Field was a walk-in freezer. It had no shelter to ward off winds or rain. I sat in open bleachers with my score sheet on my lap, exposed to boggy breezes off Irwin Creek that flowed just beyond the left field fence. The sparsely attended games were endless and raggedly played. As innings passed and scores mounted, my feet and hands—and my interest in the outcome—grew frostier. At game's end it was a warming relief to walk to the *Observer*.

Occasionally, I covered games at Highland Park, about forty blocks up Davidson Street into North Charlotte, then a separate community from Charlotte. The park offered a covered grandstand, a press box, public address system, and semi-pro players with greater-than-high-school skills. The Highland Park team played rivals from other mills in the Charlotte region. I rode the bus to and from games and made the *Observer*'s deadline every time but once.

On that night, Highland Park's game against Maiden Mills went into extra innings, causing me to arrive at the *Observer* after eleven o'clock. Ernest Hunter, the newspaper's tall, intense, shirtsleeve managing editor, known in the newsroom as "Boss," was pacing the floor.

"Hurry with that box score," he growled, and hovered over me as I filled it out. When I finished, he ran it himself to the print shop to be set in type. He returned moments later and seemed to stick his head between my eyes and the paper in my typewriter as I composed an account of the game. Each time I finished a paragraph, he ripped it off and ran it to the printers.

"Hurry, boy," he said, "Don't you know you're late?"

When I finished and the "Boss" left to terrorize others in the newsroom, my sports department colleagues, who had been tracking my torment in sidelong glances, laughed and said not to worry, that they had endured similar trials. They explained that Maiden, a town in central Catawba County, about forty-five miles northwest of Charlotte, was in the newspaper's fourth-edition territory, the deadline for which was earlier than that for the sixth edition that was delivered in Charlotte. The "Boss," they said, wanted to make sure an account of that game was in the paper for Maiden subscribers the next morning. It was my introduction to multiple-edition deadlines and the marketing of a regional newspaper.

The incident also made me aware of the *Observer*'s role in Charlotte's rising prominence in the Carolinas. The newspaper was home-delivered in seventy-seven counties across the two states and helped to make Charlotte their shopping, entertainment, distribution, and financial center.

In July 1949 WBTV went on the air as the Carolinas' first television station. It was the city's only TV station for seven years, until WSOC-TV began broadcasting in April 1956. At first only a few households had a television receiver, but almost overnight, TV sets were in show windows of appliance stores and sales were brisk. Television advertising also helped make Charlotte a regional marketplace.

While I was learning to report sports news, Slug was making it. Having played point guard on the Central High basketball team, he was the catcher and defensive leader on the baseball team. Off the playing fields, his smile and warmth brought him additional friends. Everyone wanted him to attend their party or club meeting or other social event. He was elected president of the tenth grade for the second semester, and his girlfriend JoAnn Bailey was elected class secretary and was a cheerleader.

That spring I also acquired a girlfriend. When a classmate invited me to a party at his family's house on Lake Wiley, I had to bring a date. Having worked nights at Anderson's, I was out of the dating orbit. I decided to ask Barbara Werner, who sat in front me in geometry class and had befriended me. When in frustration I had balled up my answers to a pop quiz and thrown them in the trash, she dug them out, smoothed the sheets, and turned them in under my name. I got a seventy on the quiz instead of a zero, greatly minimizing the damage to my grade point average.

When I asked if she would accompany me to the party, she said dating at the river was beyond her limits. She would have to ask her mother. The next day, she came back to say that before giving permission, her mother would have to meet me. That afternoon I walked her home—about four miles—reciting poetry much of the way. When we reached her house on Malvern Road, then the southern boundary of Myers Park, her mother was out front sweeping the sidewalk. She looked me up and down and asked about my background. She seemed impressed that I wrote stories for the *Observer*. Barbara came to class the next day saying she could go.

That party became a turning point in my life. Barbara was my steady date for the next four years. We walked or rode the bus to movies, plays, and concerts. Her family often invited me to dinner. Knowing I would see her made going to school more inviting. Suddenly, the boy who had been sleepy and sullen was alert and outgoing. As my involvement in school affairs increased, my grades improved. At the end of the spring semester, I was chosen, along with honors student Margaret Watkins, to be co-editor of the school newspaper for our senior year.

When school ended that spring, Slug got a summer job as a park counselor and coached a boys' baseball team to the finals of the city tournament. I got a job carrying lumber to carpenters framing a large apartment complex on an abandoned Plaza-Midwood golf course.

In August, my sportswriting objectivity got a stern test. The *Observer* asked me to accompany the Harding High football team to Boone and report on its pre-season training in the cool mountain air. My challenge was proving that a Central High student could fairly assess the football preparations of a rival school. The Harding team stayed in Boone two weeks. I filed stories every day, often enough to stop the Western Union clerk from questioning my credentials when I came in saying, "Send this night press rate collect, please."

Harding High coaches were so pleased with my reports that later that season, when Harding played a game in Jacksonville, Florida, they arranged for me to accompany the team, cover their game, and ride the bus home. Harding won the game easily, and its coaches were pleased with my coverage.

That fall, Slug faced a greater challenge. Over the objections of our sister Phyllis, my sister Anne plunged ahead with plans to marry the man Mother had objected to. She bought a wedding dress and set the date for a Charlotte wedding in early September. Harold, Slug, and I were to be groomsmen. On the afternoon before the six o'clock ceremony, near the end of a Central High football practice, Harold and I were dressed and waiting on the front porch when we saw Slug come dashing through the high school gate in football togs and holding a bloody towel under this chin. In muffled voice he yelled, "Tell Anne I'll be there."

A student equipment manager said that when making a tackle, Slug had suffered a deep gash under his lower lip but assured me that with a few stitches he would be as good as new. He and Slug jumped into a Jeep bound for the nearest hospital, where Slug's wound was stitched inside and out.

When he returned, his lower jaw was bound from ear to ear in thick, white bandages. Harold and I helped him into formal clothes, but as we went out the door, Slug's pallor matched the huge bandage and, in a white dinner jacket, he looked more like a zombie than a groomsman. During the ceremony, as the novocaine wore off, he was clearly in pain. We feared he might collapse, but he didn't, and his girlfriend JoAnn took him home and fed him soup through a straw.

Near the close of the year, the senior class began choosing class-day officers—poet, artist, prophet, historian, and lawyer. I had never been elected to anything but was chosen class prophet. I had fun imagining myself an Internal Revenue Service agent examining tax returns ten years in the future, projecting what many of my classmates might be doing in 1960, which at the time seemed like the dim future.

In early June, it was time for commencement, which in those days attracted generous media attention. The 425 graduates in our class were among the 30,480 North Carolinians graduating that spring, remnants of the fresh-faced boys and girls who had entered the first grade in 1938, more than half of whom had dropped out along the way.

Having attended many Central High commencements, I thought I knew how ours would go but was unprepared for the emotions swelling within me as the event unfolded. Filing into the armory, self-conscious in my cap and gown, I realized that all around were friends of long standing, many I had known since elementary school. After that night, we would scatter, just as my family was scattering. The world I had known since boyhood was about to disappear. I took my seat with apprehension.

My emotions rose higher as the ceremony progressed, and the principal began naming recipients of various awards. I had been nominated for the citizenship medal but saw it go—rightfully—to someone else. As the principal began awarding scholarships, he eventually got to the last one, the Harry Winkler Memorial, a one-year, $250 grant to a boy entering UNC at Chapel Hill. Not having applied for a scholarship, and knowing my academic record hardly qualified me for one, I was barely paying attention when he announced that the winner was "...Jack Claiborne."

I was astonished. I could barely get to my feet. I heard the cheers of classmates and felt my insides churning. My walk to the stage was an out-of-body experience. I felt the eyes of my brother Harold, his wife Tere, and my brother Slug staring down from seats in the balcony.

Accepting a certificate from Dr. Otts, I was led to a small room off stage where other honorees were waiting to be photographed for the newspapers. I accepted their congratulations, then went into a corner and quietly wept, not out of grief but in gratitude, humbled that the faculty committee that granted scholarships thought I was worthy of one. For the first time I was certain I was going to college.

The same thing happened a year later when *I* was in the balcony sitting with Harold and Tere and watching as the Slugger went through the same emotional turmoil. He had enjoyed a successful year as a starter in three sports and as president of the student body—he beat Charles Kuralt by one vote.

Still, Slug hadn't applied for a scholarship and didn't expect one. Yet, when Dr. Otts began awarding the one-year Marvin B. Smith grant to a boy entering the university at Chapel Hill, he didn't identify the recipient by the formal name stamped in gilt on the winner's diploma cover but with a pause and a big smile said, "The winner is...Slug Claiborne."

His words brought window-rattling applause, whistles, and enthusiastic cheering. It was the loudest, most prolonged response of the evening. Slug was as teary-eyed as I had been. Now he too knew he was going to college. The old Roosevelt rainbow was still working its magic.

Though the awards were small, even by 1950 standards, they fed lofty ambitions. For Slug and me, two boys barely skating by in a high school filled with privileged classmates, they opened inviting doors of opportunity.

If our stories had ended there, they would have been memorable, but the best was yet to come. With high hopes and the resilience instilled by our family, we moved out of our armory-stadium-Central High incubator into wider, more challenging worlds—but never beyond the allure of Charlotte and its increasing excitement.

Slug in football togs

PART TWO

"Becoming Adults"

Slug as Jack's best man

"Deep down I knew I was unprepared for the academic rigor I would face, but remembering my recent high school successes, I hoped I could overcome my fears."

CHAPTER

20

A Daunting Environment

The thrill of my high school graduation lasted three weeks. It faded in late June 1950 when North Korea invaded South Korea and President Truman sent American troops to intervene. All American males eighteen or older were required to register for the draft.

I registered and asked for a college deferment. A clerk advised that a deferment required my remaining a "student in good standing," which at Chapel Hill meant maintaining at least a C average. I feared that in working my way through college that might be difficult. The threat of the draft would haunt me for the next three years.

In the meantime, there were summer jobs to secure. Slug's contacts got me a job with the Charlotte parks commission umpiring boys' park-league baseball games. I borrowed a bike from a kid up the street to ride to parks that were beyond walking distance. I enjoyed the work and the responsibility of keeping games orderly, even after a furious father at Latta Park threatened me for calling his son out on an attempted steal of second base. I assured him I was closer to the play than he was and could see the fielder tag his son out. When the game was over, I didn't stay around to argue the point. I got on my bike and peddled away.

Each week I also wrote a summary of park-league baseball for the *Observer*, an example of the paper's small-town outlook, though at the time

Charlotte's population of 134,000 was the largest in the Carolinas. The *Observer* was not alone in that provincial posture. Radio station WAYS invited me to script and broadcast a fifteen-minute radio report on each week's park activities.

Slug spent that summer going door to door selling Childcraft books and *World Book* encyclopedias. His smile and engaging manner got him into living rooms not open to others. He was good at selling and earned more than he'd ever made in a summer job. His goal was to save enough money to buy a car. To increase his savings, he moved from Harold's house, where we paid a modest rent, to live for free at the home of Larry Parker, his football and golfing buddy. It was the beginning of a long separation. After that, we rarely saw each other.

In blistering July heat, I hitchhiked to Chapel Hill to apply for a self-help job in the fall. Though I had heard many radio broadcasts of UNC football games, I had never seen the university. I found the campus and the town to be all of a piece. The car culture was nibbling at the town's perimeters, but its main street was still a pedestrian's pleasure. The narrow little storefronts huddled along the town's two-block business district had the look of a European hamlet. They made me feel in touch with history. I thought of the famous people—Frank Graham, Kay Kyser, Thomas Wolfe, Betty Smith, Robert Ruark—who had walked the sidewalks I was now treading.

At the suggestion of my *Observer* mentors, I made my first call at the office of Jake Wade, the UNC sports information director who previously had been sports editor at the *Observer*. I had grown up reading his "Jake Wade's Sports Parade" column and had met him at several Charlotte Armory or Memorial Stadium events. With that in mind, I felt sure a good opportunity was waiting for me.

I found my way to Wade's office just inside the entrance to the university's Woollen Gymnasium. A bulky man with a long, oval face, a prominent nose, and a shuffling gait, he was responsible for publicizing Charlie Justice as "Choo-Choo" and promoting him to all-American football fame. He received me warmly but didn't remember meeting me in Charlotte. Even worse, he didn't know I was coming to ask for a job. My *Observer* colleagues had not alerted him. That proved to be a blessing. Had they called ahead, he might have told them what he told me, that he had just hired a full-time assistant and didn't have an opening. Then I wouldn't have met Julian Scheer, the new full-time assistant who was sitting at the next desk.

When Wade left the room, Scheer, a Richmond, Virginia, native and World War II veteran (later public relations director for the National Aeronautics and Space Administration), assured me that during football season he would need lots of help in the press box and would make sure I got some of the jobs. He suggested that in the meantime I might find more permanent work at the University News Bureau, the campus public information agency. He gave me a map showing how to get to Bynum Hall, where the bureau had its offices.

Like most buildings on that storied old campus, Bynum Hall had a fascinating history. Built in 1905 as a gymnasium, it was home to the university's first men's intercollegiate basketball team, a 1910-11 contingent that won seven games and lost four. That basketball program later lifted UNC to national prominence by winning six national championships. Bynum Hall also contained the first shower stalls on campus. In Thomas Wolfe's student days, men from surrounding dormitories often streaked across the all-male campus to shower there before breakfast. Over the years, Bynum housed other programs and by 1950 hosted UNC Press, the School of Journalism, and the University News Bureau.

The news bureau occupied four large rooms on the second floor, which on that July afternoon were smotheringly hot, even with the windows wide open and fans blowing full force. On entering, I was met by a woman who led me into the large, cluttered office of Robert W. Madry, the Bureau's bulldog director. Madry didn't waste any of his precious time with me. He listened just long enough to learn I wanted a job and sent me back to "Mid NaPeer," the woman I met at the entrance.

Elizabeth Napier, I quickly learned, was the Bureau's unofficial manager. She was small, fiftyish, and black-haired with a squirrel-like face and more teeth than her mouth could comfortably cover. She wore a headset and sat in front of an electric typewriter that clattered under her deft touch. She was quick, efficient, and friendly. My meeting with her—and the mentoring she provided—became one of my cherished memories of the university.

She sat me down next to her desk and said, "Tell me who sent you and a little bit about yourself," she said. Her gracious manner eased my anxiety.

I told her I was from Charlotte, had won a sportswriting contest sponsored by the *Charlotte News*, had co-edited my high school newspaper, received a small scholarship to attend the university, had written stories for the *Observer* and planned to make journalism a career.

She nodded appreciatively and apologized for not having a writing job to offer. "But," she said, "we have an opening in the mailroom," where dozens of news releases the news bureau produced each day were mimeographed, folded, inserted, addressed, and mailed. "The pay is fifty cents an hour," she said. "That's standard across the campus. It amounts to about twelve dollars a week, depending on the hours you work."

Then she took me to see the mailroom. It was a dusty, cheerless chamber without windows, its walls lined with dusty shelves and cubbyholes stuffed with unread weekly newspapers and other fading documents. Against one wall stood a hulking mimeograph machine. At a long, low table sat two men, one of whom I recognized as Norman Moore, a tall, lean, raffish fellow with sun-bleached hair. Norman lived three houses north of me in Charlotte. It was his younger brother from whom I borrowed the bicycle to ride to umpiring sites. I didn't know Norman, who was three years my elder, but I had seen him in our Charlotte neighborhood. Behind a fox-like face he had a keen intelligence that I quickly came to respect. Having seen my bylines in the *Observer,* he welcomed me with enthusiasm. "Come on in, Jack. We'll have lots of fun," he said.

I accepted the job—indeed was delighted to get it after my disappointment at Jake Wade's. I was told to report in mid-August before the start of freshman orientation. Pleased by that prospect, I walked down the campus main street, admiring the old buildings and sheltering trees, then happily hitchhiked home.

All that summer, in addition to umpiring, I wrote stories for the *Observer.* As I went in and out of the newsroom, reporters and editors reached out to wish me well. Some told me stories about their days at Chapel Hill. Toward the end of the summer, they passed a hat to send "the kid" to college in style. On my last night in town, Bob Page, the city editor, and Ernest Hunter, the shirtsleeve managing editor known as "Boss," presented the proceeds in a little pouch. It contained thirty-six dollars, a generous sum from newshands whose 1950 wages probably hovered between twenty-five to thirty dollars a week.

The next day, a warm Sunday, Slug, Harold, and I loaded my clothes and bedding, including Harold's old Army blanket, into his black Chevrolet for the three-hour drive to Chapel Hill. We took the old route (Interstate 85 did not exist), up US 29 through the fading textile district of Concord, then followed NC 49 through the shops and stores of downtown Asheboro, picked up US 64, which took us through pastures to Pittsboro, circled the redbrick Chatham County Courthouse, and turned north onto winding US 15 501 to Chapel Hill.

It was not a celebratory trip. Going to college was an uncertain venture for each of us. For Harold, who had sacrificed that phase of his life, it was tinged with the regret of a missed opportunity. For the Slugger, who didn't know about the grant waiting at his high school commencement, it was still a distant aspiration. For me, it was an anxious uprooting from my safe Charlotte surroundings. Deep down I knew I was unprepared for the academic rigor I would face, but remembering my recent high school successes, I hoped I could overcome my fears.

We talked little as the countryside zipped past, but on entering Chapel Hill, our heads swiveled and we blurted out comments and questions as we passed the hospital, the med school, fraternity houses, the Navy ROTC Armory, and the Carolina Inn. Our destination was the South Building at the heart of the campus. We had no trouble parking. No one else was in sight.

My instructions from the registrar were to call for a key at the Housing Office in the basement of the South Building. I was assigned to room six in the Steele Dormitory, a three-story, redbrick structure that stood perpendicular to the administrative offices in the South Building. I rang the office bell but got no answer.

To pass the time, we strolled the graveled, tree-shaded paths leading across the deserted campus to the massive, granite-columned Wilson Library. Even in the summer stillness, it exuded academic excitement. On the frieze over its porch was the university seal bearing the words "Lux Libertas," which I assumed meant light and liberty. We admired the lush lawn, the towering oaks, and the vine-covered classroom buildings. I noticed the varying architectural styles and how they differed from the uniformity I had seen at Duke. I felt an openness I hadn't sensed among the Gothic cloisters of Duke's West Campus.

When we returned to the South Building and rang the bell again, a man answered saying he hadn't expected me so soon. We got the key, unpacked my belongings, made my bed, and walked down to the town's main street for a sandwich. We ate at a place called Harry's. Except for us, its high-backed booths were empty. We dawdled over lunch and talked speculatively about the campus scenes pictured on the walls. As Harold and Slug prepared for their return to Charlotte, the conversation grew strained. They had little more to say than "good luck." I stood on the blacktop parking strip beside the South Building as their car pulled away and felt a lump ballooning in my throat. Apparently so did they. Harold later said that as they turned out of the campus gates and headed south, he told Slug, "That's the loneliest boy I think I've ever seen."

I *was* lonely. Suddenly, with my supports gone, the romance of going to college vanished. For the first time, I missed Mother's calming voice and reassuring spirit. I sensed that surviving in these surroundings was going to be a struggle. I wished I had studied more in high school. Further, I realized I would face this daunting environment without Slug, who had been my confidant and ambassador, who had introduced me to all kinds of people. That fall, the university would enroll about 5,500 students, four times more than Central High. In my lack of confidence, I would come to know few of them.

I took out my campus map and began identifying edifices and wondering what went on inside them. I stood before the tan Old East dormitory, erected in the 1790s as the oldest building at any public university in America. I thought its Federal style looked plain. I was more impressed by the ornate Greek Revival columns at the entrance to the Playmakers Theatre. I walked in the Coker Arboretum, gawked at the Morehead Planetarium, and peeked into the high-ceilinged, couch-strewn reading room of the Graham Memorial, the student center. Then I walked up the town's main street and looked in its store windows. Everything was quiet. Chapel Hill, then a village of 9,200 (by

2010 a city of more than sixty thousand), was enjoying a sleepy lull between summer school and the opening of a new academic year.

The sonorous bell atop the South Building awakened me the next morning, signaling the time for reflection was over, that now I needed a determined attitude. I showered and dressed, breakfasted downtown, and hurried to the news bureau to begin work. I was immediately sent by bicycle back downtown to the post office for a brimming basket of incoming mail. I met the rest of the news bureau staff, which included another Charlottean, Wink Locklair, a tall, lean, hollow-cheeked UNC senior who was the bureau's chief feature writer, specializing in music, drama, and art. A veteran of World War II, he was about six years older than me and had thinning black hair and a direct manner—"Who are you?" "What do you hope to become?" "What are you reading?" Yet his questions were softened by a bubbly sense of humor. As we became friends, he often called my attention to newspaper or magazine articles I should read as examples of good writing. He would hand me the sports pages of the *New York Times* and say, "Here. Read this. Louis Efrat is one of the *Times'* best sportswriters." Gradually he widened my interests from athletics to history, politics, and the performing arts.

I also learned to appreciate the eccentricities of "Colonel Bob" Madry, the Bureau's chunky director who was like a character in a Dickens novel. His desk was stacked so high with papers he literally couldn't be seen behind them. He was forever losing letters, notes, memos, or other documents that he was absolutely certain were "halfway down that corner stack." It usually took "Mid NaPeer" to pluck them out. On occasion the Colonel would complain that he'd lost his glasses, only to have one of us go into his office and find them—tilted on his forehead.

He couldn't remember our names and would summon us by calling, "Uh, uh, you there." Yet under that bumbling surface were shrewd instincts and a hidden kindness. He was well respected by editors and publishers across the state and had twice been elected mayor of Chapel Hill. Over time, he came to trust me enough to babysit his five-year-old son.

At orientation, the university's harmonica-playing chancellor Robert House looked over the freshmen assembled in Memorial Hall. In those days, the university accepted any male applicant from an accredited high school in North Carolina, knowing that half of them would flunk out in their freshman or sophomore years. The chancellor urged us to study hard, to read every assigned book at least twice and three times if possible. He asked us to look to the man on our left and to the one on our right. At the end of the year, he said, only one of them would be there. We should work hard to make sure we were among those who survived. That increased my anxiety.

When I paid the bill for the fall quarter, I discovered that my $250 Harry Winkler scholarship would cover only tuition and fees but not room, board, books, and laundry. I went to the student-aid office for help and was reintroduced to Charles Bernard, another Charlotte connection. Slug and I had met him in 1946 when he was organizing the Charlotte Center of the University of North Carolina, a night school at Central High. He was glad to see me and suggested that I apply for a job at one of the campus cafeterias that would provide my meals. I chose the sedate Pine Room at the Carolina Inn and got a job busing breakfast tables, finishing just in time for morning classes.

My life was tightly scheduled. Under the university's quarter system, I attended three hour-long classes in the morning, worked at the news bureau five hours in the afternoon, and had about five hours a night for study. Most study periods were spent in Wilson Library's oak-tabled Reserve Reading Room, where I pored over such tomes as Thomas Hobbes's *Leviathan,* Robert Malthus's essays about over-population, and Jonathan Swift's satirical *A Modest Proposal,* all required readings in my study of western civilization. I was also taking Spanish and an eight o'clock class in college algebra.

I never felt comfortable in the academic environment and usually felt less prepared than my classmates, many of whom had gone to prep schools. Forever on edge, I feared flunking out and being called up in the draft.

My social life was confined to weekends. In those years, women were excluded from the university's freshman and sophomore classes. The only female students were Chapel Hill girls, nursing students, junior and senior transfers from other colleges, and graduate students. The male-to-female ratio was something like five-to-one. To find dates, most freshmen fanned out to campuses in Durham or Raleigh or Greensboro. I opted for Greensboro, fifty miles away, where my high school sweetheart Barbara Werner was enrolled at the Woman's College (now UNC Greensboro). I could easily hitchhike there and on most weekends did. Being with her was a comfort. Each of us was struggling academically and felt at ease in our old relationship.

When the football season opened, Julian Scheer was true to his promise. He hired me to work in the press box, typing a play-by-play account of the game, and distributing it to rows of sportswriters and radio crews. At the end of each quarter, I phoned NBC and CBS radio networks with the score. For all that, which became routine for the rest of the season, I earned eight dollars a game. The university played only five home games a season, which didn't provide me much walking-around money. There were weeks when I ran out of cash on Wednesday and anxiously awaited the news bureau's pay envelope on Friday afternoon.

That improved after the football season. Julian Scheer hired me to sit at courtside during basketball games and keep statistics for distribution to the press. Though the pay was less, there were more opportunities to work because the university played many home basketball games. The work also exposed me to outstanding players from other schools, including Duke's Dick Groat, NC State's Sam Ranzino, and Wake Forest's Dickie Hemric.

As the academic pace quickened, my job at the news bureau became a refuge. There at least I felt competent. While I was struggling to absorb academic instruction, at the Bureau I was soaking up valuable information about the university, the state of North Carolina, and journalism. That was an important part of my college education. I learned who was who within the university—who was president, chancellor, and the dominant trustees, important personages in those days. I also learned who were powers on the faculty and came to know Bill Friday, then the personable dean of students who was just beginning his climb to the university's presidency. Bill and I became trusted friends. I also learned who the leaders in the state government were and who the most influential voices in the media were. All that would later be important to me as a newsman.

Mrs. Napier introduced me to a softer side of Chapel Hill life. She made me an honorary member of the village's "Ladies Lunch Club," comprised of gifted women who ran important university or town agencies headed by men. The women met monthly at a downtown coffee shop to gossip about who was drinking too much, cheating on their spouse, or neglecting their children. Occasionally, they poked fun at their bosses. Though the women's movement had yet to dawn, it was on the horizon. The ladies' behind-the-scenes information helped make the university and Chapel Hill seem less foreboding.

Throughout my years at Chapel Hill, Charlotte was never far from my consciousness. Wink Locklair and I read the *Observer* daily to keep up with hometown news. One source of our amusement was the back and forth over naming the city's new but controversial crosstown artery that slithered snake-like through the town. As it neared completion, it was suggested that because former mayor Ben Douglas had secured funding for it, the road should be named Douglas Boulevard. Knowing the uproar caused by the road's destructive impact on neighborhoods east and west, Douglas declined the honor. After much argument, the city council agreed to name it Independence Boulevard, as if nobody wanted anything to do with it.

Through the news bureau I also met important faculty members. By far the most memorable was Walter Spearman, a scrawny, unkempt but popular professor of journalism. Slight, balding, with wire-rimmed glasses, and a penchant for puns, he taught news writing, movie and drama criticism, and that most demanding of all journalistic skills, editorial writing. As he came and went from his office across the hall from the news bureau, I saw him often and discovered he was a member of the Spearman family in Charlotte to which I had once delivered envelopes containing my mother's rent money. One afternoon as we met in the corridor, Walter asked what I planned to major in. I told him journalism.

"Why?" he asked.

"Because I want to be a newspaperman," I said.

"You can do that without a degree in journalism," he said. "All journalism can offer you is practice and placement. You're getting practice here at the news bureau, and you'll get placement when you return to the *Charlotte Observer*."

He paused, as if to let that sink in. Then, with a wave of his arm, he said, "There's a whole university out there. Go sample it. Take art, take music, take history, take economics, take religion, take courses that will make you a full, *intelligent* newspaperman."

In my university career, I followed his advice. I avoided journalism, majored in English, minored in history, and took at least one course in every discipline he recommended. I have since recommended that curriculum to other would-be journalists.

Even after settling into a routine, my fears continued to override my hopes at the university. One night as I biked back across the campus, a smallish man stepped out of the darkness and asked in a soft Low Country accent, "Aren't you Jack Claiborne from Charlotte?" When I said yes, he introduced himself as Bernard Boyd. He said friends in Charlotte had told him about me, and that if I ever needed help, I should call on him. I thanked him but felt uneasy about his offer. Over the next two years, I encountered him twice more and always declined his willingness to help. Had I told anyone at the news bureau about him, I would have learned that Bernard Boyd was a former Davidson College professor who had become a celebrated Bible scholar whose UNC classes were so popular that students who couldn't get tickets to attend them often lined the hallways outside to hear his lectures.

My news bureau work also introduced me to Rolfe Neill, a supremely confident UNC sophomore who would later have a significant influence on my career. With crew-cut hair and a take-charge manner, he was managing editor of the *Daily Tar Heel,* the campus newspaper. One afternoon when the news bureau had a press release it wanted sent as fast as possible, I hurried to the *Tar Heel* office in Graham Memorial where it could be wired to the Associated Press. There I met Neill, who understood the request and immediately sat before the keyboard of a teletype machine and began sending. I knew from *Observer* experience that operating such a keyboard required a firm touch and steady rhythm, like a boxer hitting a speed bag. I watched in awe and admiration as Neill sent the message with ease and accuracy.

Afterward, he turned his attention to me, asking one question after another—"What's your name? Where're you from? What brought you to the news bureau? What kind of newspaper experience have you had?"—which I later learned was a Rolfe Neill routine. During the inquisition, I could see him filing the information in his brain. My answers must have been satisfactory because later when he needed someone to night edit the *Daily Tar Heel* at its Carrboro print shop, he offered me the opportunity. The hours were from nine till midnight, and the pay was two dollars a night. Night editing involved not only reading proof on the next day's edition but also setting type for all the headlines.

Setting type for the headlines was a special pleasure. Unlike in the unionized *Observer* print shop, where editors were forbidden to touch the type, at Carrboro l could reach into the type cases and select letters for the font and size needed and, using a Ludlow machine, mold those letters into the headline in hot metal. The tactile experience gave me a sense of ownership over the words they formed. Many times as I read proof on the next day's edition, some of the paper's senior staff members, worldly men to my innocent ears, dropped by to talk and argue whether the dour Gordon Gray of Winston-Salem, previously the secretary of the Army, should be president of the three-campus university (Chapel Hill, NC State at Raleigh, and the Woman's College at Greensboro), or whether North Carolina Governor Kerr Scott, an Alamance County dairy farmer, was liberal or conservative, or whether the university should admit Negroes who were suing for admission to the university law school. All were questions blowing in the winds at Chapel Hill.

That spring the UNC freshman baseball team played a game in Chapel Hill against Charlotte's Central High, for whom Slug was the catcher and leading hitter. The *Observer* asked me to cover the game. UNC sports publicist Jake Wade allowed me to be the official scorer, but to make sure I knew what I was doing, he sat beside me in Emerson Field's ground-level press box. About midway through the game, Slug slashed a waist-high line drive that ticked off the glove of the diving UNC third baseman and bounded down the left field line into the weeds. Slug rounded first base and cruised into second. I scored it as a double, which brought guffaws from Wade, who insisted the diving UNC infielder be charged with an error. "No wonder Slug is leading his team in hitting," he chided, "with scorers like you to help him."

The Slugger didn't need my help. About a month later, he returned to the university campus as a Mecklenburg County representative to Boys State, an annual summer program to identify potential leaders among recent high school graduates. Led by North Carolina's secretary of state Thad Eure, the week-long session gave boys a crash course in North Carolina history, legislative procedures, and politics. At the end of the week, the boys held mock elections for state offices. Slug was elected "governor." The news bureau sent out pictures of him with members of his "Council of State."

By the close of my freshman year, I felt lucky to have achieved a C average but still had to join other men of draft age in taking a comprehensive exam to maintain a college deferment. The exam contained 120 questions to be answered in two hours, averaging a minute per question. I still remember the gist of the last question: If the front wheel of a tricycle has a diameter of eleven pi over three, and every time the tricycle goes forward thirty feet the back wheels spin twenty times more than the front wheel, what is the diameter of the back wheels? I laughed at the very thought of solving that puzzle in a minute and left the answer blank. But I must have answered enough questions correctly because about ten days later, I got a card saying I passed the exam and had escaped the draft for another year.

A week later, I got a note from Wilton Garrison, the *Observer* sports editor, asking if I could spend the summer working full time as vacation relief for the sports staff. I couldn't get to a telephone fast enough to say, "Yes, sir." I wasn't proud of myself but was relieved to be "a student in good standing." I hurried home in hopes of earning enough money to return in the fall for my sophomore year. I had my foot in the university's door and was determined to keep it there.

"People would ask me, "Are you Slug's brother?" I learned to answer, "No. Slug is *my* brother," to emphasize that I was the older, though my response did not endear me to any of Slug's friends."

CHAPTER

21

"Slug Is *My* Brother"

That fall I looked forward to Slug's joining me at Chapel Hill. Outside my news bureau work, I had made few friends and longed for his company. But the boy who could chant "chook-a-lacka," who could charm Mr. Patterson at the corner grocery, who could talk us into meeting Gene Autry, was not the brother who joined me at the university. We were no longer close. Over the next two years, our relations would undergo the greatest strain of our lives.

His constant companion was his football and golfing buddy Larry Parker. While I apprenticed at the *Observer* in the previous summer, Slug and Larry palled around in Chapel Hill. An all-American running back in high school, and perhaps the best runner Charlotte ever produced, Larry had been recruited by many institutions but chose UNC in hopes he might restore its football fortunes to the glory days of Charlie Justice. Larry enrolled in the university's summer school to get a head start on course work before the strain of fall football practice.

At my suggestion, they sought rooms in the Steele Dormitory near most classrooms and dining halls. But after federal courts ordered the all-White university to admit four Black men—Harvey Beech, James Lassiter, Kenneth Lee, and Floyd McKissick—to its law school, the university Housing Office cleared one section of Steele to accommodate the Black students and reassigned Slug and Larry to rooms in a dorm across the street from Woollen Gymnasium. I wondered whether the four Black students ever knew they were given housing priority over the university's prized football recruit.

When the Slugger took a job at Finley golf course near the university, Jake Wade's Sports Information Office distributed a photo of him and Larry raking a sand trap. The caption compared them to Damon and Pithias, mythical Greek heroes immortalized for loyalty to each other. I felt displaced and envious.

With money earned by selling encyclopedias, Slug had bought a wheezing 1930s four-door Ford so rusted that from the front passenger's seat you could see the pavement passing below. With the engine running, the exhaust puffed out plumes of blue smoke, signaling that the engine was burning nearly as much oil as it was gasoline. Slug learned to stash extra quarts of oil under the driver's seat.

As decrepit as the car looked, the Slugger treasured it for the liberty and mobility it gave him. All through high school he and JoAnn Bailey had double-dated with friends who had cars. Now they could date on their own or double-date with Larry Parker and his girlfriend. In Chapel Hill that summer, the car carried Slug and Larry wherever they wanted to go—to Durham to see movies, or to the Finley golf course to improve their game, or to Charlotte to see their girlfriends. From my post at the *Observer*, I felt like an outsider.

My work in the sports department amounted to leisurely editing wire copy and writing headlines in the afternoon, composing stories from early evening phone calls about golf matches, swimming meets, and occasionally deep-sea fishing off the coast of the Carolinas. The nights were hectic, mostly devoted to taking baseball box scores over the telephone from minor league parks in surrounding counties—a total of twelve box scores a night. Though three of us were answering the phones, the pace was frantic. Most games ended just before *Observer* deadlines. Each box score required a brief account of the game and a headline. It was heady work demanding speed and accuracy. Further, we worked in a sweltering office without air conditioning. With the windows wide open, big fans blew in gnats, moths, flies, and occasionally an itinerant wasp. Frequently our copy went to the print shop stained with sweat.

Even so, it was fun. When the rush ended, each team's winning percentage had been computed, and new league standings were compiled, I went home feeling that I had accomplished something. I was learning to work and think under deadline pressure.

That summer I lived with Harold and Tere and rode the bus to and from work, often reading *Time* magazine en route. Wink Locklair, who had graduated from UNC that spring and joined the *Observer* as a reporter and arts critic, continued to coach me on good writing to emulate, good movies to see, and good books to read. He often took me to lectures, chamber music concerts, plays, and dance performances.

Occasionally, my work in the sports department brought challenging assignments. I went to Freedom Park to write about a sweating Charlie Justice as he ran, passed, and punted in preparation for joining the Washington Redskins (now Commanders) of the NFL. A few times I got to cover Charlotte Hornets baseball games at Griffith Park, where I would be not only the official scorer but also the public-address announcer. To avoid feedback of sound bouncing off outfield fences, I learned to speak in three-word phrases. I would say, "Ladies and gentlemen. Your starting lineups. For tonight's game. For the Asheville Tourists...," and so on.

When the summer ended, I returned to Chapel Hill to discover that Slug was already a big man on campus. Once freshman orientation was over and classes had begun, his magnetic grin and openhearted response to classmates won him the presidency of the freshman class. Everybody on campus seemed to know him. People would ask me, "Are you Slug's brother?" I learned to answer, "No. Slug is *my* brother," to emphasize that I was the older, though my response did not endear me to any of Slug's friends.

To replace my one-year Harry Winkler scholarship, I applied to the Student Aid Office and again encountered Charles Bernard. He arranged for me to pay tuition and fees with escheat grants derived from the estates of North Carolinians who died without a will. When the state sold assets of those estates, the proceeds went to needy students at UNC. Bernard said I could continue drawing escheats as long as I maintained a C average. Slug's one-year Marvin B. Smith scholarship paid only his tuition and fees, but he had little trouble arranging other support. He continued to work at the golf course and earned meals at Lenoir Hall, the main campus cafeteria, where his duties were depositing each day's receipts in the bank and running errands for the manager. Occasionally as I went through the cafeteria line, I would see him standing behind the cashier, watching as she collected money and made change. Neither of us had an inkling of the role that cafeterias would play later in his life.

To reduce his tuition and fees and shield him from the draft, he joined the Air Force ROTC, accepting the requirement that upon graduation he would serve three years on active duty in the Air Force and remain an active reservist for years afterward. I had considered that option but was unwilling to commit my future to military service. To cover laundry costs, Slug became the laundry agent for his dormitory, collecting dirty clothes and distributing clean ones. On Saturdays when the university football team played at home, he sold programs, usually earning twice what I did working in the press box. While I was struggling to make ends meet, I got the impression that Slug was cruising.

Our relations worsened after one of my rare visits to his dormitory. There he and Larry Parker introduced me to a novel way of polishing the big, smooth-toed, cordovan shoes that style-conscious young men were wearing. Drawing on his experience as a shoeshine boy, Slug had a wax that, when applied and lighted with a match, produced a thin blue flame. When the flame was extinguished, the remaining wax could be buffed to a high gloss. He and Larry encouraged me to try it on my shoes, which were older and more scuffed than theirs. When the wax didn't yield a high luster, they said it was because I hadn't let it burn long enough. When I blew out the flame a second time, it had burned not only the wax but much of the leather on the big toe side of my shoe. When I buffed it, the burned leather crumbled, leaving a hole about the size of a silver dollar. Slug and Larry thought that was hilarious, but I was aghast. I couldn't afford to buy another pair of shoes. As I left their room, the Slugger walked me to the door and, sensing my plight, whispered regrets but added with a grin, "You have to admit it *was* pretty funny."

To earn as much as I could, I worked every available hour at the news bureau. In addition, I bused tables at Lenoir Hall for meals, became a laundry agent for my dormitory, occasionally night-edited *The Daily Tar Heel*, and sold a few feature stories to the *Observer* about Charlotte-area students. When my news bureau partner Norman Moore graduated, his place was filled by Jim Babb, my friend from the Billy Graham dairy truck and a classmate at Central High. He proved to be even more fun than Norman Moore and took special delight in mimicking the absent-minded news bureau Director Bob Madry. One afternoon, Jim sneaked away from the bureau to look in on a track meet at a Quonset hut that university people called the Tin Can. He'd been there only a few minutes when he saw Madry walking toward him, leaving no place for Jim to hide. Madry strolled up and said, "Uh, ah, hello there. You're from the eastern part of the state, aren't you?" A relieved Babb said yes, made his manners, and raced back to the news bureau to add his story to the Bob Madry lore.

At the end of the 1951-52 school year, I stood on the outskirts of Chapel Hill with my thumb out and a valise at my feet bearing a sign that said "Charlotte?" Soon a long, black Cadillac driven by a distinguished-looking man pulled up. He motioned for me to sit up front with him and introduced himself as Granger Pierce, a Charlotte lawyer who was taking his mother home after hospital tests. When I told him I was going to Charlotte to take a summer job at the *Observer,* he brightened.

"Oh," he said, "Do you know the paper has a new publisher?"

I said yes and, showing off, went on to explain what Granger Pierce surely knew: that the previous publisher, Curtis Johnson, had died, leaving competing wills. While the wills were being contested, the bank managing the Johnson estate had hired an interim publisher named Ralph Nicholson, former owner of the *New Orleans Item*.

"Have you met him?" Pierce asked.

"No," I said, "but I have read about him." I cited a saucy headline over a *Time* magazine article that said, "New Brass for a Gold Mine."

"Well, I *have* met him," Granger Pierce said. "He called and asked if I was a good lawyer. When I told him I was pretty good, he said, 'You'd better be damned good because I'm pretty good myself.'"

Grainger Pierce and I talked all the way to Charlotte—about the *Observer,* about the university at Chapel Hill, about Charlotte's burgeoning growth, and about the new auditorium-coliseum complex under construction. We agreed that Charlotte was breaking out of its pre-war status as a big country town and becoming a bustling city.

A few days later while working in the sports department, I got a call from the publisher's secretary, who asked me to come down to Mr. Nicholson's office on the mezzanine. I hurried down one flight of stairs. A colleague later kidded that the only way I could have gone faster was to jump out the window. I took a seat outside the publisher's door until the secretary said, "You may go in now."

The office looked much as it had when it belonged to Curtis Johnson. Mr. Nicholson's desk sat in the same spot at the far end of the long, narrow room, giving the publisher plenty of time to look me over as I approached. He motioned for me to sit at the side of his desk "so I can get a good look at you." He said his lawyer Granger Pierce had suggested that we get to know each other. "Tell me about yourself," he said.

As I neared the end of my brief resume, he interrupted to ask, "What's wrong with your teeth?" I told him that, as a result of my distaste for milk, many of my permanent teeth had never pushed out my "baby teeth."

"Well, your mouth looks terrible," he said." Go to a dentist and have something done about it. Tell him to send me the bill."

I left convinced that Ralph Nicholson was firmly in command of the newspaper and even more assertive than Curtis Johnson. I also came away thinking that Granger Pierce had obviously suggested I was a young man of some promise.

I had rarely been to a dentist, but in my work at the Mercury Sandwich Shop, I had met Dr. Ernest Morris, a Navy veteran who practiced in a clinic on Elizabeth Avenue. After X-rays, Dr. Morris said my permanent teeth had grown into the roof of my mouth and would never descend. The best he could do, he said, was to pull the deciduous teeth and replace them with a bridge that would restore the shape of my mouth, improve my speech, and give me a pleasing smile. The work lasted much of the summer. Ralph Nicholson was as good as his word. He paid the bill in full.

He also improved the *Observer*. He redressed the paper typographically, air conditioned the entire plant, provided locker rooms and showers for printers and pressmen, and created a pension system that enabled several seventy-year-olds to retire. When the dispute over wills was resolved in favor of Curtis Johnson's widow, Nicholson moved on and bought a newspaper in Dothan, Alabama.

By the fall of 1952 I had completed the core curriculum at Chapel Hill and was beginning to take courses leading to a major in English. By then my zest for academics was waning. I was tired of taking courses I wasn't interested in, tired of working several jobs, tired of not having any money, and tired of taking tests to avoid the draft. Days of reckoning were ahead.

"I was relieved to think I could put aside the discomforts of my academic life but was distressed at the thought of postponing my quest for a college degree and a journalism career."

CHAPTER

22

Big Decisions

On Christmas 1952 Slug gave JoAnn Bailey a ring and asked her to marry him. She and Slug had been dating since the eighth grade and had long assumed they would marry as soon as possible. After completing a one-year secretarial course at the Woman's College in Greensboro, JoAnn had taken a job as secretary for a prominent Charlotte executive.

On learning of their wedding plans, the *Observer*'s Dick Pierce asked if they would participate in the annual June bride and groom promotion by the *Charlotte News*. They would appear in ads for household goods needed by most newlyweds. Slug and JoAnn agreed and soon were pictured in almost every edition of the *News*, admiring a store's china and crystal one day and fingering another merchant's sheets and towels the next. They didn't earn any money, but they got nice gifts and a month of public notice.

They were married at Caldwell Presbyterian Church with Harold as best man and me as an usher. After the wedding, I went back to work at the *Observer,* but exciting things were happening at Harold's house. He had agreed to let the Slugger use his black, four-door Chevrolet for a honeymoon trip to Fontana Lake deep in the North Carolina mountains, provided Slug made sure his friends didn't soap it up with "Just Married" graffiti.

After dressing in going-away clothes, Slug and JoAnn rushed out the front door under a hail of rice, but at the curb they bypassed Slug's rusty old Ford parked prominently on the street and hurried to Harold's shiny Chevrolet safely sheltered up the block. Their getaway appeared to be perfect.

After about an hour's drive, Slug stopped for gas and watched as a service station attendant raised the hood and checked the oil and water. As he finished, the attendant looked at JoAnn, smiled, and winked. Slug thought the attendant was a little cheeky but paid the bill and drove off. Farther down the road, Slug stopped at another service station and again an attendant raised the hood to check the oil and water. He too smiled and winked at JoAnn. That made Slug angry. He got out and asked the attendant, "What in hell is going on here?" The attendant laughed, raised the hood, and pointed to a piece of white tape stretched across the radiator cap. There in Harold's unmistakable handwriting was a note saying, "Newlyweds. Wink at the bride."

Slug and JoAnn had better luck later when they applied for housing in Chapel Hill's Victory Village, a complex of prefabricated cottages for married students. Built during World War II for the Navy preflight program, the village consisted of one-story, sand-colored apartments, each attached to the other and strung along a winding road south of the university's medical school. Vacancies in Victory Village were rare, but just as Slug and JoAnn arrived to apply for a unit, a fellow Charlottean, Herbert Spaugh Jr., and his wife were moving out. Herbert Spaugh was the son of Bishop Spaugh, pastor of Charlotte's Moravian Little Church on the Lane (later chairman of the Charlotte-Mecklenburg school board). Young Spaugh knew Slug only by name, but in vacating the only available unit in Victory Village, he and the Slugger became fast friends. So did Slug and most of his Victory Village neighbors. The apartment walls were so thin that everyone came to know each other—and most of their secrets.

JoAnn got a job in the ticket office of the university's Athletic Department. Later she served as secretary to Chuck Erickson, the university's athletic director. Slug continued to work at Finley Golf Course and the manager's office at Lenoir Hall. In addition, he became a campus representative of Reynolds Tobacco Company, handing out free samples of Winston cigarettes to anyone who would accept them. With cigarettes lying around their tiny home, Slug succumbed to temptation and began to smoke.

The fall of '52 also brought me some luck. Red Smith, the nation's most literate sportswriter—the Grantland Rice of his generation—was covering Walker Cup golf matches at Pinehurst and planned to attend the UNC football game against his alma mater Notre Dame and write his Sunday column from Chapel Hill's Kenan Stadium. I had read Smith's writings often and was thrilled at the opportunity to meet him in the press box and watch him work. In addition, the Notre Dame radio network asked UNC to provide a real time play-by-play account of the game for announcers in South Bend, Indiana, who would recreate it over a radio network for Notre Dame faithful across the country. I knew a little about such recreations. As a boy I had stood before show windows in Efird's department store in uptown Charlotte and watched as Russ Hodges, then a WBT sports announcer, mixed telegraph accounts, prerecorded crowd noise, and the sound of a screwdriver hitting a bat to recreate MLB games. His broadcasts sounded as if they were coming from a ballpark.

Julian Scheer of the UNC Sports Information Office arranged for the Notre Dame network to receive the play-by-play summary I routinely provided the Kenan Stadium press box. As I typed, a telegrapher with a dot-dash key sat at my right shoulder transmitting every word. Conscious of that, I added more color to my play-by-play, referring occasionally to the weather, team uniforms, cheerleaders, bands, and crowd reactions.

The Slugger was at the stadium that Saturday, hawking programs before the game and afterward sitting in glum admiration as Notre Dame quashed every effort by his buddy Larry Parker to generate a UNC offense. Led by burly Paul Hornung, Notre Dame easily won the game, but I had a great time describing it and was paid a whopping forty-five dollars for my efforts. During the game, I got to witness Red Smith put aside his professional impartiality to cheer openly for Notre Dame.

Turning twenty-one that October, I made sure I exercised my right to vote. Before leaving Charlotte, I had registered at the elections board. Having read about the opposition of Southern Democrats to progressive legislation, I knew I didn't want to be associated with them, so I registered as a Republican.

I was unaware that in doing so, I was forfeiting my right to vote in Democratic primaries that usually determined local and state elections. Further, in following the 1952 presidential campaign, I found myself identifying more often with the progressive spirit of Democrat Adlai Stevenson than with his Republican opponent, Dwight Eisenhower. I wrote the elections board requesting an absentee ballot. When it came, I voted for the Democrats.

Slug couldn't believe what I had done. "You're crazy," he said. "How could you vote against Eisenhower? He won the war in Europe." Actually, the same might have been said of Winston Churchill or George Marshall or George Patton or Bernard Montgomery or other Allied commanders.

Like most athletes, Slug liked military regimentation. To him, having a general at the helm of the national government was a little like having a football coach there. That was the beginning of what became fifty years of political dispute between us. I was always too progressive for the Slugger, and he was too standpatish for me. On my next trip to Charlotte, I changed my voter registration to Democratic.

During the winter of 1952-53, as Slug was sailing along, I was stumbling into a crisis. As part of my English major, I was taking a novels course taught by the distinguished C. Hugh Holman, a star of the university's English faculty. The course required that I read a hefty book—a long, windy novel such as *Tom Jones, Tristram Shandy,* and *The Mayor of Casterbridge*—every two or three days. In addition to working at the news bureau, I was a laundry agent, a dry-cleaning agent, a statistician at basketball games, and a bus boy in the Lenoir Hall dining room. In struggling to read those books and keep up with assignments in two other courses, I was staying up late and getting up early.

One morning as I cleared tables in Lenoir Hall, I sensed I was feverish but knew I had to work to eat. Suddenly I blacked out and awoke in the car of the Lenoir Hall manager, who took me to the student infirmary. I was confined there almost a week. The doctors said I had a virus and was dehydrated and physically exhausted. By the time I was released, I had run up a sizable medical bill and, because I hadn't worked in a week, had no money coming in.

There weren't many places I could turn for help. I knew Slug had no money, and neither did Harold. I was hopelessly behind in the novels course and didn't see how I could catch up. I went to see my faculty adviser, a squat, avuncular biologist named Claiborne Jones, with whom I had a warm relationship because we shared the same name. He was a kindly man with an ironic sense of humor and often kidded me about making going to college too hard. "It's not supposed to be so difficult," he'd say. This time he listened to my woes and suggested I take some time off.

"They've stopped shooting at each other in Korea," he said. "Why don't you take this opportunity to volunteer for the draft, serve your two years in the military, and come back under the GI Bill? Then your life will be easier."

He added that even after all my striving, I shouldn't think of withdrawing as a defeat. He had long believed, he said, that it was a good idea for students to take a break at some point between high school and college to gain maturity and a wider perspective. The number of kids who flunked out after a year or two of college buttressed his belief. He suggested that in the long run, serving two years in the military might be good for me.

I left our conference with mixed feelings. I was relieved to think I could put aside the discomforts of my academic life but was distressed at the thought of postponing my quest for a college degree and a journalism career. I went to see Slug, who was shocked to hear of my situation and lectured me for getting into such a predicament. Finally, he agreed I didn't have much choice but to follow my counselor's advice.

I called Harold, explained my situation, and asked if I could live with him until I was taken in the draft. He expressed disappointment and asked whether there was any alternative. I told him no, that I was in debt, mentally and emotionally drained, and needed to take a break. He said I could live with him temporarily and offered to help me find a job in Charlotte. I hung up feeling ashamed to have let him down.

The one person I didn't call was Barbara Werner, my girlfriend in Greensboro. I knew she would be deeply disappointed. After withdrawing, I wrote her a long letter explaining my situation and promising to see her soon. She immediately wrote back, angrily alleging I should have called on her father, who would gladly have advanced me the money to stay in school. I told her I didn't want that kind of relationship with her father.

Once back in Charlotte, Harold got me a menial job at Lassiter Press, running a round-cornering machine that trimmed corners of thin cardboard sheets, around which women's stockings would be wrapped before packaging. At first it was fun, then the job got repetitious, and the days got long. The younger men among my fellow workers jeered me as "the college boy" and made fun of my every mistake. A couple months later, sports editor Wilton Garrison called to ask if I would again work vacation relief at the *Observer*. I quit the Lassiter Press job and resumed my apprenticeship in the sports department. My duties were the same, but after my round-cornering experience, I appreciated them all the more.

Early in July I scored a small triumph. Vic Seixias, a former UNC Chapel Hill tennis player, had celebrated July Fourth in England by winning the 1953 men's singles championship at Wimbledon. The next day, I wrote a feature story about him based on wire service reports and what I knew about his days in Chapel Hill. When the first edition of the *Observer* bearing the story came up from the pressroom, the curmudgeonly "Boss" Hunter charged into the sports department, his outstretched arms holding an open newspaper in front of him.

"Who wrote this tennis story?" he demanded.

For a moment, everything in the office stopped as members of the staff looked quizzically at each other. Finally, Herman Helms said, "The kid did."

Whirling to return to his corner of the newsroom, the "Boss" said over his shoulder, "Well, it's damned good." The office erupted in laughter.

"As I was stumbling out of the university and into the Army, significant events were occurring in Charlotte."

CHAPTER
23

Entering the Army

In early September the long-awaited draft notice arrived, ordering me to report at six in the morning on September 23 to the top floor of the Coddington Building on West Trade Street, four blocks from the town square. The notice said I should bring only the street clothes I would be wearing.

Harold set the alarm for five o'clock in the morning to make sure we arrived on time. He let me out at the curb, laughed at my anxiety, and said, "You'll be all right. Millions of guys have survived it. Just do as you're told."

I took the elevator to the Coddington's top floor and arrived before the induction station opened. Other draftees, some White, some Black, all looking miserable and avoiding eye contact, leaned along the walls resignedly. Among them were two high school classmates, Jack Guion and Ralph Rowe, the son of Oliver Rowe, a Charlotte industrialist. Like me, they had decided to take a break from school. I greeted them and laughed uncomfortably at their gallows humor. Then I joined others lining the walls.

When the doors to the induction station opened, we were ushered in and told to take off our clothes, including rings, watches, and other jewelry, and place them in cloth bags hanging on the wall. Then we walked in single file from table to table where doctors took our medical histories, checked our vital signs, looked at our eyes, ears and noses, and listened to our hearts and lungs.

They also checked for hernias, skin diseases, and flat feet. Having us parade naked around the examining room was the first step in the Army's effort to strip us of our personal identity and turn us into anonymous soldiers.

Those of us who cleared all the examining stations were told to line up in ranks along parallel lines painted in the floor. Gradually the lines filled, and an officer in crisp khakis stood before us—rows of nude wretches, maybe thirty in all. He called us to attention and said he was going to read the soldier's oath. When he finished, if we agreed, we should take one step forward. After that, we would be in the United States Army.

He read the oath about defending the United States against all enemies, foreign and domestic, upholding the Constitution and obeying the nation's laws, ending with "so help me God." Then he asked us to take one step forward. As we did, someone way in the back said, "Holy Mary, mother of God, pray for us sinners now."

We got into our street clothes, then were fed breakfast and led downstairs to an Army bus. Soon we were cruising up and down the forested hills of US Highway 21 headed for Fort Jackson, South Carolina. Sharing a seat with me was Ralph Rowe, who had spent the summer acting in the Barter Theatre in Abington, Virginia, where he had played in the sword-slashing, verbal-bashing comedy "Cyrano de Bergerac." He recited lines from the play, including the plaintive "Roxanne...Roxanne," all the way to our destination.

At Fort Jackson's massive induction center, we were herded into classrooms and given intelligence and aptitude tests. Afterward, we received metal "dog tags" containing our names, serial numbers, blood type, and religious preference, Protestant, Catholic, or Jewish. We were taken to barbers to have our hair shorn to Army standards—shorter than crew cuts—and afterward we went to the supply center to get duffel bags and sets of dress and fatigue uniforms, shoes, and combat boots. We boarded another Army bus and were taken to a row of tents and told to get out of our street clothes and into the green fatigues, including combat boots—"on the double."

The tents were like sauna baths. Their canvas roofs absorbed heat and held it. I dressed and was lacing my boots when a soldier wearing sunglasses and stiff khakis came charging through the screen door. "Anybody here named Claiborne?" he yelled.

Meekly I answered, "I am."

"Come with me," he barked in a commanding voice.

" Oh, God, I've done something wrong," I thought.

Outside I saw an olive-green Army sedan with official-looking white lettering on the sides and in the back seat an ominous figure in khakis and sunglasses, sitting ramrod straight and staring intently ahead. For all I knew, he might be the fort's commanding general.

The soldier who had ordered me outside opened the sedan's rear door and commanded, "Get in." The only seat available was next to the man sitting ramrod straight. Timidly I got in. Then the ramrod-straight man slowly removed his sunglasses and turned full face to me. I recognized him as Jim Babb, my milk-truck riding, high school classmate and former news bureau colleague. Babb whooped in laughter, saying, "You should have seen your face, Claiborne. I've never seen a rabbit look as scared as you."

Like me, Babb had grown weary of going to school, working long hours, and not having enough money. He had left Chapel Hill, entered the Army, and was nearing the end of his two years' active duty. As a private first class in the Fort Jackson Public Information Office, he had seen my name on the list of inductees and wanted to make his commanding colonel and the major who led the fort's Troop Information and Education program aware of my availability.

"These guys are always looking for talent," he said, "and will be interested in your background and how you might fit their operations. Just answer their questions. Chances are you won't go to Korea. You might spend your entire two years right here, just as I have."

I could hardly believe my good fortune. Though fighting in Korea had ceased, that battleground, like Vietnam would become twenty years later, was not a place a soldier wanted to go. It was either too hot or too cold. Though Fort Jackson was hardly alluring, it beat being assigned to Seoul.

I met the spit-and-polished PIO (Public Information Officer) colonel, who said he didn't have an open slot but might have one by the time I completed sixteen weeks of basic training. The major at Troop Information and Education, who was less formal, said he would soon need someone to replace the base newspaper editor, who was about to complete his two-year hitch. When the major asked if working on the base newspaper interested me, I assured him it would.

Babb and his driver returned me to my tent to await my assignment to a basic training company, where I would be physically and emotionally challenged. I knew that tough days lay ahead, but for the moment, the Army seemed a lot less foreboding.

As I was stumbling out of the university and into the Army, significant events were occurring in Charlotte. They grew out of the city's effort to annex the Park Road Shopping Center, built in the early '50s as the first major retailing complex outside uptown. It served a sprawl of neighborhoods that when added to the city's population would push Charlotte over the two-hundred-thousand mark in the 1960 census.

When bills authorizing a referendum on the annexation went to the state legislature in Raleigh, protests immediately arose from people in the target areas just beyond the city limits who didn't want to pay city taxes. For days, busloads of them overwhelmed the legislature, which then met in the old capitol's narrow corridors and cramped committee rooms. As soon as they left, busloads of annexation advocates arrived to further jam the tiny capitol. Besieged legislators began asking, "Why are we in this fuss? This is Charlotte's business."

Out of their frustration came a study commission headed by Senator Pat Taylor of Wadesboro. The commission held hearings and decided there was no fair way to hold a referendum; residents of targeted areas would vote "no" but would be overwhelmed by city residents who voted "yes." It issued a final report saying what was urban in population should be municipal in government. No referendum was needed; people who moved into areas to be annexed had voted with their feet. A law based on that report was upheld by the courts.

Hailed as a model for other states, the law became a major means of making Charlotte a big city. For the next fifty years, Charlotte's used it repeatedly to extend its boundaries. If Atlanta, Georgia; Richmond, Virginia; or Greenville,

South Carolina; had had such a law available, the modern South might look far different.

Jack at the Jackson Journal

CHAPTER

24

Glimpsing Our Futures

While I was enduring the indignities of Army basic training, Slug was completing his business studies at Chapel Hill and thinking about his future. By age twenty, he had starred as a three-sport athlete, been president of his high school student body, governor of Boys State, won a scholarship to the university at Chapel Hill, been president of his freshman class, and married the girl of his dreams. He had reason to think he could be anything he wanted to be.

During the summer of '53, he completed six weeks of ROTC boot camp at the Keesler Air Force Base in Biloxi, Mississippi. Afterward, he joined his father-in-law W.W. Bailey in opening Wilma's, a new cafeteria amid the neon glitz of Myrtle Beach, South Carolina. Slug oversaw the dining room, making sure customers were comfortable and content. It was like leading a bear to a honey pot. He met people with ease and warmth, chatting up patrons, making people laugh, and often sitting at family tables. He rediscovered what he had experienced at our mother's boarding house: that dining in the company of friends is one of the satisfying acts of human life. More importantly, he discovered that doing so fed a socializing hunger within him.

Even so, his eyes were on loftier goals. On his return to Chapel Hill for his junior year, he began making plans to study law. In the back of his mind he could see himself ultimately entering politics. In his senior year at the university, he applied for admission to the UNC law school and was accepted pending completion of active-duty service in the Air Force.

Meanwhile, as a lowly recruit in basic training at Fort Jackson, I was learning to march, wax and buff floors, clean latrines, and follow orders that often seemed absurd. I remember the shock of being told to display items in my footlocker in an exacting way: so many centimeters between razor and blades, so much distance between socks and underwear.

The Army also wanted us in good physical condition. It got us up at the hint of dawn to take pre-breakfast calisthenics. One morning as I struggled on frost-encrusted sand to complete the assigned number of push-ups, I felt a weight in the middle of my back. "How old are you, soldier?" a man asked.

Turning my head slightly, I saw a captain wearing green fatigues, a superior snarl, and a combat boot in the middle of my back.

"Twenty-one, sir," I said.

"How in twenty-one years did you get so weak, soldier?" he asked, without removing his boot.

Risking a saucy answer, I said, "I've lived a charmed life, sir."

Removing his boot, he replied acidly, "We'll *charm* your life, soldier. You'll soon wish to hell you were back in your charmed life." Mercifully, he moved on to torment some other recruit.

As training progressed, I was given a nine-and-a-half-pound, grease-impacted M-1 rifle capable of hitting a target three hundred yards away with a .30-caliber bullet. I was told to clean it and learn to disassemble and reassemble it blindfolded. All that was relatively easy. Knowing that soon I would have to fire the thing became a secret concern. Having never wielded a weapon more lethal than a cap pistol, I worried about the M-1's reputed recoil.

Before going to the firing range, we were drilled in ways to absorb the rifle's kick. We learned to lodge the gun's stock firmly against our shoulder, wrap its leather sling around our supporting hand, and sight our target. It all seemed simple, but on the rifle range, in the din of continuous firing, with bullets flying through the air and red-and-white targets bobbing up and down in the distance, any skills I might have acquired vanished.

When it came my turn to lie in one of the sandy firing pits, I donned a steel helmet and stretched out beside a somnolent sergeant who after training recruits for weeks looked as if he was bored to the bone. He coached me through the firing routine, saying my goal was to hit the black bull's-eye in the red and white target several hundred yards away. After leading me a number of times through the firing routine, he gave me a clip of three bullets and told me to load and fire when ready.

I thought I had done everything he taught me, but when I squeezed the trigger—BLAM!—the rifle butt leaped from my shoulder, struck my jaw, and nearly blacked my right eye. I didn't know where the bullet went, but the target puller down range waved a red flag, signaling that I not only had missed the bull's-eye but also the entire target.

The mentoring sergeant retrieved my rifle, braced it more firmly against my shoulder, wrapped its sling even tighter around my supporting hand, and told me to relax and try again. I took a deep breath, aimed, and squeezed the trigger. BLOOEY! Again the rifle jumped from my grasp, sideswiped my jaw, and knocked the steel helmet off my head.

As I reached from the pit to recover the helmet, my sergeant-mentor was preparing for a third try, but an alarmed captain, red-faced under a Smokey the Bear campaign hat, came dashing down the line of sandy pits, gesturing and shouting, "Get that man off the firing line before he kills somebody!"

Embarrassed, I picked up my rifle and ran my tongue over my teeth to make sure they were all there. When I handed the clip with its one remaining bullet to my sergeant-instructor, he didn't say a word. Another recruit was waiting to take my place.

I was ashamed to have failed at something most soldiers enjoyed. After more practice, I qualified on the rifle range and did even better firing carbines, which were lighter and had less recoil. I even fired a .30-caliber machine gun.

As if my firing range failures were not disheartening enough, they were compounded a few days later by an emotional lashing I got from Barbara Werner, my high school and college sweetheart. In a letter, she coldly said our four-year romance was over. "Now we need to date other people and get on with our separate lives," she said. I felt sick inside. Sitting on the curb outside my barracks I reread the letter several times, wondering what had gone wrong. For four years I had been her emotional bulwark, but now I needed her support. I gathered up all the pictures I had of her and sent them back with a note saying, "I'm sorry."

My first eight weeks of basic training ended on Thanksgiving. I went on leave to Charlotte with orders to report back—not to my basic training unit but to the fort's Headquarters Company as a member of the *Jackson Journal* staff for eight weeks of on-the-job training. It meant I wasn't going to Korea or Japan or Germany. I was to remain at Fort Jackson practicing journalism.

The *Jackson Journal* was an eight-page tabloid distributed every Friday across the sprawling fort. On a base where training was routine and breaking news scarce, filling it with lively copy was a challenge. Our five-member staff sought out stories about soldiers who had interesting backgrounds, including musicians, actors, poets, singers, jugglers, and athletes. One of them was Wilmer "Vinegar Bend" Mizell, later a pitcher for the St. Louis Cardinals and even later a congressman from the Salisbury district of North Carolina.

Unlike basic training, which was physically challenging, life on the *Jackson Journal* was mentally stimulating. It exposed me to Headquarters Company colleagues who were graduates of rigorous institutions, including Emory, Davidson, Vanderbilt, Dartmouth, and Boston College. They helped fill gaps in my education by encouraging me to read, giving me a firmer foundation on which later to return to the university at Chapel Hill.

The *Journal* office was a square, four-room hut isolated on a pine-shaded hill about a mile from Headquarters Company. I bunked there rather than in the company barracks and from there often made weekend trips to Charlotte. On one of them, Wink Locklair, who had become the *Observer*'s arts critic, drove me out to see pile drivers sinking steel beams resembling spikes in the crown of the Statue of Liberty. They were supports for the new coliseum's aluminum dome that for many years was a Charlotte icon.

Two months after I joined the *Jackson Journal*, the paper's editor completed his Army hitch and went off to graduate school. I was named to succeed him, though as an E-1 I was the lowest ranking soldier on the premises. The major who ran the Troop Information and Education program was a soft-voiced soldier with the manner of a college professor. From him I got a notion of what was appropriate—or more important, what was *inappropriate*—to put in an Army newspaper.

The *Journal*'s officer-in-charge was Wiley C. Conner, an easy-going, battlefield-commissioned second lieutenant from Roanoke Rapids, North Carolina. He won his commission in Korea when his platoon leaders were casualties and as the ranking noncom, he successfully took over. He had no newspaper experience and showed little interest in acquiring any. He left producing the newspaper to us, provided we did nothing to get him in trouble.

The only time we came close to trouble was the day Fort Jackson got a new commanding general. I sent our photographer to take the general's picture as he arrived by plane, then ran his photo three columns wide on the front page, with a story about his background. Within an hour after the paper's fifteen thousand copies were distributed across the fort, I got a call from the new commander demanding, "Who authorized that photo?" When I said I did, he ordered me to retrieve every copy of the newspaper, remove his photo, and never again publish a picture of him in profile. Looking again at the picture, I understood why. The general had a long and jagged nose.

Our staff hurried to the motor pool for trucks and fanned out across the base, but retrieving all fifteen thousand copies of the paper proved impossible. Many were already in troops' hands. After gathering all the copies we could, we had to fill the space occupied by the offending photo and have fifteen thousand copies of the new edition printed and distributed. I alerted the civilian print shop in Columbia to be ready to reproduce the last issue. When I told the shop foreman why, he said, "You've got to be kidding."

We never ran another picture of the commanding general—except when he was awarding the *Jackson Journal* a Department of Defense citation for publishing one of the best base newspapers in the Army. The picture showed the back of his head as he extended an arm to present the award. That was one of two Defense Department citations the *Journal* received during my tenure, which on reflection was not exactly a compliment. It meant we had done nothing to antagonize the Army, though the years 1954 and '55 offered inviting opportunities to do so.

That was when the French were defeated at Dien Bien Phu and driven from Vietnam, prompting the United States to send economic aid and military advisors to support an anti-Communist government in South Vietnam, embroiling America in a prolonged war. That was also when the Army-McCarthy hearings were televised from Washington, exposing the demagogy of Wisconsin Senator Joseph McCarthy's anti-communist witch-hunts. Radios and black-and-white televisions all over the fort were tuned to those hearings. The *Jackson Journal* ignored them. Further, 1954 was the year the Supreme Court handed down its first *Brown v. Board of Education* decision, declaring segregated public schools unconstitutional. The ruling did not affect the Army—US Armed Forces had been desegregated in 1948 by executive order of President Truman—but the court decision threatened segregated schools around Columbia, South Carolina, where many soldiers and civilian personnel maintained homes. The *Jackson Journal* did not delve into that issue either, though it was a major factor in Strom Thurmond's successful write-in campaign for one of South Carolina's seats in the US Senate.

About midway through the summer of 1954, Lieutenant Conner called me over and said he needed to discuss some billing errors by our printer "Go to the motor pool, get a sedan and drive me into town," he said.

I responded, "I'm sorry, sir. I don't drive."

"What do you mean you don't drive?" he asked.

I said, "For most of my life no one in our family had a car, sir. I've never had a chance to learn."

"That's the damnedest fool thing I've ever heard," he said. "Go to the motor pool, get a sedan, and I'll teach you."

His tone suggested he would brook no argument, so I got my overseas cap—the kind that looks like an upside-down envelope—and in the heat of a July afternoon walked to the motor pool about two miles away.

There I asked a soldier at the front desk where to go to get a sedan.

"At that desk over there," he said. "You got a driver's license?"

"No," I said.

"You'll need a license," he said. "Go see the guy behind the typewriter in the next room."

I went to the next room, found the guy behind the typewriter, and said, "They sent me here to get a driver's license."

He put down the magazine he was reading, put a blue card in his typewriter, and asked, laconically, "What's your name?... Rank?... Serial number?... Date of birth?... Color of eyes?... Color of hair?" etc. He typed each of my answers on the blue card, pulled it from his typewriter, stamped it with some officer's signature, and handed it to me. "That license is good anywhere on the base and in Columbia," he said. He didn't ask if I could drive.

I went to the desk of the soldier who dispensed sedans, showed him my license, and said, "Lieutenant Conner sent me to get a sedan."

He handed me a clipboard with a long list of signatures under a note saying, "Sign In Here." I signed in. When I handed back the clipboard, he gestured to a line of sedans angle-parked in the yard behind him. "There they are," he said. "The keys are in them. Take any one you like."

I walked among the sedans, all olive-drab green, all with official white lettering on their doors, all gassed and waiting to be driven. Also, all had stick-shift transmissions, meaning that to drive one, I'd have to use a clutch and shift gears. I'd seen that done many times but had never mastered doing it myself. I selected a sedan, found the key, pushed in the clutch, and started the engine. I shifted the gear to neutral, then started searching for reverse so I could back into the motor pool street. Twice I let the clutch out too fast or too slow and stalled the engine. Finally, I eased the car out of its parking slot, turned the wheel, pushed in the clutch, and ground the transmission until I found low gear.

When I tried to go forward, I stalled the engine again. I stalled it a second time, then a third. Finally, I got the clutch out at just the right moment, and the car sprang forward. With that success I dared not make any changes.

Alternating use of the clutch and accelerator, I lurched the car—stop-go, stop-go, stop-go, like a goofy carnival ride—out of the motor pool, and onto the main road, all in first gear. Frantically, I bobbed unnoticed past the Military Police headquarters and down the hill toward the little frame hut that was the *Jackson Journal* office.

As I neared the *Journal,* Lieutenant Conner and my colleagues were on the porch, laughing and cheering as I came bucketing toward them. Turning into the incline that led to the *Journal* office, my foot slipped off the brake and the car nearly crashed into the porch, forcing my colleagues to leap out of the way.

Battle-hardened Lieutenant Conner was unperturbed. Before I could get out of the car, he took the rear, right-hand passenger's seat and ordered, "Now drive me to Columbia."

I had visions of disaster, but calmly, in a soothing voice, the lieutenant coached my every move. His key word was always "easy." Under his tutelage, I got the car into reverse and back into the street, then into low gear, into second, and finally into high. We cruised serenely past MPs at the fort's main gate and onto the major highway leading to Columbia. Along the way were lots of stop signs and stoplights where I had to brake and repeat the gear-changing maneuver. I stalled the engine several times, but Lieutenant Conner never lost his cool.

At the print shop, he resolved the billing problem and came out telling me to drive him back to the fort. I was sweating but no longer flustered, and driving was easier. I had passed an important test. In succeeding weeks, I often went to the motor pool for sedans, Jeeps, pickup trucks, and once for a six-by-six in carrying out the *Journal's* mission.

In early September 1954, as Slug was entering his senior year at Chapel Hill and drilling with the Air Force ROTC, I was ordered to attend the Army Information School in Fort Slocum, New York, on a rocky spit of land in the Long Island Sound. During the Civil War, the fort had been a prison for captured Confederates. The assignment gave me easy access to New York City through New Rochelle and Grand Central Station, opening new doors in my life.

Jack editing the Jackson Journal

CHAPTER
25

Pivotal Events

As my Army stint was ending, the ever-ebullient Slugger finished his schooling at Chapel Hill and hurriedly entered the Air Force to begin his three-year commitment to active duty. Over those three years, unexpected events would greatly alter the course of both his and my careers.

At the same time, events in Charlotte were raising its status as a welcoming place to live and do business. In July 1954 a new terminal for Douglas Airport was dedicated, lifting the facility out of the drab, olive-green makeshift barracks it had inherited from the Army Air Corps. The new terminal off West Boulevard (later the airport's freight depot) positioned Charlotte to become a major stop on the nation's developing air routes.

A year later, in September 1955, with a dedicatory address by Charlotte evangelist Billy Graham, the aluminum-domed Charlotte Coliseum and neighboring Ovens Auditorium were opened, replacing the armory auditorium and strengthening the city's appeal as an entertainment center.

Meanwhile, I was still in the Army and, in preparation for Fort Slocum, was gathering phone numbers for people I knew in New York. The first to answer was Margaret Watkins, once my co-editor on the high school newspaper. She had finished Duke with a Phi Beta Kappa key and taken a job with the Prentice Hall Publishing Company, helping produce *The PH Report*, a guide to stock market trading.

"Where are you?" she asked.

"At the Thirty-Fourth Street Y," I said.

"What are you doing *there*?"

"I'm staying here. It's a place Wink Locklair recommended because it offers low rates to servicemen. I'm in the Army."

"Have you had dinner?" she asked. It was about six in the evening.

"No," I said.

"Well come on down, have some wine with us and we'll all go to dinner in the neighborhood."

Within a half hour I was sitting on a sofa in her walk-up apartment in Greenwich Village, drinking sherry with her and her roommate, Laurie Ann Vendig, a Duke classmate who had an acting role in *Search for Tomorrow*, a televised soap opera. The Margaret Watkins I saw that evening was nothing like the grade grind I remembered from high school. She was witty and fun and informed about events around the world. The three of us talked, walked to a nearby chophouse for dinner and more animated conversation. On my way back to the Thirty-Fourth Street Y, I told myself the next time I had a free evening in New York, I should spend it with Margaret.

One afternoon when I called Prentice Hall and asked to speak with Margaret, the switchboard operator said in clipped New Yorkese, "Sir, repeat that, please?"

In the clearest voice I could command, I responded, "I said I would like to speak with Margaret Watkins. She works there—on *The PH Report*, I think."

The operator laughed, dropped her professional tone, and said conspiratorially, "I know exactly who she is and where she works, honey child. I just wanted to hear you say that again in your sweet Southern accent."

We had several dates. Once we went to the Brooklyn Academy of Music for a performance of Gilbert and Sullivan's *Pirates of Penzance*. Another time we went to Eddie Condin's jazz club and heard a number of famous musicians drop in for impromptu jam sessions.

At Fort Slocum I joined Jim Carson, a fellow soldier from Bristol, Virginia-Tennessee, for a delightful encounter after a late-night event at Madison Square Garden. As we entered all-but-deserted Grand Central Station to catch the last train to New Rochelle and the ferry to Fort Slocum, workmen were mopping the terminal floors and squeezing a filthy black liquid into buckets. Suddenly, out of one of the tunnels came a pretty, raven-haired girl about our age. She wore a white dress with a great splash of purple down the front. As she saw us, she said with chirpy surprise, "Oh, look. They're mopping the floors! I've never seen that before."

She said she had been to a party, had wine spilled on herself, and, abandoning her date, hoped to catch the last train home to Stamford, Connecticut, several stops beyond New Rochelle. As we introduced ourselves, she asked where we had gone to college. When Jim Carson answered, "Emory and Henry," she thought that was the funniest name she'd ever heard and accused Carson of making it up. He assured her it was a real institution nestled comfortably in the mountains of East Tennessee.

With equal doubt, we couldn't believe her name was Smith, "Kit Smith," she said." Nobody in New York was named Smith, we said, and accused her of making that up. She insisted she had come from a long line of Smiths and that her father was a famous New York newsman.

"Your father is not the sportswriter Red Smith, is he?" Jim Carson asked, laughing at the implausibility of such a thought. Indeed he was, she said. When we quizzed her about Red Smith's background, she answered each question correctly, prompting Carson to say, "Either you're Red Smith's daughter or you're one helluva a Red Smith fan."

We caught the same train and talked until reaching New Rochelle. As we got off, she said, "Come see me tomorrow," an invitation Jim and I interpreted as the Yankee equivalent of the Southern "Come see me sometime." As previously planned, the next day, Carson and I went to Brooklyn to see the Dodgers play baseball at Ebbets Field, our first visit to that storied old ballpark. It was a memorable experience, but I have often wondered what would have happened had we gone instead to visit Kit Smith.

In finishing the Fort Slocum program at the top of my class, I gained greater confidence in producing Army newspapers and found on my return to Fort Jackson that I needed it. Staff departures had brought the *Jackson Journal* a new photographer, a new sports editor, and a new features writer. I had to reorganize the staff.

At the same time, reorganizations were occurring at the *Charlotte Observer*. The court had resolved the dual-wills issue by awarding the newspaper to Curtis Johnson's widow. She served as publisher for a year and, after fighting off efforts to unionize the newsroom, sold the paper to the Knight brothers, John S. and James L., publishers of dailies in Akron, Detroit, Chicago, and Miami. Shortly after the Knights bought the *Observer*, I made a weekend trip to Charlotte and with Wink Locklair visited Julian Scheer, who had left Chapel Hill for a job on the *Charlotte News*. Scheer assured us that the Knight brothers had a reputation for quality journalism and would make the *Observer* a better paper.

After finishing his studies at Chapel Hill in May 1955, Slug accepted an Air Force commission and scurried to Wright-Patterson Air Force Base in Dayton, Ohio, where his duty was selling surplus Air Force property. Mastering bureaucratic procedures for such sales took little of his time. Mostly he played golf. His golfing buddies were captains, majors and colonels who urged him to make the Air Force a career. They could see him rising as an Air Force star, but his wife JoAnn said no. Pregnant with their first child, she paled at the thought of constantly moving from one military base to another. She wanted her family to have roots.

Later that summer I had a distressing phone call with Julian Scheer, who whispered that Wink Locklair had been arrested in a Charlotte police sweep and was charged with crime against nature. Neither Julian nor I were aware that Wink was gay. I remembered his frequent dates with a pretty actress who often starred at the Charlotte Little Theatre.

Wink appeared before a judge and pleaded guilty. He was sentenced to five years in prison. Five years! He might have held up a liquor store and gotten a lighter sentence. The penalty reflected the 1950s homophobia. Though I had heard whispers of him being homosexual, Wink's case exposed me to the cruel injustices endured by the LGBTQ community.

Wink served two and a half years as a librarian at the state's Central Prison in Raleigh, then was paroled in the care of Harry Golden, who guaranteed him a job collecting back advertising bills for the *Carolina Israelite*. After earning enough to pay his debts, Wink moved to New York and took a job with the

American Newspaper Publishers Association. Later he became assistant to the president of the Julliard School. He died in 1984 after suffering a heart attack on a Manhattan subway platform. He was fifty-nine.

In August 1955 before leaving the Army, I stopped by the *Observer* to check on developments. To assure the paper's local autonomy, John Knight and his brother Jim had hired thirty-nine-year-old C. A. "Pete" McKnight as its editor. A native of Shelby, North Carolina, McKnight had finished first in his class at Davidson College and joined the *Charlotte News*, where he had demonstrated such talent that at age twenty-nine he became the *News*'s editor. His editorials once won first, second, and third place in the state's annual assessment of outstanding journalism.

Following the Supreme Court's 1954 ruling that segregated schools were unconstitutional, McKnight left the *News* to help organize the Southern Education Reporting Service as a source of reliable information about Southern desegregation. He returned to Charlotte in 1955 as the *Observer*'s editor and began turning the paper into a revolving-door journalism school.

He brought intelligence and enterprise to a dull newspaper that *Time* magazine once dismissed as "a typographical mishmash with the editorial voice of a whisper." Tall, thin, and a bundle of twitches, McKnight had only one good eye but great civic vision. Before matters crucial to the city's advancement became public issues, he would be on the telephone to local business leaders pointing the way forward.

As the *Observer*'s managing editor, McKnight recruited soft-spoken Tom Fesperman, another former *Charlotte News* visionary. Together they began hiring bright, young staffers to give the *Observer* an aggressive edge. Each spring McKnight and Fesperman recruited graduates of communications schools across the country and began turning them into professional journalists. Over succeeding years, the paper's lively editorials, its aggressive reporting, and its openness to public comment created a community dialogue that made Charlotte a more progressive city.

My purpose in visiting the *Observer* was to meet one of the paper's new hires, Walter Kelley, nicknamed "Whitey." He was a spare, exuberant sprite from Miami, who had leaped over Wilton Garrison to become the paper's executive sports editor. A live-wire competitor, Whitey was committed to more aggressive coverage of sports news and stronger commentary. But with offices 150 miles from the state's Big Four athletic powers—UNC at Chapel Hill, Duke at Durham, NC State at Raleigh, and Wake Forest in Wake County and later in Winston-Salem—the *Observer* was at a disadvantage. Rival papers in Raleigh, Durham, and Greensboro carried more timely stories.

I told Whitey I could remedy that. From Chapel Hill I could drive to the Big Four schools and find a story or two every day. My *Observer* colleagues ·Dick Pierce and Herman Helms assured Kelley I was capable of doing that. Whitey was hesitant, then said, "Let's try it and see how it goes."

I invested my Army mustering out pay in a 1949 Chevrolet and applied for government-backed GI Bill benefits. Once enrolled, I began going to classes in the mornings and driving in search of sports stories in the afternoons. I found many. After a month, Whitey Kelley elevated me from correspondent to a full-time staff member and paid me a generous stipend that with the GI Bill enabled me to resume my college studies without the constant burden of worries about money.

I covered memorable events. I saw quarterbacks Don Meredith of Southern Methodist and Sonny Jurgensen of Duke clash as collegians long before their Hall of Fame careers with the professional Dallas Cowboys and the Washington Redskins. But my presence often offended coaches, athletic directors, and sports information officers who didn't like having a student from a rival school dropping in on their football or basketball practices.

One Sunday morning as I drove past the athletic complex at Chapel Hill, I heard the sound of footballs being punted and a lot of loud chatter. I pulled into a parking lot, entered Kenan Stadium and saw the UNC football teams running through a variety of drills. I took a front row seat and watched. "Sunny Jim" Tatum, UNC's celebrated new coach, spotted me and came over. A UNC alum who had starred as a Tar Heels lineman in the 1930s and after World War II had won renown as a head coach at Kentucky and the University of Maryland, he had been brought "home" to restore North Carolina's football fortunes. A large man with gargantuan appetites for food, football, and glory, he was wearing sweat clothes, a baseball cap, and around his neck a whistle.

As he sidled up, he also wore a sheepish grin. After an exchange of pleasantries, he said he hoped I would not make an issue of his holding a Sunday morning practice, that he didn't want the mothers of his players to think he was keeping them out of church services.

I told him I had not intended to write a story about the practice, but now that he had challenged me about it, I was afraid I had to. So I wrote a terse little piece saying that Coach Tatum was so anxious to return UNC to football prominence that he was holding Sunday workouts.

The next day, I got a call from the UNC football office inviting me to lunch with Coach Tatum at the training table for UNC athletes. I arrived on time and waited for Coach Tatum, who came in late and, as always, a little breathless. I chose a modest lunch, but he ordered a big meal with several bowls of black-eyed peas. With a spoon, he ate and talked rapidly, accusing me of abusing my student privileges by spying on athletic activities. He asked why I was not being as fair to UNC as other sportswriters in the state. I told him I was as loyal to UNC as any other journalist, but I was also obligated to report what I had seen. I said that any other sportswriter who witnessed that Sunday practice would have written a story about it. We amicably agreed to disagree and, having finished the last of his black-eyed peas, he left. We got along well after that.

I had similar confrontations with athletic officials at Duke and NC State, but in time they were pleased to see my stories about their teams in the *Observer* and let me cover their activities.

The reporting experience that most absorbed my imagination and ultimately changed the course of my career was covering the 1956-57 UNC men's basketball team that went undefeated in thirty-two games to win the national championship. Over the years, the significance of that feat has paled as UNC basketball teams have won six national championships, Duke five, and NC State two. But in 1957 no Carolinas team had won a national championship in any major sport. The UNC team was coached by Frank McGuire, an Irish charmer with deep roots in New York.

North Carolina's 1957 basketball team starred four Irish Catholics and a Jew, all New Yorkers. As the team's winning streak grew and the Tar Heels rose to number one in national rankings, a frenzy, now known as "March Madness," arose across the Carolinas. When the team advanced to the NCAA tournament, a television network was hastily arranged to bring the games into homes in the Carolinas, creating a broadcast tradition that endures to this day.

Televising those games made that tournament the biggest sports event in Carolinas history up to that time. It was bigger than the 1942 Rose Bowl that was moved from Pasadena, California, to Duke Stadium in Durham after the Japanese bombed Pearl Harbor.

Having seen most of UNC's regular season games, I accompanied the team to Madison Square Garden in New York to see it defeat Yale, then to the Palestra in Philadelphia for a victory over Canisius and a bruising conquest of Syracuse. That qualified it for the Final Four tournament in the cavernous Municipal Auditorium in Kansas City.

As one of the youngest sportswriters (I was twenty-five) covering the national tournament, I was often on national radio and TV shows to talk about the Tar Heels and their undefeated season. I explained that North Carolina had an indomitable scorer in jump-shooting Lennie Rosenbluth, but its greatest strength was a dogged defense.

In the Final Four tournament, the Tar Heels had to win two of the most incredible games in the history of NCAA finals, first a heart-stopping, triple-overtime victory over Michigan State in the semifinals, and a second gut-wrenching triple-overtime clash with seven-foot Wilt Chamberlain and the Kansas Jayhawks for the national championship. There hasn't been a Final Four to equal it since.

Played in the Central Time Zone, the championship game didn't end until well after midnight in Charlotte, minutes before the *Observer*'s Eastern Time Zone deadline. I had to have two stories ready to give the telegrapher, one if North Carolina lost and another if it won. On my portable typewriter at courtside, I wrote both while frantic overtime play was underway in front of me. Every dribble, every pass, every shot might determine the outcome.

When their leading scorer Lennie Rosenbluth fouled out in overtime, the Tar Heels relied on their defense and finally won a low-scoring game, 54-53. After the last shot, North Carolina's Tommy Kearns grabbed the rebound and flung it high into the rafters, knowing time would expire before it came down.

As I typed the opening paragraphs onto my game-winning story and gave it to the telegrapher, my ears rang with the words of a comic song from the musical *Oklahoma*, "Everything's up to date in Kansas City. They've gone about as far as they can go..."

I also thought about the Slugger, knowing he probably watched the game on television and was envious of my being there to witness it and afterward talk to the players and coaches. That added to my satisfaction, but for me the event held even greater significance. During the jubilant flight back to the Raleigh-Durham airport, where a carpet of cheering faces covered the tarmac as far as you could see, I made up my mind that I would get out of sportswriting. I thought I would never cover another sports event as historic, as suspenseful, or as satisfying. Also, I had begun to see sportswriting as seasonal and shallow. So much more news beckoned my interest.

Unlike my anxiety-fraught early years at Chapel Hill, my final years there were marked by great confidence and intellectual growth. No longer was I intimidated by course titles or famous professors. For the first time, my goal shifted from earning a degree to getting an education. I fulfilled the prediction of Claiborne Jones, my former faculty advisor, who said a little maturity would improve my outlook.

Despite warnings about hard quizzes, I stood in line to get tickets to Bernard Boyd's Bible classes, the first on the Old Testament and the second on the New. Both took me behind scriptures I had memorized as a boy and showed where they had come from and how they were assembled into a single volume. As a result, the Bible became a more fascinating document.

Also, I was learning things that deepened my understanding of our culture—about the New South and its struggle to overcome strictures of the Old and about North Carolina politics, characterized by author V. O. Key as a "progressive plutocracy" in which leaders of tobacco, textile, and furniture industries pushed the state ahead industrially and educationally.

When I could, I spent weekends in Charlotte seeing Margaret Watkins, who had come home to join the staff of the *Charlotte News*. Her parents began inviting me to dinner at their home and introducing me to Margaret's aunts, uncles, and cousins, substitutes for the scattered family I had lost.

Unexpected events were altering Slug's life too. Shortly after UNC won its national championship, his father-in-law, W. W. Bailey, suffered a heart attack just as the Bailey Company was opening a cafeteria in West Gate, a new Asheville shopping center. He called on the Slugger for help. Through the Red Cross, Slug got a hardship discharge from the Air Force, moved his family to Asheville, and took over the cafeteria's operations. By the time his father-in-law recovered, Slug and his wife were expecting their second child. Anxious to bring his daughter and grandchildren closer to home, Bailey transferred Slug to Charlotte to manage Bailey cafeterias there.

As the deadline for Slug's law school admission approached, he let it lapse without lament. He said he'd had enough of going to school and scrimping by on part-time jobs. He liked the responsibility of managing cafeterias and was ready to put into practice many of the methods he had learned in business school.

I regretted his decision. I could envision Slug as a lawyer and thought that for once in his enchanted life, he had muffed an opportunity. With his discipline, wit, and powers of persuasion, he could have been a successful attorney and, in time perhaps, a popular elected official.

After completing my studies for a bachelor's degree in English in July 1957, I joined the *Observer*'s Charlotte sports staff and ate at Slug's cafeterias often enough to hear him complain about his father-in-law's resistance to his business-school ideas. At the *Observer* I faced similar frustration. Senior members of the sports staff asserted their claim on major events, leaving me to find stories on my own. Drawing on my park-league umpiring experience, I wrote a series of stories on the pluses and minuses of Little League baseball. I quoted recreation experts who frowned at parental participation at Little League games and charged that Little League imposed adult rules on children's play. My *Observer* colleagues belittled the series—until it won first prize in the North Carolina Press Association's first ever sportswriting competition.

All that summer, officials of Charlotte city schools, under court orders to desegregate their schools, were quietly collaborating with counterparts in Raleigh, Greensboro, and Winston-Salem. If schools in all those cities were desegregated at the same time, public protests might be minimized.

Blacks applying for admission to Charlotte's Central High, Harding High, and Alexander Graham and Piedmont Junior Highs were secretly accepted for an early-September enrollment.

At that moment, I had other interests. On the last day of August 1957, after a two-year courtship, I married Margaret Watkins. In tux and tails, my best man was the Slugger. But on the first day of our honeymoon in New York, Margaret and I were horrified to read about the effort to desegregate a Charlotte high school. There on the front page of the *New York Times* was a photo of Dorothy Counts, a Black teenager, being spat upon by a raucous crowd as she entered Harding High. Charlotte had successfully desegregated other schools, but the Harding High stain took Charlotte years to live down.

Jack with Coach McGuire

CHAPTER

26

Reaching Takeoff Points

As the 1950s drew to a close, Charlotte approached what urban planners called a "takeoff point," by achieving a critical mass that would propel steady growth. One of those takeoff points occurred in November 1957 when American Trust Company merged with its next-door neighbor Commercial National Bank to form American-Commercial, beginning the bank's long climb to become Bank of America, once the largest banking company in the United States. The climb was made under the drive of successive leaders, the visionary Addison Reese, the strategic Tom Storrs, and the aggressive Hugh McColl, all ambitious for the bank and for Charlotte.

At the same time, Union National Bank, under the crisp leadership of Cliff Cameron, was also expanding. Cameron's zeal was handed down to his successor Ed Crutchfield, who with Bank of America turned once-sleepy Charlotte into a national financial powerhouse.

Another launchpad move occurred in 1958 when, at the insistence of the business community, voters in Charlotte and Mecklenburg County approved plans for merging the city and county school systems into one big district. The 1959 merger signaled that all Charlotte-Mecklenburg schools, urban or rural, would be on the same financial footing and offer high-quality education. Many families interpreted the merger as an invitation to move to the suburbs.

The pace of Charlotte's growth was accelerated after a 1960 search for a city manager to replace the icy disciplinarian who had resigned. Many on the city council wanted to appoint a folksy in-house successor who would be less demanding than his predecessor. That annoyed investment banker Rush S. Dickson, then one of the city's wise men. It was said that you shouldn't start a new enterprise in Charlotte without having Dickson look over your business plan.

The city had often relied on Rush Dickson's acumen. In 1940, after building Memorial Hospital with more beds than the community could fill, the city council appointed Dickson to head an authority that would assure the hospital stayed solvent and beyond the reach of local politics. During World War II, to save on food costs, Dickson bought a mule and planted a large garden on hospital grounds. When the war ended and the hospital was filling its beds, Dickson discontinued the garden and sold the mule—at a profit.

As the city council squabbled over appointing a new city manager, Dickson looked on its squint-eyed politics with impatience. He recruited four prominent businessmen—lawyer Gibson Smith, builder Brevard Myers, chemist Randy Babcock, and engraver Herbert Hitch—to seek seats on the seven-member council. Running as the "Better Government Four," the businessmen won and used their majority to hire as city manager Bill Veeder, a tough-minded young man with a brisk manner and suffer-no-foolishness discipline. He brought polish and professionalism to every city department and quickened life at city hall. He emphasized planning and the timely execution of plans. A decade later, when Veeder left to supervise the building of Carowinds as an regional amusement park, he was replaced by other professionals like him—David Burkhalter in the 1970s, Wendell White in the 1980s, and Pam Seifert in the 1990s. With each, Charlotte's stature grew.

Throughout the summer of 1958, Slug and I were reaching our own takeoff points. I left the *Observer* to go to graduate school, and Slug left the cafeteria business to try his hand at real estate.

Slug's move resulted from increasing friction with his father-in-law. When Slug suggested greater efficiencies in cafeteria operations, W.W. Bailey balked. His resistance typified the era's generational clash as World War II veterans came home from college and sought leading roles in family businesses.

From my post at the *Observer*, I could appreciate Slug's situation. In a sports department dominated by senior colleagues who claimed the best assignments, I felt hemmed in. Further, I missed the intellectual excitement I had enjoyed in my last years of college. When I asked for a leave to attend graduate school, *Observer* editor Pete McKnight made me promise to return when my year's study ended.

I entered the University of Chicago in the fall of 1958 in pursuit of a master's degree in literary criticism. It was a bold leap into a rigorous institution in a distant part of the country, but I was buoyed by the confidence gained in my final years at Chapel Hill.

With Pete McKnight's help my wife and I got jobs on the *Chicago Daily News*, plum assignments for two Carolinians with little exposure to big city nightlife. My wife Margaret became the writer-reporter for *Weekend*, a *Daily News* magazine suggesting things to do on a Friday night, Saturday, or Sunday in the city. She combed Chicago's cultural calendars, theater schedules, and museum exhibits for good ideas. Her job got us tickets to all manner of cultural and entertainment events.

My job resulted from an interview with "Stuffy" Walters, the *Daily News*'s portly, bug-eyed, and raspy-voiced managing editor. He asked if we had nightclubs down South. In answering no, I assured him that where we came from you couldn't even buy mixed drinks. He said I was just what he was looking for, someone with fresh eyes who could visit nightclubs and describe what I saw. Compared to graduate school, the job was easy and the pay supplemented my GI Bill benefits. In addition, I got to see such musical innovators as Dave Brubeck, Sarah Vaughn, Miles Davis, and John Coltrane. Meeting and interviewing them and others gave me new confidence as a reporter. But after six months of driving Chicago's snowy streets at night, my interest in watching routine and sometimes bawdy floor shows waned. That and the pressure to produce graduate school papers persuaded me to give up the job.

While I was enjoying Chicago, the Slugger split with his father-in-law and joined real estate developer Lat Purser in assembling shopping centers. One of those centers became Amity Gardens, a strip of one-story shops on newly completed Independence Boulevard east of the new Ovens Auditorium and Charlotte Coliseum, then at the eastern edge of town. It is all but deserted now, but back then that stretch of Independence Boulevard was known among planners and developers as the "Gold Coast," a hot spot for new enterprises.

Among Slug's duties in filling Amity Gardens was finding an operator for a cafeteria, one mandated by the lender to assure the shopping center a steady flow of traffic. Slug turned to his father-in-law, who agreed to open a Bailey's Cafeteria there. Before papers could be signed, however, Bailey got a competing offer from the developer of a shopping center in the Cotswold neighborhood about two miles away. Assuming the Cotswold site would be better, Bailey withdrew his commitment to Slug.

As Slug sought another option, the hour for planning the Amity Gardens cafeteria drew near. Lat Purser gestured toward a calendar and said, "Looks to me, Slugger, like you're about to run a cafeteria."

Seizing the opportunity, the twenty-seven-year-old Slug replied, "Only if I can own it."

When Purser and the lender agreed to let Slug buy the enterprise over time, he began planning the cafeteria building and its furnishings. Drawing on his marketing studies, he made sure the structure had a distinctive look. Set back from a row of innocuous, one-story shops, the two-story cafeteria looked like something from an Arabic oasis, with rows of tall, arched windows on each side and a canopy over its entrance. Its golden-hued dining room was bright and cheery. Its second floor included a large private room for special events. Slug named the cafeteria "The Barclay" after a New York hotel he admired.

On my return from graduate school in the fall of 1959, I rejoined the *Observer* as a reporter rather than a sportswriter. It was an opportune time to be writing news. The city's planning positioned it for rapid growth. I reported on the unveiling of many proposed expansions, including the 1960 Thoroughfare Plan that laid out much of the street and expressway system Charlotteans use today. Other plans called for the building of high-rise housing for senior citizens. I often wrote several stories a day.

It was also an opportune time for the Slugger. As his Barclay cafeteria neared completion. he led me with brotherly pride on a tour, emphasizing the smallest detail. He took every opportunity to show that this was a big deal. Truly, it was. No one in our family had ever embarked on such an ambitious venture.

The Barclay opened in late 1960 to big crowds and rave notices. People flocked to enjoy the food and exchange banter with Slug, who over the next nine years was there for almost every serving. As he had earlier at Myrtle Beach and Asheville, he endeared himself to patrons by learning their names and treating them like family.

One of those patrons was bulky, fast-talking Paul Buck, a one-of-a-kind character who ran the auditorium and coliseum like an old-time impresario. He looked something like a penguin with a small, round head, slicked-back hair, dazzling eyes, and a bubbling playfulness. He loved to tell stories about show-business people he had met. With his help, Slug opened the Barclay's private dining room to casts from the Charlotte Summer Theater, then filling Ovens Auditorium with weekly revivals of popular Broadway plays. The Summer Theater brought big city glamour to Charlotte and the surrounding region. People could see in person such stars as Andy Williams, Debbie Reynolds, Jimmy Durante, Betsy Palmer, and Tom Poston. During the week, Summer Theater casts climbed the Barclay stairs to catered lunches and dinners in Slug's private dining room. Soon the Barclay became a popular dining destination, eclipsing the Bailey Cafeteria in Cotswold.

As products of Charlotte's exploding growth, the Barclay and Amity Gardens gave Slug a higher profile. He moved his family into larger, upscale quarters on suburban Folger Drive, part of a new subdivision on what was then the southeast rim of the city.

As Slug was opening the Barclay, I was assisting the hard-charging Rolfe Neill, a friend from my Chapel Hill days. After a fling at weekly newspapering, Neill had become the *Observer*'s business editor and daringly put himself on the same plane with local corporate leaders by calling them all by their first names. I remember the day he placed a call to the august Charles Cannon, then lord of the Cannon Mills sheets-and-towels empire in Kannapolis. When Cannon came on the phone, Rolfe said, "Hello, Charlie....Rolfe Neill here..." I expected the offended Cannon to hang up in a spluttering rage, but the two enjoyed a long conversation.

Shortly after I joined the business desk, Neill left for a stint in the newspaper's Washington bureau, leaving business reporting to me at an auspicious moment. The site of the World War II shell-loading plant southwest of town had begun to lure large manufacturers to Charlotte. In addition, along Tryon Street bankers were speculating over when First Citizens Bank of Smithfield, a financial power in eastern North Carolina, would plant its flag in Charlotte to be near the clearinghouse of the Charlotte branch of the Federal Reserve Bank. It did so on my watch, enlivening competition among the big banks that were beginning to dominate the city's economy.

Other stories I covered included the 1959 opening of Charlottetown Mall, envisioned by famed city-builder Jim Rouse as Charlotte's first enclosed shopping center. The mall was built on what had been a pasture on the Thompson Orphanage farm. I met the unpretentious Rouse as he sat on a keg of nails in the raw, unfinished mall, wearing a three-piece suit, an orange tie, and talking on the telephone to a banker in London. When that conversation ended, he stood up, shook my hand, and said, "Now let me tell you why this mall will be an exciting asset for Charlotte."

As a business reporter, I also broke the story of the Charlotte City Club's plan to move from the aging opulence of the old Buford Hotel at Tryon and Fourth Streets into elegant quarters in a new building at Second and Tryon. There it achieved its peak influence on Charlotte's commercial, civic, and political affairs. Over countless private lunches in a dining room that excluded women, civic leaders discussed how to improve the city, how to expand its economy, how to manage racial unrest, and what to do about the increasing prominence of women in political, cultural, and business affairs.

It was there, over countless private luncheons, that leaders of Belk's and Ivey's department stores and Sears Roebuck agreed to create a new, upscale shopping center on what had been former governor Cameron Morrison's model dairy farm in Sharon Township southeast of town. The center opened in 1971 under the name SouthPark and attracted a new city of shops, offices, apartments, and medical facilities, all siphoning energy from uptown Charlotte.

While I was covering business, my wife and I bought our first house, an idyllic, white-framed cottage high on a terraced yard with a white picket fence.

It was from that little house on a low-traffic street that I taught my son Jacky and my daughter Margaret to ride bikes and often pedaled with them on long jaunts to their grandparents' house on Beverly Drive, where they were treated with milk and cookies.

While my wife and I were buying that house, John F. Kennedy was sprinting through Democratic primaries in quest of his party's nomination to become the first Catholic president of the United States. After a narrow victory over Richard Nixon in the 1960 election, he became a glamorous figure. His youth (only Theodore Roosevelt was younger in becoming president), his eloquence, his attractive wife Jackie, and the vigor of his sprawling family excited many Americans to think the nation had reached its own takeoff point. Earlier evidence of that excitement had come in 1958 when South Carolina elected Ernest F. Hollings of Charleston as the first of a series of progressive governors. That excitement was felt in North Carolina in 1960 when Governor Terry Sanford was elected to bring "a new day" to North Carolina. Sanford began that "new day" by inviting "Fritz" Hollings to participate in his inauguration. One of my favorite images is of Hollings leaning over the Sanford inaugural viewing stand and seeing rows and rows of National Guard units marching up Raleigh's main street. The sight moved him to prod Sanford and crack, in his heavy Charleston brogue, "Aye, looka heah, many more troops an' this and we secede again." It was a funny line but no measure of Hollings' politics, which were more New South than Old.

"With the Kennedys in power—
Jack in the White House, Robert
in the Justice Department,
and Teddy in the US Senate—
Washington was the world's most
glamorous news center."

CHAPTER

27

Schools and Race

When Rolfe Neill returned from Washington, I shifted to covering the public schools, always a sensitive subject. It was especially prickly in 1960 because, while improving many schools, the city-county merger bred simmering jealousies over whose methods and traditions, city or county, would be adopted by the consolidated system. Further, record enrollment by "baby boom" children required the rapid building of new schools and raised questions about desegregation. City schools had begun token integration in 1957, but county schools remained racially segregated. To retain White support, leaders of the merged school system were in no hurry to desegregate further.

My reporting again put me in touch with Dr. Elmer Garinger, the former Central High principal who became superintendent of the consolidated system, and with his deputy Dr. John Otts, my former Central High principal. Their guidance gave my stories clarity and authority, resulting in my winning the North Carolina Education Association's 1961 School Bell award for excellence in reporting.

I also covered the elevation of Charlotte College into a full-service state university. When the college, a locally funded, two-year institution spawned by the temporary CCUNC, moved from its closet-like quarters in Central High to a new campus ten miles north, I was there to witness its move and talk with Bonnie Cone, the Charlotte College president. Of all the marvelous people I met in my journalistic career, she was the most memorable. A stocky woman with dark hair and piercing eyes, she walked leaning slightly forward, as if pushing against prevailing winds, which was often the case. She took in everything around her and was relentless in encouraging students. She wouldn't let them give up on themselves. For eighteen years her vision and optimism kept Charlotte College alive. Miss Cone wanted to anchor the college in the old Central High buildings and expand into the surrounding neighborhood through imminent domain, as Central Piedmont Community College had done, but state officials objected. They said the Central site was too close to the South Carolina line. They wanted a commuter school at a safer distance north.

Oliver Rowe, a leading Charlotte industrialist and backer of Bonnie Cone, used to laugh at the way she assembled the college's new campus, which fronted both US 29 and NC 49 ten miles north of town. In addition to the farmland that had once fed the county home for the poor, Bonnie sought adjoining acreage owned by friends of the college, including Tom Belk of the Belk department stores family. Oliver Rowe joked that if Bonnie kept asking for "that next little piece of land" adjacent to the campus, and after that the "next little piece of land," the college grounds might extend to the Catawba River. To Miss Cone's credit, the campus wound up covering about a thousand acres, enough to support a large research university.

I attended the college's first event on its new campus, a picnic of ham biscuits and fried chicken served on red-and-white gingham tablecloths in the loft of an abandoned dairy barn. There, on worn, hay-strewn planks, Bonnie Cone looked over the rolling hills and shared her vision of the university she was certain would soon arise. She pointed out where the student union would be, the physics and chemistry labs, the arts and science classrooms, the gymnasium, and administrative buildings. Having known Bonnie Cone since her teaching days at Central High and having watched her transform a lost-and-found closet into a burgeoning college, I knew better than to doubt her. Almost everything she envisioned that night later came to pass, helping to transform Charlotte into a big city. Once the nation's largest metropolitan region without a major university, Charlotte used its growing influence to help Charlotte College became a four-year state institution in 1964. A year later, with the help of Oliver Rowe, Pete McKnight, lawyer L. P. McLendon of Greensboro, and others, including Bill Friday, then president of the state university system, Charlotte College became UNC Charlotte, the fourth branch of the state university system, along with UNC Chapel Hill, NC State, and UNC Greensboro. Its subsequent rise to research university status made Charlotte more attractive to high-tech companies.

In the summer of 1961, as I was driving home from a weekend conference in Raleigh, I heard on the radio that Ernest Hemingway had died. Knowing I would soon pass Chapel Hill, I thought I might try to interview Dr. C. Hugh Holman, the professor who taught the novels course I had taken four years earlier, about Hemingway's place in American literature. I found Dr. Holman's phone number and caught him at his office in the ivy-covered confines of Bynum Hall. I asked if he would talk with me about Hemingway, knowing I intended to write a newspaper story about our conversation. I warned that he would be putting his reputation in the hands of a former student to whom he had once given poor grades. He laughed and said, "Oh, I remember you. Come on. I'll risk it."

In his book-lined office he looked the same as I remembered: his black hair slicked back, his dark-rimmed glasses shading his face and emphasizing the puffy bags under his eyes from having read so many student papers. He talked with a soft Southern accent (he was from Cross Anchor, South Carolina) and tended to smack his lips as he finished a sentence. He said Hemingway's greatest influence on literature was probably his minimalist writing style that was intended to make readers not only see but also feel the intensity of what he was writing about. That style inspired many imitators, including North Carolina's Robert Ruark of Southport. He talked of Hemingway's masculinity and of his great respect for personal courage but said there was also a feminine side of Hemingway, as evidenced by the heroines of his novels. He said his favorite image of Hemingway was of a great hairy fist holding a delicate red rose.

By the summer of 1962 my performance on a number of assignments earned me the opportunity to monitor the Democratic primary in South Carolina between incumbent Senator Olin D. Johnston and the state's sitting governor, Ernest F. Hollings. In those days, winning the Democratic primary was equivalent to winning the office. Republican opposition in the general election was rarely a threat.

In accepting the assignment, I was made aware of a previous South Carolina primary between a sitting governor, Strom Thurmond, and an incumbent senator, Olin D. Johnston. Johnston later told me that Thurmond, then a celebrated physical fitness buff, had been pictured in *Life* magazine standing on his head. Johnston said he effectively used that picture in telling audiences that "what South Carolina needs is a senator who can stand on his feet, not one who can stand on his head," helping Johnston win the primary.

In carrying out my assignment, I drove around South Carolina and wrote daily stories about what people said they were hearing in the Johnston-Hollings campaign. Shockingly, as popular as Governor Hollings was, most people said they were more impressed by what Senator Johnson was saying. My stories soon became a pain to the Hollings team. At the time, the *Observer,* with fifty thousand subscribers in South Carolina, was an influential newspaper in the state.

On election night, as radio reports indicated Hollings was losing two to one across the state and had even lost Charleston, his home county, I was standing with a large group on the porch of the Hollings headquarters in Columbia. When the governor and his aides arrived, Hollings walked briskly past, then took a few steps back to look squarely at me and said, "You were right. There's more mass than class." Then he strode into his headquarters.

In time Fritz Hollings would win the Senate seat once held by Olin Johnston and in Washington would win great respect for his brains and wit, but his Charleston accent was always a source of amusement. An admiring Ted Kennedy once quipped that Hollings was "the only member of the US Senate "who doesn't speak English."

In January of 1963, a few months after the South Carolina primary, I was appointed to represent the *Observer* in the Knight Newspaper's Washington bureau, a plum assignment for any reporter but especially so in those circumstances.

Beyond public education and state politics, more ominous issues were rising across the South. In many places, Freedom Riders and others protesting segregation were met with anger and violence. When protests arose in Charlotte, Slug played a critical role in advancing the city's profile as a racially tolerant place.

Charlotte protests began on May 20, 1963, usually a quiet holiday commemorating Mecklenburg's 1775 declaration of independence. Students from all-Black Johnson C. Smith University came clapping and singing out of the Smith campus on Charlotte's west side, led by Dr. Reginald Hawkins, a bantam-size dentist impatient for racial reform. The protesters looped through the town's main square and down East Trade Street to the County Courthouse. They halted on the courthouse plaza before an obelisk memorializing Mecklenburg's revolutionary quest for freedom from Great Britain. There Dr. Hawkns observed that even after 188 years, the county's Black citizens were still not free. Unless barriers to Black equality were lifted, he warned, future marches would be longer, louder, and angrier.

At the time, the ugliness and humiliation of racial discrimination were evident in daily newspaper stories. One was of *Observer* columnist Kays Gary's description of interviewing jazz trumpeter Louis "Satchmo" Armstrong in a Black hotel because, despite his worldwide fame, Armstrong was refused lodging at Charlotte's White hotels. There sat Armstrong, grumbling bare-chested in his under shorts as a small electric fan blew over a block of ice, the best "air-conditioning" the hotel, once the refuge for White unwed mothers, had to offer. Another was the fury of the Boston Celtics' great Bill Russell, the most valuable player in the National Basketball Association (NBA), who couldn't accompany his Celtics teammates to a White hotel because it wouldn't accept Blacks. Stories out of Atlanta told of Harry Belafonte, whose "Calypso" album had topped the *New York Times* bestseller list for thirty-one weeks, being refused service at several White restaurants.

Charlotte mayor Stanford R. Brookshire understood Dr. Hawkins' warning. The next morning, he phoned Chamber of Commerce leaders and urged them to do something, lest headlines about racial unrest mar Charlotte's image as a progressive place. Over the next few weeks, chamber directors met privately at the City Club and persuaded hotel and motel operators to desegregate as they had two years earlier during a federally supported trade fair.

Subsequent meetings with White restaurant operators were less harmonious. Most restaurateurs feared that serving Blacks would drive off their White clientele. At one of the meetings, thirty-year-old Slug proposed a strategy that would lessen those fears and leave offended White patrons few other places to dine. Pointing to members of the all-White chamber board, he suggested that each director invite a counterpart from the Black community to lunch at a White restaurant. If such pairs spread themselves all across town and on the same day, no restaurant would be hurt. His suggestion drew a spontaneous endorsement from Dr. Carlyle Marney, pastor of Myers Park Baptist Church and a voice of gravitas among chamber directors and the religious community.

On the appointed day, chamber directors and Black business leaders broke the color line at dozens of restaurants. It wound up taking them two days to cover the whole town, but it was a bold move, wiping away lifetimes of segregation. Coming on the heels of the desegregation of the University of Alabama over the objections of Governor George Wallace, the Charlotte success further emboldened the Kennedy brothers to submit to Congress a massive civil rights bill calling for ending segregation in public accommodations, education, and employment. In praising Charlotte, the Kennedys sent a message across the country suggesting that the city was a stable, open, New South community without many of the barriers of the Old South.

I began my Washington assignment on January 1, 1963. I moved from reporting on education to covering the Carolinas contingent in Washington. With the Kennedys in power—Jack in the White House, Robert in the Justice Department, and Teddy in the US Senate—Washington was the world's most glamorous news center. My job called for keeping tabs on four US senators—Sam Ervin and Everett Jordan from North Carolina and Strom Thurmond and Olin Johnston from South Carolina—and on seventeen congressmen from the Carolinas, including Harold Cooley and Herbert Bonner from North Carolina and Mendel Rivers from South Carolina, each of whom was a committee chairman. In addition, I had to report on numerous Carolinians who held senior posts in the Kennedy administration, including former North Carolina governor Luther Hodges, who was secretary of commerce, Charles S. Murphy of Wallace, North Carolina, who was undersecretary of agriculture, and Henry Hall Wilson of neighboring Monroe, North Carolina, a Kennedy liaison to the House of Representatives. I worked long hours and was often on call for congressional comment on weekend developments.

Every week, I wrote a column on Washington events for the Sunday editorial pages. My column about the passage of the Elementary and Secondary Education Act, which, among other things, initiated head start programs in kindergartens across the country, brought me a warm thank-you note from President Johnson.

Our seven-member Washington staff was led by Edwin A. Lahey, a *Chicago Daily News* reporter famed for mordant humor. His story on a suicide began, "She was neat. She hanged herself in a closet." When he covered the H-bomb test in the Pacific, he skipped the scientific measures in writing "Mega tons, smega tons, it was a helluva blast." Lahey said he wrote for "people who move their lips when they read."

Yet, in person Lahey, a little larger than a leprechaun, was a softie. He took a personal interest in each of his bureau hands, often asking about our wives and children. He seemed to know everybody of consequence in Washington and usually got information for his stories over the telephone.

After I had been in Washington several months, he called me into his office with carbon copies of my stories stacked in front of him. "I've been looking over your black sheets," he said, "You're working too much. Slow down. This isn't the Continental Can Company. We don't get paid at piece rates."

Later it dawned on me that what he was really saying was I wasn't digging deep enough, wasn't asking enough questions, wasn't getting to the bottom of congressional affairs. If I had followed his advice, I might have avoided what soon became an embarrassment.

A few weeks later, I met a young man from Pickens County in the rural hills of South Carolina. He had come to Washington as a page and, as a lackey for majority leader Lyndon Johnson, had risen to be secretary to the US Senate. He bragged that he knew the secrets of many senators. Impressed by his story and knowing that few Carolinians had heard of him, I sought few other sources and wrote a glowing story of his climb to prominence. The *Observer* displayed it prominently in a Sunday edition. Months later, that former Senate page was the target of a lawsuit in Washington's US District Court and the subject of what became the Bobby Baker scandal. Washington correspondents from across the country dropped by our bureau to read—and take notes on—my story and laugh at my naivete, as if they had known all along who Bobby Baker was. After weeks of hearings, the scandal proved to be less than advertised, but Bobby Baker was indicted for theft, fraud, and income tax evasion. He was convicted on the tax charge and served sixteen months in a federal prison.

It took a while for me to regain my perspective, but even from Washington I could appreciate the example Charlotte had set in desegregating its restaurants. One afternoon, I stood on the grassy White House front lawn having a friendly chat with Frank Sherrill, owner of S &W Cafeterias from Washington to New Orleans. He had just come from hearing President Kennedy urge him and other restaurateurs to support the civil rights bill before Congress. Like most of his peers, Sherrill was wary of desegregating his cafeterias, though he confessed to admiring what Charlotte had done at Slug's suggestion.

It took a massive civil rights march on Washington, the assassination of President Kennedy, and Lyndon Johnson's rise to the presidency before the Civil Rights Act of 1964 could extend Charlotte's example across the country. I was in Washington to report on all those events.

I made up for the Bobby Baker blunder by becoming one of the few correspondents to report in depth on Kennedy's 1963 civil rights proposals. When North Carolina senator Sam Ervin, then chairman of a subcommittee of the Senate Judiciary, began holding hearings on the bill, he summoned as a witness Attorney General Robert Kennedy. The two men knew and liked each other—Kennedy had once worked as a staff lawyer on the Senate Judiciary Committee—but their long colloquies before the subcommittee were often barbed. They were lawyers from different eras. Ervin would quote interpretations of the Constitution from *Blackstone's Commentaries*, a staple of nineteenth-century legal scholarship, and Kennedy would respond with quotations from Supreme Court rulings on New Deal legislation, most of which Ervin dismissed as "bad law."

I attended every hearing and wrote stories about them, including as much of the Q and A as possible, to alert Carolinians how far the proposed law might reach. Question: "Will the law cover Mrs. Murphy's boarding house?" Answer: "Yes, if Mrs. Murphy serves food that moved in interstate commerce."

My editors in Charlotte played the stories on the front page under the heading "The Sam and Bobby Show."

Soon, rival papers in the Carolinas were petitioning wire services for fuller reports on the Ervin hearings. Ultimately, reporters from big city dailies, including the *New York Times*, were attending, though most of us knew the Kennedy civil rights bill was going nowhere in that divided Congress.

Even so, evidence that the Ervin hearings had attracted national attention was apparent on August 28, 1963, during a massive march on Washington for jobs and freedom. As gathering crowds passed a temporary stage on the mall, folk singer Joan Baez was belting out, "Ain't gonna let nobody turn me 'round, turn me 'round, turn me 'round," and, in subsequent verses sang, "Ain't gonna let ol' Sam Ervin turn me 'round, turn me 'round, turn me 'round," signaling that the Ervin hearings had penetrated national consciousness.

Plans for the Washington march had aroused alarm that it might provoke violence, but it turned out to be the most memorable political gathering I ever witnessed. Even with half a million people present, it had the atmosphere of a vast and joyous old-time singing on the grounds, with a great variety of soaring speeches, concluding with Dr. Martin Luther King's thrilling "I Have a Dream" oration.

Within the cloaked corridors of Capitol Hill, wary congressmen and senators watched and even admired the televised event, but the march did not persuade them to pass the Kennedy civil rights bill. The assassination of President Kennedy and Lyndon Johnson's rise to the presidency brought that about.

I was in Washington on November 22, 1963, when Kennedy was slain in Dallas. Our seven-member bureau had just finished our weekly staff luncheon in the National Press Club. As we returned to our office two floors below, our United Press printer began dinging, dinging, dinging, signaling urgent news. I ripped off a terse advisory that said shots had been fired on Kennedy's Dallas motorcade and the President had been hit. It quoted Secret Service agent Clint Hill saying Kennedy might be dead.

Our bureau chief sent me to Capitol Hill to get reactions. At the time, nobody knew who the assassin was or whether the shooting was part of a larger coup. As my taxi cruised down Pennsylvania Avenue, I saw crowds strolling happily along the sunny sidewalks. I wanted to stick my head out the window and shout that the world had just turned upside down.

When I asked Senator Ervin for his response to the shooting, he paled, slumped heavily against a doorjamb, and said, "A thing like this just makes you sick." Then he added, "I just hope the shooter wasn't a Southerner," a remark he immediately asked to be off the record. I stopped by the Capitol office of the vice president and found Lyndon Johnson's chief aide George Reedy, a fellow University of Chicago alum, talking on the phone and making notes on a yellow legal pad. He kept saying, "Yes, sir....yes, sir.... yes, sir..." I assumed he was taking orders from LBJ. When he hung up, he said, "Sorry, Jack. Don't have time to talk," and was on the move.

After gathering other reactions, I took a taxi back to the bureau and hastily wrote several stories. As I handed them to our telegrapher, I was told to hurry to the White House and catch a press bus for Andrews Air Force Base, where President Johnson and the body of President Kennedy would be arriving. I ran four blocks to the White House but arrived just as the press bus pulled away.

I climbed the West Wing stairs to the office of Henry Hall Wilson, a tall, slow-talking former state legislator from Mecklenburg's neighboring Union County. Henry Hall had once been an oboe player in the Charlotte Symphony, distinguished by the red socks he wore with his tuxedo. He was as shaken by the assassination as the rest of us. Knowing he was fully informed about the president's record in getting legislation passed, I asked how he would assess the Kennedy presidency. He waved me off, saying, "This is not the time for that." Instead, he recalled some of his Kennedy memories, then suggested that we go down to the back lawn and witness Lyndon Johnson's arrival at the White House for the first time as president.

The area around the White House helipad was cordoned with gold ropes, behind which stood a scattering of executive staffers. As we waited, still trying to comprehend the enormity of the Dallas events, Henry Hall marveled that under the US Constitution, despite the sudden loss of a beloved leader, the nation could still expect a peaceful transfer of power.

In the gloom, the White House, usually flooded with light, was completely dark out of respect for the fallen leader, as were most other buildings in

Washington. Through the barren trees, only the majestic dome of the Capitol was bathed in white light. Suddenly, over the dark Virginia horizon, a winking red light arose from the belly of the Johnson helicopter, like a beating heart bringing new life to the government. Watching it glide over the spire of the Washington Monument, pass the dome of the Jefferson Memorial, and descend over the cornice of the Lincoln Memorial, I said to Henry Hall, "He's certainly coming down the corridors of history."

At the far edge of the White House south lawn stood a little fountain that, unaccountably, was still lighted on this otherwise doleful night. As Johnson's descending helicopter swooped over them, the fountain's dancing fingers of water curtsied under the copter's downdraft, as if assenting to the power passing overhead. When the helicopter landed, a rumpled Johnson got out, trudged over to the few of us strung out behind the gold ropes, and, moving from person to person, said in a husky voice, "Pray for me.... Pray for me.... Pray for me..."

Less than a year later, Democrats, under intense pressure from Johnson, forced a subdued Congress to pass the Civil Rights Act of 1964, opening public accommodations across the country to all races and mandating equality in employment and education. Though most Southerners despised it, Johnson predicted presciently that the law would cost Democrats the South's loyalty for generations. The law proved to be the beginning of the gradual transformation of the South, wiping out the Jim Crow laws that forbade citizens from attending integrated schools, dining at restaurants of their choice, entering public libraries, drinking from public water fountains, using public restrooms, and a great number of other humiliating customs sanctioned by law. While Black and White citizens were slowly struggling toward a more equitable and open society, economic opportunities expanded for all. For the remainder of the twentieth century, the South outgrew the rest of the country.

Slug with Restaurateur of the Year plaque

CHAPTER

28

Widening Our Reach

In the summer of 1965, as the House was passing proposals for a national health insurance program called Medicare, it became obvious that news from Washington was being increasingly overshadowed by the Vietnam War and angry protests against it on streets and campuses across the United States. Further, the freewheeling Ed Lahey had been replaced as our Washington bureau chief by a man with a different agenda for generating news. Instead of seeking stories of interest to our hometown papers, we were expected to compete with wire services, television networks, and newsmen from big metropolitan dailies in gathering national news. The new bureau chief and I clashed often. Despite warnings by Washington colleagues that I was crimping my career, I asked the *Observer* to bring me home.

As I called on congressional sources and thanked them for the help they had given me, I stopped at the office of Senator Strom Thurmond, about whom I had written many stories but none favorable to him. Ever the Old South gentleman (you could not write him the last letter; he would always respond), Thurmond looked shocked at my desire to leave Washington and go back to Charlotte. He rose from behind his desk and began patting his jacket and vest pockets and opening desk drawers in search of a suitable farewell gift for me. Finally, he reached into his pants pocket and handed me his pearl-handled pocketknife with a gilt-lettered "Strom Thurmond" printed on one side. Before handing it to me, he said I would have to give him two pennies, one for each of the knife's two blades, "lest they cut our friendship."

Back in Charlotte, I went on what *Observer* editor Pete McKnight called a "management escalator," assuming a variety of newsroom responsibilities, first as copy chief, then as Carolinas editor, then city editor, and finally as an editorial writer. I looked on it as an inviting opportunity, though the move from reporter to editor all but ended my public exposure. There are no bylines for copy chief, city editor, or editorial writer, but I saw management as a path to fulfilling my dream of becoming editor of the paper.

Meanwhile, Slug's emergence as Charlotte's premier restaurateur was underway, beginning in 1969 when the Barclay Cafeteria was running smoothly and steadily drawing crowds. One morning as Slug arrived at work, a kitchen helper asked, "What's all that cooking equipment doing on the curb across the street?"

Slug crossed Independence Boulevard and found the innards of a bankrupt restaurant waiting to be auctioned. He examined the pile of stainless steel and the vacant building from which it had come. Then he hurried uptown to seek a bank loan. He had been looking for such an opportunity and was confident that with the equipment in that building, he could create the stylish new restaurant he had envisioned.

It would be a white-tablecloth place with two distinctions—it would serve only roast prime rib of beef and it would offer a salad bar, something new to the Charlotte market but one he had read about in restaurant magazines. He planned to call it "Slug's Rib."

When he learned that financing his dream would require more collateral than he could command, Slug went to see his friend Charles Ervin, Charlotte's busiest and boldest homebuilder whose subdivisions were extending boundaries on all sides of the city. With offices nearby, Ervin often lunched at the Barclay and enjoyed kidding around with the Slugger. But when Slug finished presenting his plan, Ervin, a builder widely admired for savvy marketing, was aghast.

"Let me get this straight," he said. "You want to open a restaurant that serves only one item, and you intend to call it 'Slug's Rib'? Are you crazy? Who in their right mind would want to eat in a place named for a slimy worm? You'll go broke in no time."

Slug had answers for those objections. He knew of successful restaurants across the country that served only prime rib. Further, he said, the name Slug was well known in Charlotte. Its distinction would make his restaurant the object of curiosity and word-of-mouth comment. Once people tasted the food and enjoyed the service, they would tell friends about it. In time Ervin and others agreed to back the venture. It was another example of the generous support that helped propel Slug to prominence.

As chef for the new restaurant, Slug chose Reinhold Frank, a gruff, portly German he had met through the Chamber of Commerce. With a Teutonic accent and a brusque manner, Frank proved to be a stickler for quality and consistency. In the kitchen, cooks and servers learned to perform with Prussian precision, but in the dining room, Slug created a relaxed, convivial atmosphere.

As the front man, Slug's mission was to make people comfortable and happy. He didn't do it entirely out of good business practices. It fed his genuine affection for people. He liked meeting them and treating them like family. That led Slug's Rib and all his later restaurants to be known not only for their cuisine and ambiance but also for the chance to chat with the garrulous, good-humored Slugger.

Painted a deep red and accented in gold, the Slug's Rib dining room didn't glisten as much as it glowed. Its symbol was a gilt-edged black shield topped by a medieval crown much like one King Arthur might have worn. In addition to a salad bar and roast prime rib, its menu also included baked potatoes and creamed spinach.

In March 1970, Slug invited my wife and me and about fifty of his friends to a trial dinner at the Rib to work out glitches, something he did before opening each of his restaurants. Dressed in a tuxedo, he was on top of his game. He circulated among the guests as if he had invented roast prime rib. When he came to my table he asked, "What do you think?" Before I could answer, he said, "Isn't that good?" Indeed it was. Of all Slug's restaurants, many Charlotteans best remember the Rib. It moved the Slugger to the forefront among Charlotte's fine-dining establishments.

Often college basketball teams preparing to play in the Charlotte Coliseum would eat their pregame meals in the Rib's private dining room. To Slug's great joy, that included teams coached by North Carolina's Dean Smith. Slug's serving staff marveled at the amount of prime rib the UNC players could put away only hours before the tip-off of a big game. Occasionally, the Rib staff hauled the restaurant's delicacies down Independence Boulevard to feed crowds attending events on the kitchen-less mezzanine of Ovens Auditorium. The Rib quickly became the first of Slug's beloved places to enjoy fine dining and celebrate special occasions.

Impressed by the Rib's success, other businessmen began inviting Slug to bring his magnetism to their ventures. Over the next ten years, he was asked to open ten additional restaurants or cafeterias scattered over three cities and two states, giving him twelve in all. Slug did not seek those opportunities. They came to him.

The first invitation was from tall, syntax-mangling John Belk, head of the sprawling Belk department store chain and from 1968 to '76 a popular Charlotte mayor. Belk was notorious for uttering non sequiturs. During a bond campaign to expand the Charlotte airport, critics of aviation noise asked why the airport was built where it was. Belk answered, "Because that's where the planes come in."

Slug and I had known John Belk since our boyhood at Caldwell Presbyterian Church. When Slug went into the restaurant business, Belk began referring to Slug as "Toots," as in Toots Shor, the ebullient New York restaurateur famed for hospitality. In 1971 Belk asked Slug to take over the cafeteria at his Belk store in SouthPark, thinking Slug's presence would increase traffic through his dry goods emporium. As soon as Slug assumed operations there, it did.

That cafeteria, also called the Barclay, developed a clubby atmosphere and became a place for Charlotteans to have lunch or a weeknight supper and meet friends and neighbors. There you might see public officials or the president of a local college or chairman of an arts group. Later Slug was asked to take over the three varying restaurants in Belk's big uptown store where hundreds of shoppers and uptown workers dined daily.

Noting Slug's impact at Belk's, managers of the SouthPark mall asked him to take over a losing restaurant at the mall's entrance. Slug responded by creating

"Slug's Choice," with a dining room larger and more glamorous than Slug's Rib. It offered a wider menu that included such delicacies as snails and roast duck. The Choice was an immediate success. Many Charlotte business deals were closed over lunches or dinners there. Wedding anniversaries, graduation dinners, marriage proposals, and high school proms were celebrated around its tables.

In recognition of his success and his leadership in championing restaurant interests before the state legislature, the North Carolina Restaurant Association named Slug Restaurateur of the Year for 1975-76. At the time, Slug was forty-two.

Slug's Choice opened at an opportune time. For many years, Slug and others, including me as a writer of *Observer* editorials, had been prodding state legislators to pass laws allowing North Carolina restaurants to sell mixed drinks. That would end the hypocrisy of restaurant-goers bringing their booze in brown bags, a tradition that offended sophisticated diners and made Charlotte look like a backwater burg.

Just as Slug's Choice was opening, the state legislature passed laws allowing cities and counties to hold referenda on whether to permit the sale of liquor by the drink in their jurisdictions. Charlotte, which in 1904 had been the first North Carolina city to vote itself dry, in September 1978 became the first North Carolina city to vote itself wet. The Slugger got the seventh liquor license issued by the state. Almost overnight, restaurants in other cities across North Carolina sought the privilege of serving mixed drinks.

New restaurants, hotels, and convention halls representing national chains began coming to Charlotte. The city built a new, larger convention center and created a regional Conventions and Visitors Bureau to promote it. Slug became a founding member of that bureau.

Slug's Choice drew all kinds of celebrities. One memorable night when Slug's daughter Priscilla, a pretty elementary school teacher, was waitressing there during her summer break, a table of eight arrived at her station. Among them was architect Harvey Gantt, a handsome Black man who with poise and grace had desegregated Clemson University, had won a seat on the Charlotte City Council, and had just been elected Charlotte's first Black mayor. After Gantt and his friends gave Priscilla their drink orders, Slug stopped by to welcome them. When Priscilla returned, he proudly introduced her as his daughter and a schoolteacher.

Impressed, Harvey Gantt said, "You don't *look* like a schoolteacher."

Priscilla, replied "No, and you don't *look* like a mayor, either." Everybody laughed.

While Slug's reputation was echoing across the Carolinas, my prominence was growing in the *Observer* newsroom. It was a great time to be a hometown journalist as landmark events were occurring. In addition to Charlotte's growth, the daily headlines reflected the racial revolution, protests over the Vietnam War, the rock-and-roll craze, the drug culture, debates over abortion and gun safety, and the rise of feminism. The bitter divisions between rich and poor, Black and White, urban and rural, Republican and Democratic that mark America in the early twenty-first century had their origins in the 1960s.

Three times editor McKnight came to me with job offers from other Knight newspapers. Each time I asked whether declining would lessen my chances of becoming editor of the *Observer*, and each time he said no. I wanted to stay in Charlotte to experience firsthand the events shaping the city and the region. I thought knowledge of the community was a prerequisite for any newspaper editor.

I also did well in my new managerial assignments. Over the next few years, my work twice won me the honor of leading week-long seminars at the prestigious American Press Institute at New York's Columbia University, one for copy editors from across the country and another for city editors. As an editorial writer, I was chosen chairman of the North Carolina Editorial Writers Conference.

Running the copy desk challenged everything I knew about English grammar and good journalism. Seated in the slot of a horseshoe-shaped desk, I was the last gatekeeper to see copy before it was set in type. I doled out stories to be edited and headlined by six copy editors seated around the rim. We often quibbled over the accuracy or appropriateness of headlines. I rejected as too flippant the proposed headline on a story about a farmer seeking relief for an accident that destroyed his dairy truck. The headline said, "Farmer Cries Over Spilt Milk." I also rejected as too clever a headline about a mine disaster that said, "Tons of Soil Buy Sons of Toil."

I urged my colleagues to remember when writing headlines that they had read the story and the next day's readers had not. Often that could make a big difference in the meaning of headline. As an example, I recounted a headline I had once written on a story about Marilyn Monroe marrying playwright Arthur Miller. As the New York press pursued the fleeing couple into Connecticut, one reporter's car missed a turn and slammed into a tree. My headline said, "Reporter Killed Tailing Marilyn." The copy chief working that night giggled and showed my headline to other copy editors, drawing laughter from each. I didn't get the joke until he handed me back my headline with an *r* penciled in to make the new headline, "Reporter Killed Trailing Marilyn." My response was, "Oh, I didn't get the sexual implication because I had read the story and knew the reporter killed was a woman."

During my time as copy chief, the *Observer* found it difficult to hire copy editors, so I began training my own. I taught a former glass salesman to edit copy and write headlines. He later moved on to reporting and wound up as an editorial writer on another newspaper. I also taught a Black teacher from Second Ward High to be a copy editor. He did so well he would end up on the staff of *Time* magazine.

My most satisfying success came from teaching my laundry agent to edit copy and write headlines. One morning as he delivered clean shirts to my house, he noticed books on the coffee table about North Carolina history and poetry, some of which he had read. We talked a few moments and he confessed that his daughter had been embarrassed at school when her teacher asked students to state aloud their father's occupation. When she said her father was a laundry man, the class laughed.

I invited him to come by the *Observer* newsroom each afternoon after his workday and let him edit wire copy I knew was not going in the paper. After several months of those tutorials, I suggested to the managing editor that we offer him a job. He accepted and worked on the *Observer* copy desk until his retirement.

When time came for me to move to the state desk, a crisis was occurring in my home. Before we left Washington, our pediatrician there had described Jacky, then about nine months old, as a "special child" who would require distinctive care. Later, when Jacky was about two and we were back in Charlotte, our pediatrician there, the astute Carlton Watkins, diagnosed him as autistic. Though still a mysterious malady, autism then was even less understood. Dr. Watkins went to a research institute in Philadelphia to learn all he could about it, then helped Margaret and me work with Jacky in floor exercises that opened new paths between his body and his nervous system. He also referred us to Christopher Carmichael, a distinguished but gentle child psychiatrist. After treating Jacky for two years, Dr. Carmichael arranged for him to be a patient at the North Carolina Children's Psychiatric Unit, an experimental facility on the sprawling state hospital and mental health center in Butner, North Carolina, about fifty miles north of Durham. Sending Jacky there was heartbreaking. He was a beautiful boy, but his autistic tantrums were uncontrollable. Dr. Carmichael warned that without intense treatment, Jacky would have little chance in life.

During those years, Jacky's sister Margaret Louise was born with no sign of disability but a hunger for food and affection. After closing the final edition of the *Observer* each night. I came home to give her a two o'clock feeding and in a rocking chair sing her back to sleep.

When Jacky reached age five and was admitted to the Children's Psychiatric Unit, I arranged to have Fridays off so my wife Margaret and I could have weekly visits with Jacky in Butner. In his first several weeks there, we could see him only through a two-way mirror without his knowing we were there. We saw him play alone, oblivious to the other children playing around him. Later we began taking him off campus for lunch, and still later taking him home for weekend visits. I drove him back to Butner every Sunday afternoon.

After four years, as Jacky, then age nine, was discharged, his Butner psychiatrist advised us to let him "battle his own battles," but warned that Jacky's greatest challenge was developing social skills. I remain grateful to the state of North Carolina for providing that forward-looking facility that helped us and other families at a critical time in our children's lives.

Even as I was dealing with these delicate family matters, important events were altering the course of Slug's and my careers. After two years on the state desk I was moved to the city editor's chair, where I supervised a staff of thirty, including twenty-four reporters, six of whom were women. When I first worked in the *Observer* newsroom there was one woman there. When I left the city desk there were eight, indicating that the women's movement was well underway and soon would be the dominant gender in journalism.

As city editor, I directed *Observer* coverage of several historic Charlotte events. The first was the explosive *Swann v. Mecklenburg* lawsuit resulting in the desegregation of all Charlotte-Mecklenburg schools. As the suit was being argued in the US District Court before Judge James B. McMillan, I knew our coverage had to be factual and fair because elsewhere in the paper, *Observer* editorials were strongly supporting desegregation. Anti-desegregation protesters often crowded the sidewalks outside our building at the corner of Stonewall and Tryon Streets.

Acknowledging that for years buses had been used to segregate public schools, Judge McMillan ruled that buses should be used to desegregate them. Each public school was ordered to seek an enrollment matching Mecklenburg's White-to-Black population ratio: 70 percent White, 30 percent Black. The decision outraged many people and gave rise to a number of private or parochial academies that drained support for public education.

When the *McMillan* decision was appealed to the US Supreme Court, I was sent to Washington to report on oral arguments before the justices. From a press table in the shadows of the small courtroom I heard attorneys for Charlotte-Mecklenburg schools present their case against desegregation. Their presentations drew few questions from the black-robed justices who had heard similar arguments many times before. But when Charlotte attorney Julius Chambers, representing the Black plaintiffs, coolly began defending busing as a means of desegregating schools, a relatively new idea, the jurists came to life with frowns and finger-pointing interruptions. Justice Hugo Black, a former Alabama klansman turned civil liberties champion, rocked back and forth in his big leather chair and peppered Chambers with questions. Chambers, who was no stranger to the high court, having already won several cases there, never lost his cool. Unlike the school board attorneys who offered carefully crafted arguments based on case law, Chambers presented facts. It took the justices months to grapple with all the relevant issues, but in time they unanimously upheld Judge McMillan's order, setting off a national debate over busing as a tool for desegregating schools. For the next twenty years Charlotte was often cited as a city that had made busing work. Unfortunately, in the 1990s another federal judge, Robert Potter, decided Charlotte-Mecklenburg was desegregated enough and rescinded the McMillan mandate. Charlotte-Mecklenburg schools resegregated almost overnight.

During the uproar over school desegregation, a second landmark event occurred, one that still dogs local government in Charlotte and Mecklenburg County. With approval from the state legislature, Charlotte business and political leaders launched an all-out effort to consolidate the city and county governments into a single unit, an idea that had been knocking on local doors since the mid-1920s. The merger promised to reduce friction between the city and county governments, improve local services, coordinate public spending, and through comprehensive planning better accommodate growth. It also would enable the unified government to speak with one voice throughout the county, to the exploding region beyond, and to the state legislature.

With help from the Institute of Government in Chapel Hill, a commission representing all parts of the county began drafting a charter for a single government. I attended the commission's meetings and wrote stories explaining each provision of the proposed charter. My stories attracted the attention of the American Association of Political Scientists who awarded me a national prize, but local voters were less impressed. In a referendum, they defeated the proposed charter two to one. Anger over school desegregation had so soured the electorate it was unwilling to look objectively at anything.

Even so, many elements of that proposed charter have been adopted, the most significant of which was district representation after the discovery that all five members of the Board of County Commissioners were members of the same Myers Park church. While district representation assured each citizen an equal voice in local affairs, the cacophony of neighborhood voices has weakened the public-private coalition that had promoted Charlotte's progress for many years. Among the charter proposals not adopted was the merger of the Board of County Commissioners and the city council into one governing body. Though the city and county have divided up responsibilities for local services—the city will do this, the county will do that—the separation of powers continues to sap strength and efficiency from local government. For instance, in speaking with one voice the city-county government might have avoided many errors in land-use planning—the ill-advised location of Eastland Mall is a good example—and might have improved relations with the six county towns, the state legislature, and other governments in the burgeoning metropolitan region.

After the charter vote, I was moved from the city desk to the *Observer's* embattled editorial board, essentially from gathering facts to writing opinion. The analytical skills honed at the University of Chicago would prove invaluable. My instructions from Pete McKnight were to temper *Observer* editorials that he thought too often got into the gutter with the opposition. He wanted the *Observer* to stay on the high road, but he gave me no authority to edit proposed editorials.

The editorial staff was led by David Gillespie, a Gastonia native who had won a Silver Star for gallantry during World War II. As editorial-page editor, he needed all that bravery in confronting protests, from readers and from within the Knight Newspapers management over *Observer* support for desegregation and a long list of other hot-button issues, including women's rights, gun safety, and the separation of church and state. Though well-read and conscientious, Gillespie let his combative instincts lead him into confrontations.

In time I discovered that writing persuasive editorials required having not only an opinion but also the facts to support it. The *Observer* had many sources from which to draw in enriching the popular discourse. Among them were government professionals, the Institute of Government at Chapel Hill, professors at various universities, and Charlotte lawyers. Talking with them made editorial writing more fun than news reporting.

One Saturday about a year after my move to the editorial pages, as I arrived at the office to read proof on the Sunday pages and produce pages for the Monday edition, the news editor handed me a piece of copy and said, "I thought you ought to see this before it goes into tomorrow's paper." The copy said that Reese Cleghorn, a veteran Atlanta newsman, had been appointed to succeed David Gillespie as editor of *Observer* editorial pages. I was astonished. I had assumed that in time I would become editor of the editorial pages.

After meeting Reese Cleghorn I understood why he was chosen. A tall, elegant, soft-spoken man in his late forties, Cleghorn became the best editor I ever worked with. Under his sensitive eye and sharp pencil, *Observer* editorial pages expanded their perspective beyond government and politics to include cultural, financial, sports, and literary topics. When one of us wrote an editorial using high-flown language, Cleghorn would remind us of a grizzled Atlanta copy chief he once knew who claimed "the average Georgian is below average." We assumed Cleghorn meant that applied to average Carolinians as well.

When one of my colleagues consistently misspelled accommodate, Cleghorn typed a copy sheet full of *m*'s and left it in his typewriter with a note saying, "Accommodate always takes two *m*'s. If you're afraid of running out, here is a reserve supply." None of us misspelled accommodate thereafter.

As a newcomer to Charlotte, Cleghorn relied on my knowledge of the city. When Fred Alexander, the first Black elected to the Charlotte City Council, won a seat in the North Carolina Senate, the city council was responsible for appointing his successor. Cleghorn allowed me to write an editorial suggesting that the council appoint Harvey B. Gantt, the young Black who had won national notice for his poise in desegregating Clemson University. Within a week or so after the publication of my editorial, Gantt was appointed to the vacant seat, propelling him to a political career that eventually would make him Charlotte's first Black mayor.

Cleghorn also encouraged me to write editorials reflecting local history and in the fall of 1972 suggested that I write a signed Saturday column modeled after the "Talk of the Town" essays in the *New Yorker* magazine. My response was to take a current event in Charlotte and relate it to a similar incident in the city's past, giving readers a sense of permanence in the midst of change. As he edited my first installment, Cleghorn called, "Hey, Jack, what do you want to call this thing?"

I thought quickly, then in a moment of inspiration said, "Let's call it 'This Time and Place.'" Part history, part nostalgia, part reporting, the Saturday morning columns defined what the Rev. Doug Oldenburg, pastor of Covenant Presbyterian Church, called "the ethos of the city." Even after Reese Cleghorn left the paper, his successors Ed Williams and Jerry Shinn encouraged me to continue writing them. The columns let me step back from the whirl of daily news and, by focusing on a single event, provide perspective on life in Charlotte and the Carolinas. The result made the community more conscious of its past and opportunities for its future. They also afforded me a rare but prominent byline on the editorial pages.

My columns helped enliven interest in preserving historic landmarks, beginning with "Mr. Dewey's Bank," a small Tryon Street structure where, following the South's defeat in the Civil War, the fleeing Confederate cabinet held its last full meeting. The building also hosted the founding of the Mecklenburg Medical Society, the Charlotte Public Library, and the Southern Manufacturers Club, a forerunner to the City Club. The little bank building was about to be demolished to make room for a surface parking lot. We brought in an Atlanta architect to show how it could be saved by incorporating it into a larger structure. We lost that battle but in the struggle won community support for saving other landmarks. A column on preserving the Latta Arcade and its distinctive architecture won a first-place award from the North Carolina chapter of the American Institute of Architects. The arcade was later designated a local historic site.

My columns prompted the founding of a city Historic Properties Committee, which was later morphed into the Mecklenburg Historic Landmarks Commission. Under the leadership of UNC Charlotte professor Dan Morrill, those two bodies goaded Charlotte and Mecklenburg County, once known for obliterating everything in their past, into identifying and protecting more historic properties than any county in the Carolinas.

My columns helped preserve the James B. Duke mansion in Myers Park, the McNinch House on North Church Street, the Carr House on North McDowell Street, and the conversion of the old sanctuary of First Baptist Church on North Tryon Street into an arts center called Spirit Square. They also built support for the founding of two local history museums.

Among readers of my columns was the Slugger, who responded with occasional praise—and often complaint. I was still too liberal for him and so was the *Observer*. When we were together he invariably brought up some

Observer item that had annoyed him. After repeated complaint, I asked how he would like it if every time I saw him I groused about the food or service at one of his restaurants. He got my point and reduced the frequency of his criticism—for a while. He couldn't entirely put aside our rivalry.

After two years of "This Time and Place" columns, Pete McKnight suggested that I publish the most popular ones in a booklet to be called *Jack Claiborne's Charlotte*. One of them traced the multiracial origins of Johnson C. Smith University, a century-old Black institution on the west side of town that few Charlotteans Black or White knew much about. Another traced the women's movement and featured Gladys Tillett, a gentle but determined feminist who in the 1920s had founded the Mecklenburg League of Women Voters. She talked of going door to door among women in her privileged Charlotte neighborhood, encouraging them to exercise their newly won right to vote. "Oh, Gladys," the neighbors would say, "I couldn't possibly do that. I love my husband." My paperback book came out in 1974 and sold five thousand copies.

Meanwhile, the Slugger, buoyed by his restaurants' success, had joined the Carmel Country Club, which had carved eighteen-hole golf courses out of thick woods in Sharon Township. He became part of a double foursome of golfing buddies known as "the Mafia." They played to win and after toting up their scores each Saturday went to the bar to review their performance and laugh at their errors. In the process they became lifelong pals. Three of them joined the Slugger on a trip to Scotland to play in a four-ball tournament on one of the craggy old courses that gave birth to the game of golf.

Slug served on several Carmel Country Club committees before being elected to consecutive terms as the club's president. He worked to improve the club's appeal to families by improving its food service, accounting process, and amenities.

In those years golf's Kemper Open was an annual Charlotte attraction. Slug often played in the pro-am match that preceded the tournament. One year he was paired with Lee Trevino, one of the pro tour's best golfers and a crowd-pleasing cutup. Followed by a large gallery, they laughed their way through eighteen holes, exchanging quips with people in the crowd. Walking down the fairway, Trevino said in a voice loud enough for everyone to hear, "Hey, Slugger, did you hear about Billy Graham getting hit by a boat?"

In his best straight-man mode Slug answered, incredulously, "By a boat?"

"Yeah," Trevino said, "He was out walking his duck."

Slug came to know many other big-name golfers and after their Kemper Open rounds dined with some of them at Slug's Rib or Slug's Choice.

Those were years when Arnold Palmer was the brightest star in the golfing heavens. One afternoon after a pro-am event at the Carmel Country Club, Slug was standing with Palmer and others just off the eighteenth green, talking about their play. One Carmel member who knew Slug but didn't recognize his companions, whispered to a man at the edge of the group, "Who's the guy standing next to Slug?" When Palmer heard of the query, he laughed and often retold the story himself. After being elaborately introduced in Charlotte or elsewhere in the Carolinas, Palmer would go to the microphone, tell the story, and add humbly, "I'm the guy standing next to Slug Claiborne."

Slug golfing at Carmel Country Club

CHAPTER

29

Slug Hits a Peak

Opportunities in the 1970s and '80s came at Slug in waves, enabling him to open seven more restaurants, including a Slug's Rib in Myrtle Beach, South Carolina, and a Slug's Choice in North Myrtle Beach. Both establishments became popular beachgoer retreats. He also took over two distressed restaurants in the cultural district of Winston-Salem, one of them partially owned by Billy Parker, a former Wake Forest point guard who became a nationally renowned basketball analyst for CBS television. In addition, Slug breathed new life into uptown Charlotte by opening two glamorous places that enhanced the appeal of a resurgent center city.

After years of decline, uptown Charlotte was entering a prolonged boom. Its North Carolina National Bank (now Bank of America), First Union National Bank and Wachovia Bank and Trust (both now part of Wells Fargo) were expanding fast, attracting new talent and racing to see which could erect the most soaring office towers. Slug's restaurants contributed to that surge by offering high-rise vistas for glamorous uptown dining.

In 1974 officers of First Union National Bank asked him to enliven an anemic piano bar on the twenty-ninth floor of the Jefferson-First Union tower at College and Second Streets, four blocks from the city's center. In less than a year Slug turned that space into Slug's Tower Suite, creating Charlotte's only high-rise dining room open to the public. From its windows diners could look down on a sprawling carpet of twinkling lights in a dramatic urban setting. On most nights you could see the broadcast towers of WBTV on Crowder's Mountain and beyond it the historic Revolutionary War battleground of King's Mountain. On clear nights you could see the North Carolina mountains. Before its opening, Slug showed me the dining room with a sense of joy. Certain of its success, he said with a big grin, "You may think you're at the top of the heap at the newspaper, but I'm at the top of the heap in the whole city."

Indeed, the setting gave Slug, whose previous uptown operations had been limited to cafeterias, a prominent profile in the inner center. He became something like uptown's unofficial host. People from surrounding cities— Gastonia, Rock Hill, Monroe, Kannapolis, Concord—were soon coming to dine at his white-tablecloth restaurant, marvel over Charlotte's increasing eminence, and enjoy joking with the Slugger. Among them was George Shinn of Concord, who brought Charlotte an NBA franchise that repeatedly put the city's name on television screens and sports pages across the county.

The entire uptown area was being redeveloped, thanks to decisions made a decade earlier when suburban shopping centers were draining life from the corridors of Tryon and Trade Streets. City leaders had hired architect A. G. Odell, slim, elegant, and mercurial, to draw a plan for reviving the central business district. His design of the aluminum-domed Charlotte Coliseum and neighboring Ovens Auditorium had won plaudits all across the Carolinas and parts of Virginia.

After many meetings with local leaders over private City Club lunches, Odell issued the Central Area Plan in 1966, calling for more trees, more uptown housing, a convention center, more hotels and restaurants, and more cultural amenities. Among his most daring suggestions was a seventy-four-thousand-seat uptown stadium that had to wait thirty years to be fulfilled, but in 1994-95 it was built to house the NFL's Carolina Panthers, which put Charlotte in the major leagues of spectator sports.

As associate editor at the *Observer,* I wrote editorials supporting the Odell plan, especially the revival of the inner city's northwestern quadrant known as Fourth Ward as an in-town residential area. Research by UNC Charlotte professor Dan Morrill showed that many of the old houses still standing were part of a once affluent neighborhood. As those houses were refurbished for "urban pioneers," entrepreneurs like Reitzel Snyder of Synco Properties saw a business opportunity and joined others like Hugh McColl at NCNB (now Bank of America) in building new apartments and condominiums there. Suddenly, an area once dismissed as a wasteland of weeds and winos was a flourishing in-town neighborhood. Over the next twenty-five years Fourth Ward's renaissance spilled into neighboring Third Ward, First Ward, and South End. Uptown living became a prestigious privilege.

To attract suburbanites, uptown citizen groups staged big street events with Slug as an enthusiastic supporter. Cyndee Patterson, a leader in promoting Springfest as a street fair that brought thousands to the inner city, listed Slug as a gung ho member of her advisory board. Later, when promoters sought to create The Taste of Charlotte, another popular midtown event, Cyndee said Slug was an outspoken advocate. "Sure, we can do that," he said, and took the lead in encouraging other restaurateurs to offer samples of their menus to strolling uptown visitors.

According to his son Clay, Slug at that stage of his career was the quintessential entrepreneur. "He didn't rely on market studies or focus groups or anything of the sort. He relied on his experience, his reading of the community, and his sense of the opportunity. He shot from the hip."

After three years Slug's success at the Tower Suite persuaded First Union Bank to offer him an even larger, more elegant space on the tower's top floor, previously the bank's executive dining room. He closed his twenty-ninth floor suite and created a distinctive, surreal dining room that he, borrowing from his brother's newspaper argot, named Slug's Thirtieth Edition. (In journalism, the number thirty is a symbol for the very end.) The place became his signature restaurant, a magical, sophisticated space, more dramatic than any other dining room in Charlotte.

As the restaurant neared completion, Slug invited me to see it and talk with its award-winning architect, Harry Wolf. After a walk-through, I was impressed and thought the project was worthy of a "This Time and Place" column, the first sentence of which warned readers that I was about to describe a place operated by my brother. Literally and figuratively, it offered the city a higher level of public dining. I didn't mention the restaurant's food or service but focused on its design and decor. The dining room was as formal as a tuxedo, all black and white and lined by rows of black columns that didn't quite reach the ceiling, creating an illusion that the restaurant was floating in space. The frames of its tall, narrow windows were lined inside and out with mirrors that brought views of the outside in and the inside out. Lights from surrounding towers and sparkles from traffic on the streets below made Charlotte look like a fairyland.

To help celebrate the restaurant's opening, Slug and JoAnn invited Dot Gunnells, a friend from JoAnn's secretarial days in the Athletic Department at Chapel Hill. As Slug, Jo, and Dot exited the elevator and neared the restaurant entrance, they spied a huge spray of flowers. Dot paused to read the card that said, "From Your Friends in The Mafia." Visibly appalled, she turned to Slug and said, "I never thought you'd have anything to do with those thugs in the Mafia," referring to the infamous Sicilian crime family.

Slug laughed, then told her that in this instance the Mafia was a group of his golfing buddies. "Their only crimes," he said, "are their Saturday golf scores."

That wasn't the first time Slug and Dot Gunnells had occasion to talk about golf scores. Earlier, in compliance with Title IX of federal civil rights laws, colleges and universities had to offer women opportunities to participate in intercollegiate athletics equal to those offered men. When the university at Chapel Hill began organizing a women's golf team, the athletic director put Dot Gunnells in charge. Knowing a lot about golf but nothing about organizing a team, she turned to Slug for help. With his assistance, she drew up a plan that included a scholarship program for which Slug raised money. In appreciation, the women's golf program at Chapel Hill began awarding an annual Slug Claiborne Cup to its most promising player.

Slug's investment in the Thirtieth Edition's decor was further evidence of his imagination and willingness to take calculated risks. At the time, the redevelopment of uptown Charlotte as a place to live, eat, and entertain was still a gamble. Efforts to attract art galleries uptown and a drive to create a center city performing arts complex to replace Ovens Auditorium were barely underway. With its glamorous setting, the quality of its food, and the personal magnetism of the Slugger, the Thirtieth Edition helped to strengthen uptown's appeal. People who lived in the suburbs and rarely went uptown had more reason to do so after hearing about the Thirtieth Edition.

By that time the Slugger, who was around food every day and constantly nibbling, had put on weight and was letting his hair grow long enough to curl at the ends. People said he looked like a sad-faced comedian often appearing on television. Both had fat faces and the rheumy eyes of a clown. That resemblance was evident one night in New York when Slug and JoAnn attempted to dine and dance at the Starlight Roof of the Waldorf Astoria. They were standing in a long line waiting for a table when the maître d' beckoned them forward, escorted them down front next to the orchestra, and had a new table set up and a white tablecloth spread over it. As Slug and JoAnn took seats, the orchestra leader looked down and smiled. The food was good and the waiters couldn't have been nicer—until it was time to pay the bill. When Slug submitted his credit card, everyone discovered he was not Jackie Gleason.

Though Slug liked playing the clown, he had a very serious side. He read newspapers carefully and talked about stands he would have taken had he been in charge of national or local affairs. Under all his comedy, the Slugger still wanted to be a public official with a voice in setting policy. As a member of the Chamber of Commerce board, he was repeatedly disappointed when fellow directors who looked upon him as a fun guy failed to put him on the escalator to become the chamber president. If he could attain that office, Slug could see himself entering politics.

His ambitions were exposed when, to heighten interest in an upcoming election, the Chamber of Commerce and the Charlotte Women's Caucus staged a mock presidential nominating convention. Neighborhoods were designated as "states" and sent delegates to a political conclave at Charlotte's first Convention Center, a glossy white building at Trade and College Streets topped by pyramids. Slug was among three people competing for the presidential nomination. The others were Emmie Alexander, a White woman active in civic programs, and "Rocking Ray" Gooding, a popular Black disc jockey on WBT radio.

Ever the showman, Slug went all out to win the nomination. He put together teams to stage "spontaneous" demonstrations when his candidacy was put in contention. He rode onto the convention floor wearing a white suit and waving to the crowd from the back of an open convertible, accompanied by rousing music from a high school pep band. His jubilant followers threw confetti, released helium-filled balloons, and carried placards bearing his caricature. Some of them said, "I Tug For Slug."

When the roll call was completed, Slug finished first but fell a few votes short of the majority needed to clinch the nomination. On succeeding ballots, his opponents joined forces to nominate Emmie Alexander instead. Slug was shocked. He had wanted that honor.

Whether he was up or down in public perception, the Slugger never lost his touch as the genial host. His goal had always been to make people happy. A good example occurred one Saturday night when Slug's son Clay was working the front desk at the Thirtieth Edition. Things were not going well. It was raining, the place was packed, the kitchen was running behind, and people stood at the entrance waiting to claim their reserved table. When Slug arrived, he sensed the situation and began working the dining room, moving from table to table, chatting up guests and assuring them their dinner was coming. Gradually the atmosphere calmed.

During his table-hopping, Slug encountered a young Marine and his date. The Marine was about to be shipped to the Middle East. Slug came back to Clay at the front desk, handed him twenty dollars and said, "Go get me some flowers."

Clay protested, "Dad, it's eight thirty on a Saturday night. Where at this hour can I buy flowers in uptown Charlotte?"

Unmoved, Slug persevered. "Just get me some flowers," he said.

Clay left his post and, in his best suit and Sunday school shoes, ran in the rain up Tryon Street, looking for a place that might be open. Nine blocks north at a small stall, he found a bouquet of roses, bought them, and hurried back to the restaurant.

Noting that the Marine's date had gone to the ladies' room, Slug hid the flowers behind his back, handed them to the Marine, and said the rest was up to him. When the date returned, the Marine presented the roses, knelt at the edge of the table, and asked her to marry him. The restaurant erupted in applause. Months later, Slug and Clay got a thank-you note from the Marine and his wife saying what a marvelous night that was and how much they appreciated Slug's and Clay's contribution to their happiness.

Such things occurred frequently at Slug's restaurants, especially at the Thirtieth Edition. It was the place people dined on special occasions. Weekend nights might witness two or three marriage proposals. And if a couple got engaged there, they frequently came back to celebrate the memory of it. If Slug was there for their return visit and heard their story, he might pass them up when presenting the bill.

"That was vintage Slug," his son Clay said, "making a memorable moment even better. Dad gave away a lot of meals. He liked people and wanted them to like him. He also wanted them to come back to eat at his restaurants. He liked his position as the city's most visible host."

"You may think you're at the top of the heap at the newspaper, but I'm at the top of the heap in the whole city."

—Slugger

CHAPTER

30

Slug's at the Pines

In the same year that Slug opened the Thirtieth Edition, he was invited to take over The Pines restaurant on the outskirts of Chapel Hill. For years The Pines' rustic steakhouse atmosphere and the hospitality of its managers, Leroy and Agnes Merritt, had been a haven for friends of the university, especially on football weekends and big basketball nights. For Slug, who rarely missed a Tar Heels home football game and had been a consistent contributor to the Rams Club that funded UNC athletics, taking over a landmark like The Pines was a special privilege. He turned it into Slug's at the Pines, an elegant, sophisticated, white-tablecloth dining room that became an even greater attraction for Chapel Hill visitors, including governors, legislators, business leaders, famed academics, and star athletes. One night a waitress looked up and there was historian David McCullough sitting at one of her tables.

On some nights Dean Smith, North Carolina's famed basketball coach, would call ahead for a dinner to take home. He would enter through the back door, pick up his order in the kitchen, and exit undetected. He didn't dare enter the dining room, where he knew he would be mobbed.

Sometimes UNC players came in. When tall Sam Perkins, a UNC basketball hero, and his date finished their meal at the Pines, the waiter tried to make their dinner complimentary. Perkins knew that was against national intercollegiate rules and declined the offer. A couple days later Dean Smith stopped by to tell Slug and his staff that such favors would be serious infractions of recruiting rules and could bring severe penalties to UNC.

Since opening Slug's Rib, the Slugger had taken over nearly a dozen other restaurants, averaging about one new opening a year and tried to be the front man at each of them. He hadn't anticipated operating on such a scale. From the outside he appeared to be riding high, but inside he knew he was spread dangerously thin. He was often on the road by day and in the office late at night going over reports and accounting summaries. He was also smoking more, downing more vodka martinis, gaining weight, and generally neglecting his health.

He created a cadre of managers that looked like a United Nations roster of chefs, maître d's, waiters, waitresses, and secretaries, all loyal to the Slugger. In addition to Reinhold Frank, they included the quiet but efficient troubleshooter Eddie Gell. Later he hired Matt Henny, Kirk Johnson, Ken Kohout, and Roberto Gonzalez as managers.

In adding the Pines to his enterprise, Slug needed to expand his managerial staff. Tony Marder, a fifth-year senior at UNC, was working at the Pines as a server and occasionally a kitchen helper. He recalled the night Slug offered him a management job.

As Marder was waiting tables, Slug, his wife, and the high command of UNC basketball, coaches Dean Smith, Bill Guthridge, Phil Ford, and their wives, took seats at his station. After filling their drink orders, he went back for their food choices and heard Slug ask in a husky voice, "Marder, what are you going to do after you graduate?"

He replied, "Mr. Claiborne, I hope someday to open a restaurant as fine as this and compete with you."

As a competitor himself, Dean Smith, sitting beside Slug but outside his line of sight, was bobbing his head in approval.

Slug answered, "Why waste all that time. Why don't you just join my managerial staff now?"

Again, Dean Smith's head was bobbing up and down in the affirmative.

Marder thought for a second, then asked what terms Slug was offering.

"Can you begin Monday?" he said. Again, Dean Smith was signaling yes.

After all that coaching, Tony Marder joined Slug's staff as the youngest of his team. "I learned more from Slug than from my American studies classes," he said. "I learned never to go to a table and ask if everything thing was all right. Inevitably something was likely to have gone wrong. Slug taught me to ask, 'Are you having a good time?' I worked for him fourteen years and have since managed four other companies. That's the greatest lesson he taught me: make sure your customers are having a good time."

Among those Slug added to his staff at the Pines was my daughter Margaret, then an undergraduate history major at the university who wanted to earn a little extra money. She learned to wait tables, memorize drink and food orders, and uncork wine bottles.

At one point Slug had more than four hundred people on his payroll. He viewed them as his extended family and tried to know the names of their spouses and children. He trusted them and they repaid him in loyalty. A good example dated from the early days of the Barclay Cafeteria in Amity Gardens. One morning a young Black man named Ray came in looking for a job. He told Slug he had just been released from prison for driving the getaway car in an armed robbery. He said he knew he had made a stupid mistake but had served his time and was asking for a second chance. Slug listened to his plea, felt his desperation, and told him the cafeteria carpet needed vacuuming. "Let's see how you do with that," he said. Soon afterward, Slug added Ray to the payroll.

On the morning of September 22, 1989, after Hurricane Hugo had laid waste to much of Charlotte and blown out windows in uptown towers, Slug hurried to the Thirtieth Edition to assess the damage. When he arrived, he found Ray already there, vacuuming up the shattered glass.

Slug in the Thirtieth Edition

CHAPTER

31

I Reach a Pinnacle

As Slug's fortunes took flight in the 1970s and '80s, so did mine. Each Saturday's "This Time and Place" column told readers something they didn't know about Charlotte, winning me a large following. The columns aroused interest in creating a regional farmers market and persuaded the city to build a new sports arena uptown rather than in the suburbs. I wrote columns that saved trees, preserved neighborhoods, and promoted uptown development.

My columns talked about the A-Model plant the Ford Motor Company operated on Statesville Road in the 1920s, about the Bantams, a semi-pro football team that represented Charlotte in the same era, and about a turn-of-the-century medical school at Church and Fifth Streets that trained doctors and set Charlotte on the path to becoming a medical center. Associated with the medical school was the newly established Presbyterian Hospital housed on the upper floors of a four-story building at West Trade and South Mint Streets. Back then hospitals were scary places. Sick people were treated at home; those hospitalized were thought to be near death. Accordingly, on the building's ground floor was a liquor dispensary called the "Last Chance Saloon."

Often at Christmas I called prominent Charlotteans to ask for their best memory of Christmases past. I'll never forget the response of Colonel J. Norman Pease, an engineer and beloved civic statesman who, after serving in World War I, was recalled to duty in World War II to help build ports and air strips in the South Pacific. He remembered a Christmas Eve on a lonely atoll as he tried to sleep but felt a long way from home and family. Suddenly, natives of that island gathered in the dark at the edge of the jungle and in the best English they could command began singing "Silent Night." The colonel said he wept out of both joy and sadness.

The success of *Jack Claiborne's Charlotte,* the booklet Pete McKnight had suggested, brought me an invitation to write a history of the Alexander Children's Center, about which I had a special interest. The center was an outgrowth of the Alexander Home, the orphanage to which my vexed mother often threatened to send Slug and me. My history, *Unto the Least of These,* became one of the center's fund-raising tools.

My world widened one afternoon when William Snider, editor of the *Greensboro Daily News,* called to ask if I would replace him as a member of the North Carolina Humanities Council, a subsidiary of the National Endowment for the Humanities. I accepted the offer and joined the council at the same time as Liz Hair, the first woman to chair the Mecklenburg Board of County Commissioners and a fierce feminist. We often drove together to the council's quarterly meetings, gossiping all the way about public affairs and local politics.

The council's mission was to bring scholarship in the humanities—history, literature, languages, anthropology, archaeology, philosophy, and religion—to bear on local problems or opportunities. Pursuing that mission became a mind-expanding experience and the most enriching, non-newspaper affiliation of my career. Under federal mandate, the staff serving each state council had to include a retired humanities scholar. During my time on the humanities council, that retired scholar was Dr. John Caldwell, former chancellor at NC State and before that president of the University of Arkansas. A broad-shouldered, thick-chested man with thinning gray hair, bright eyes, and a smile to equal that of Dwight Eisenhower, he had grown up in Yazoo City, Mississippi, and accumulated an endless store of tales about people and places. He told them with great animation and mirth. Just getting to know John Caldwell was a joy, but the humanities council offered much more.

It exposed me to the diversity of cultures in North Carolina and to the scholars who studied them. At each meeting we reviewed twenty or more grant requests and awarded seed money to maybe a half dozen that were sustainable and likely to make an impact. The discussion of each proposal was usually vigorous and stimulating.

One request came from a shrinking community of Blacks on the outskirts of Pittsboro in Chatham County. Every year more of that community's young people were leaving for opportunities in bigger places. The remaining townspeople submitted their request on brown wrapping paper. It opened with none of the formalities of academic proposals but said something like, "Here's what we want to do..." Essentially, their goal was to save their community by teaching themselves, their children, and grandchildren how the community was started and what kept it going, who had dug the ditches, felled the trees, pulled the stumps, built the church, and maintained the cemetery. We argued long and loudly over the merits of that proposal, about whether it was a humanities project, and whether it would make a difference in preserving the community.

Ultimately, after a series of narrow votes, we provided seed money for the project, provided it was matched several times over with support from other sources. With great interest we watched the project develop. As residents young and old began working with scholars and discovering things about their environs, they felt a growing sense of pride. Sons and daughters who had moved away came home and gained a greater appreciation for the community, their parents, and their grandparents. It was one of the most rewarding proposals we funded.

I served on the humanities council five years, two of them as chairman, and discovered that North Carolina owes much of its progressive spirit to the legions of scholars, writers, historians, and philosophers whose teachings transcend the classroom and echo across the state. Those teachings have raised hopes and aspirations within the population and attracted many newcomers. Thanks to such scholars, as well as visionary foundations, informed business leaders, and a few vigilant newspapers, North Carolina has acquired a positive image.

One humanities council grant placed an ethicist in a Charlotte hospital and led to the establishment of the Charlotte-Mecklenburg Bioethics Resource

Group, of which I became a founding member. The Group promoted ethics in medicine and especially in care for the dying. Our work included drafting "No Code" policies for hospitals and encouraged senior citizens to write and adopt living wills. Our group, one of the earliest local bioethics organizations in the country, brought eminent ethicists from across the nation to speak in Charlotte.

In 1984 *Observer* managers gave me the opportunity of a lifetime. Noting that in 1986 the *Observer* would celebrate its one-hundredth anniversary, they asked if I would take a year's leave from editorial writing to research and write a book on the paper's history. It was a flattering assignment, one that entrusted me to interpret the paper's past. Though I had never read a newspaper history, I assured my bosses I could write one. After examining several, I discovered I had accepted a difficult assignment.

A good newspaper history must reflect the interests of the audience the paper served and tell the paper's story in context with news of past life in that community. The trouble was there was no reliable history of Charlotte to measure the *Observer* against. Even worse, I discovered that the *Observer* lacked records of its operations prior to 1955. To find out who its early editors, reporters, and columnists were and what stands they had taken on public issues, I had to read miles of microfilm of back issues. I also learned that the *Observer* began publishing earlier than 1886. Its first issue appeared in January 1869, as Charlotte was recovering from the Civil War. It briefly disappeared in the early 1880s but was revived in 1886.

Reading *Observer* microfilm from 1869 onward took two years but immersed me in the day-to-day developments of Charlotte. As I read each day's edition I felt as if I were living through those times. Like *Observer* readers from past times, I endured the Panic of 1873, mourned the 1876 massacre of the Seventh Cavalry at Little Big Horn, celebrated Thomas Edison's 1879 invention of the electric light, marveled over the Wright brothers' 1903 flights, and wept over the 1912 sinking of the Titanic.

I also felt excitement over the 1927 opening of Charlotte's First National Bank as the tallest structure in the Carolinas, topped on its twenty-first floor by the Charlotte branch of the Federal Reserve Bank, an institution that made Charlotte the financial capital of the Carolinas. The Federal Reserve was there because a Charlotte banker, Ward Wood, a co-founder of American Trust Company and a garrulous poker player, entertained Carolinas bankers for several years and persuaded them that Charlotte was the best site for such an institution.

I was surprised to see that *Observer* stories about the First National Bank's opening were written by Stanford R. Brookshire, a young Iredell County native fresh out of Duke University and later to become a Charlotte industrialist and one of the city's most effective mayors. Many years later, during his tenure as mayor, Brookshire recalled that he discovered he had little stomach for the rough and tumble of competitive reporting and on the advice of his city editor broke off his career in journalism.

My review of microfilm showed Charlotte emerging from a humble farmers market into the leading commercial center of the Carolinas and finally into a financial power. I saw its boundaries expand, its economy burgeon, and its skyline rise. I also saw the impact of its various leaders. Over and over at critical junctures, a businessman, a preacher, an educator, or a private citizen would step forward to turn the community dialogue in a positive direction.

As I was completing my *Observer* research, Slug invited me to join him and his lawyer for lunch at a new hotel just off Charlotte's main square. I assumed we would be discussing one of Slug's new restaurant ventures. When I arrived, there wasn't one lawyer present but a dining room full of them. It was the Mecklenburg Bar's annual observance of Law Day.

During the ceremonies, a speaker began talking of the Bar's Liberty Bell Award given annually to a non-lawyer whose work promoted respect for law and justice. Previous winners included some of Charlotte's most beloved citizens, including Dr. Frank Graham, former president of UNC; Dr. Bonnie Cone, founder of UNC Charlotte; and Dr. Warner Hall, pastor of Covenant Presbyterian Church and chairman of the Community Relations Committee, which sought racial harmony. When the speaker talked about the next recipient as someone who had lived on Jackass Lane in Newell and grown up on Charlotte's East Fifth Street and Park Drive, I instantly assumed I was there to cheer as the Slugger was honored for his service to the community.

When the speaker went on to talk about editorials and "This Time and Place" columns, I felt the eyes of six lawyers at our table staring at me. When the speaker summoned me to the dais to accept the award, I was glad I wasn't asked to say anything because I was numb and speechless. For the first time in a long time, I felt the Slugger was proud of me.

Later that year I finished writing the *Observer* history and submitted the manuscript to UNC Press, which accepted it for publication, giving the book an academic imprint that greatly enhanced its prestige. The book showed how the *Observer*'s development followed that of many other newspapers—from birth under a founding printer, to growth under an owner-editor, to purchase by a wealthy publisher, to control by a large corporation, and finally as part of a huge media conglomerate. In most instances, each step up the ownership ladder took the newspaper farther from local control and community focus.

Entitled *The Charlotte Observer, Its Time and Place*, the paper's history amounted to a post-Civil War history of Charlotte. My friend Rolfe Neill, who had risen to become the *Observer* publisher, bought a copy for every *Observer* employee—about 1,500 people. The book enjoyed strong sales and, judging from calls I got from college students across the country, it was used in many journalism schools.

Slug and JoAnn celebrated the book's publication by presenting me with a handsomely framed copy of the book jacket and a favorable review by Burke Davis, once an *Observer* rival at the *Charlotte News* and the author of seventy-five books of his own. Again, it made me feel that the Slugger was as proud of me as I was of him.

Meanwhile, serious trouble was brewing at the *Observer*. With his eyesight failing, Pete McKnight was neglecting the paper's day-to-day operations. Corporate managers in Miami began grooming as his replacement James K. Batten, a Virginian and a Davidson College graduate that McKnight had recruited and developed into a star reporter. I liked Jim Batten and, in asking to be brought home from the Washington bureau in 1965, had suggested that he be appointed to take my place, which he did. I also suggested that he ask for a higher salary, warning that he could not live in Washington on the *Observer*'s pay scale.

In replacing me in Washington, Batten did exceptional work, especially in covering Israel's lightning victory in the 1967 Six-Day War. In preparation for his return to Charlotte, he was assigned to the *Detroit Free Press,* where he worked in a variety of management slots, preliminary to taking over operations at the *Observer.*

On a quiet Saturday before donning his *Observer* mantle, he flew into Charlotte for a round of discrete conferences. Knowing he was coming, I arranged to meet him and talk about my future at the newspaper. As I waited outside a conference room in the *Observer's* deserted business offices, I could hear voices behind closed doors but couldn't make out what was being said. Finally, Batten came out to greet me.

Our meeting was brief and shocking. Without preliminaries, he asked what I wanted to do at the *Observer.* I said I wanted to be editor or managing editor. He said my value to the paper was as a writer and editorialist, not as a manager. For that reason I would never serve in a management position at any Knight newspaper. If I wanted to pursue one of those options, I would have to leave the Knight organization. That comment led me to believe the assessment came more from the cautious human resources managers in Miami than from my record at the *Observer.*

That appraisal seemed as hard for Batten to deliver as it was for me to hear. He kept taking great gulps of air between sentences and seemed anxious to get the whole encounter over, leaving me little time to respond before returning to his conference room.

I went away in a daze, shattered by the realization that an ambition building since my teen years had just been bludgeoned. I thought his assessment was all wrong and contrary to my experience in ten years of managing in the *Observer* newsroom. Even so, it took me several months to regain any sense of value to the newspaper.

Mercifully, Jim Batten helped. When he moved to Charlotte and replaced McKnight, he greeted me warmly and was always cordial in our encounters, including an occasional lunch together. Though that startling confrontation was never mentioned again, I was not offered any post above being an associate editor. I swallowed my disappointment and concentrated on writing, leaving managers to deal with office politics and outraged readers.

It helped that one afternoon when Lee Hills, editor of the *Detroit Free Press* and chief executive of all Knight newspapers, was in town, he stopped by my cubicle in the *Observer's* editorial corner to tell me that good managers were relatively easy to train but good writers were hard to find. I was surprised by his visit but took his message as a welcome vote of confidence.

Fortunately, other opportunities were in the offing. One of my colleagues on the North Carolina Humanities Council was William S. Price Jr., then director of the North Carolina Division of Archives and History and a scholar steeped in the state's colonial past. At humanities council meetings we often swapped stories about heroes and scoundrels in North Carolina's past. When friends at UNC Press encouraged us to collaborate on an anthology that would reflect the character of the state, we accepted the challenge. Working independently, he in archives in Raleigh and I in libraries in Charlotte, we looked for newspaper, magazine, or book excerpts that were representative of the state. We chose one hundred pieces, including John Lawson's 1709 account of life among Native Americans in the Carolinas; Jonathan Daniels' delightful Depression-era essay defining North Carolina's Coastal Plain, Piedmont, and Mountain regions; and Elizabeth Smith's little-known story of how a teenage George Herman Ruth won the nickname "Babe" and hit his first professional home run during spring training with the Baltimore Orioles at Fayetteville, North Carolina. When the anthology was published 1991, Charles Kuralt called it "the most interesting book about North Carolina I've ever read."

After the success of *Discovering North Carolina*, UNC Press often sent me unpublished manuscripts to evaluate. My suggestions for improvement saved a number of them from rejection, including an atlas of North Carolina, a book about Charlotte as portrayed in picture postcards, and a biography of Harry Golden.

Early in the twenty-first century, the director of UNC Press asked me to write a history of North Carolina focusing on the twentieth century. Previous histories, she said, put such emphasis on the state's early development, the Civil War, and Reconstruction that there was little space left for the century in which North Carolina earned its progressive image. I told her that, as much as I would love doing so, I could not. By then I had an advanced case of macular degeneration that would soon leave me legally blind. On a computer I could write in large type, but I could not read the small print essential to good research. Still, it was thrilling to think the press director recognized that I was capable of writing a book that would stand beside those of Hugh T. Lefler and William S. Powell, two giants of North Carolina letters. That idea led me to think the Roosevelt rainbow was still working its wonders, that the Claiborne boys, with the help of many people, had achieved a prominence beyond any expectations.

Slug as a Happy Campaigner

CHAPTER

32

Declining Fortunes

While *Discovering North Carolina* was in production, my life and Slug's began spiraling downward, mine after a series of unexpected phone calls and Slug's over a period of several years. Afterward, neither of us quite recovered the prominence we had once enjoyed.

It all happened without warning. I was looking forward to promoting *Discovering North Carolina* and, with twelve restaurants or cafeterias to manage, Slug sought to create a thirteenth. Until then almost everything he touched had turned to success, but in the tremulous dot-com economy of the early 1990s, things began going awry.

A "me generation," unaffected by the Depression or World War II, had come of age, bringing a change in attitudes and lifestyles. Young people were less anchored, less community-minded, wanted casual settings, lighter food, and louder music. At the same time, the fabric of Charlotte's collaborative ethos was fraying. People were dividing along class, neighborhood, economic, or racial lines. Fewer helping hands were being extended.

The first blow came when operators of the SouthPark mall, ignoring Slug's role in enhancing the early days of their enterprise, doubled the rent on Slug's Choice. Rather than pay it, Slug chose to open a new upscale restaurant across town in the Shoppes at University Place, a proposed mall across North

Tryon Street from UNC Charlotte. The center's promoters envisioned University Place as a northern counterpart to SouthPark. Like John Belk, they thought Slug's presence would help generate business.

They gave him the choicest location, a fourteen-thousand-square-foot space overlooking a large lake. As a complement to his restaurant, Slug planned to open an adjacent wine cellar, a novel venture in Charlotte, which was still mostly a beer and cocktails town.

It looked like a great opportunity except that the site, ninety blocks from midtown Charlotte, was largely rural. Though UNC Charlotte was growing rapidly, most of its ten thousand students were commuters. Few houses or apartments were in the area and almost no commercial outlets. University Place was expected to be the neighborhood's first shopping hub. As it turned out, a rival center on NC 49 near the university's south entrance preempted it.

During planning for the new restaurant, to be known as Slug's at University Place, Slug came down with double pneumonia and was hospitalized in intensive care for seventeen days. In his absence, developers made decisions about the new shopping center, the restaurant, wine cellar, and parking that were difficult to remedy later.

Still, the venture had some comic elements. According to Tony Marder, who had joined Slug's management staff, the Slugger asked him to oversee the new place and promised, "You won't have to show a profit for three years." As costs of opening the restaurant rose, Slug amended that forecast by telling Marder he wouldn't have to show a profit for two years. Still later, after the installation of an indoor waterfall, that profit deadline was reduced to one year. By opening night, after a national recession had bankrupted the shopping center's developer, Slug advised Marder he would need to "show a profit next week."

Unfortunately, Slug's at University Place was never profitable. The shopping center was way ahead of its time. It would be twenty-five years before that area of Charlotte, now known as University City, was bustling enough to support such an elaborate enterprise. The major department stores that planned to open there withdrew their commitments, leaving the developers scrambling to find new tenants.

Slug's resources were insufficient to endure a long wait for profits. As dining tastes changed, most of his other restaurants faced problems. The public desire for white-tablecloth service was waning. Diners were no longer drawn to lingering around tables with a chance for conversation. Instead, they wanted more casual food with music often blaring in the background. Tax-law changes reduced expense-account dining. National chains that could do market studies, match menus with local tastes, and buy in bulk moved in to undercut Slug's prices.

As revenues fell, Slug's creditors began pressing him for payment. Instead of seeing him as the civic asset he had been for thirty-five years, he was treated as a guy who might not pay his bills. By 1995, at age sixty-three, he was slowly ceding ownership of his cafeterias and restaurants like peeling off pieces of his soul. The big heartbreak came when he had to give up Slug's at the Pines in Chapel Hill and later the exquisite Thirtieth Edition in Charlotte.

He fought back briefly by opening four smaller places, two in Charlotte and two beach places, one in Litchfield, South Carolina, and the other in Emerald Isle, North Carolina, both known as "Little Sluggers." But by then the tide that had once flowed in his favor was running against him. Even so, the dining innovations he introduced at Slug's Rib, the Tower Suite, and his glamorous Thirtieth Edition had set off a culinary movement that lifted Charlotte to national attention as an attractive place to live or visit.

About that time Slug saw what he thought was a new opportunity. Charlotte was creating a sports authority to attract athletic events to the region—football, basketball, soccer, swimming, tennis, and golf, as well as auto racing. Slug applied for the job as its executive director. He knew most members of the selection committee and felt that he knew Charlotte's sports history and potential better than any other candidate. When the post was awarded to a young man from out of town, Slug was shocked. Reflecting on his efforts to promote Charlotte, his work with the Chamber of Commerce, and his service on the regional conventions bureau, he said, "I thought I had paid my dues."

After relinquishing the last of his food-service enterprises, Slug joined Lat Purser Jr., the son of the man he had worked for in the late 1950s. Again, his job was helping recruit restaurants and other tenants for shopping centers.

He renewed contacts with people across the country and for a while enjoyed the job. But at the dawn of the twenty-first century, having turned sixty-eight, he retired from that too, saying he had become "an old dog unwilling to learn new tricks."

My troubles also began in 1990 when a Central High classmate persuaded me to organize a fortieth anniversary reunion of our 1950 class, which hadn't met in many years. After gathering names and addresses, I sent out a letter announcing that the class planned to gather in Charlotte in August. Among the many letters returned for insufficient addresses was one to Barbara Werner, my former high school sweetheart. I finally found her in Dallas, Texas, sent her the announcement, and got a response saying she not only planned to attend but would arrive a couple days early to visit a sister who lived in Charlotte.

Figuring we wouldn't have time for a private talk during the reunion, I invited her to lunch a day ahead to talk about what caused our 1953 split. When she arrived at a crowded uptown Charlotte corner, she missed the restaurant entrance and entered the building next door. In retrieving her, I kidded that she was "still going in wrong doors," which didn't amuse her. She looked about as I remembered her, but her reticence about our breakup was more pronounced. She blamed me for deserting her by joining the Army. I blamed her for not having patience enough to find out where I would be assigned after basic training. We talked a long time about our lives since the breakup and agreed to stay in touch.

My greater downfall began in a phone call from Rudy Pate, a gregarious alumni secretary at North Carolina State University. He alerted me to a job opening at Park Communications in Ithaca, New York, which he said owned seven television stations, fourteen radio stations, and 134 newspapers. Roy Park, the corporation founder, was a North Carolinian and an NC State alum looking for an assistant who could "speak his language." As much as I admired Rudy Pate, I had to tell him I wasn't interested.

A couple days later I got a call from Bill Friday, president of the seventeen-campus UNC, saying in his soft, reassuring way that I should reconsider, that Roy Park was a man of considerable wealth who was looking for ways he might use it to benefit North Carolina. "You could do yourself and North Carolina a noble service by going to talk with him," Friday said. As much as I loved Bill Friday, respected his judgment, and admired the reach of his intelligence network, I said I could do more good from my editorial perch in Charlotte.

Two days later I got a call from Roy Park himself, who said, "Young man (I was fifty-nine), you'll be making a great mistake if you don't at least get on a plane and come talk with me." I flew to Ithaca and met Park on his eightieth birthday.

A square-framed, raw-boned man with a flinty jaw and a high forehead, he had the look of a once handsome fellow. Under a shock of unruly salt and pepper hair, he had deep-set eyes and bushy eyebrows that flitted up and down as he talked. Wearing a red NC State blazer, he greeted me warmly and talked glowingly of the assistantship he was offering.

Park was a product of upward mobility. Raised in rural Surry County north of Winston-Salem, he finished NC State in 1931 at the bottom of the Great Depression when jobs were nonexistent. He took an orange crate as a desk and his own typewriter to the Raleigh offices of the North Carolina Cotton Council, offering to work for free until he proved his worth. From there he rose to become a billionaire.

I dined with him and other company officers, walked through the four-story corporate headquarters that overlooked Ithaca, and went home impressed by the opportunity. I would be vice president and assistant to the chairman in a highly profitable, tightly held corporation. I was led to believe I would have a voice in corporate decisions. The salary would be nearly twice what I was earning at the *Observer*. Having worked for newspaper wages most of my life, I saw an opportunity to accumulate some savings before retirement.

Back in Charlotte, I visited Slug at his Thirtieth Edition office to discuss the job offer. He listened patronizingly, nodding and occasionally asking questions. He wanted to know more about Roy Park. When I finished, he encouraged me to make the move. He said he thought I was under-appreciated at the *Observer*, which was probably true. When informed of the Park offer, the paper's editors made no effort to keep me.

Leaving the *Observer* after more than forty years stirred emotions, not only within me but also within many readers. I got stacks of mail and dozens of phone calls telling me not to go. Dr. Paul Hardin, then chancellor at the university in Chapel Hill, sent a card with a one-word protest: "Phooey." One woman called and, unable to speak, simply wept. Fellow journalists who knew the reputation of Park Communications warned that I would be a misfit in that profit-driven organization. But by then it was too late. I had already accepted the job.

In departing I was putting aside things I held dear—my knowledge of the city and its region, my contacts across the Carolinas, and the respect of colleagues at the *Observer* and of readers who trusted me. It was like pulling up deep roots. Further, it was an exciting time to be in Charlotte, which was then on the cusp of becoming a big city. Between 1990 and 2010 Charlotte exploded in all directions. Having won an NBA franchise for its new coliseum on Tyvola Road, Charlotte's name was being put before national audiences almost every night. In addition, through restaurant franchiser Jerry Richardson of Spartanburg, South Carolina, the city was aggressively pursuing an NFL franchise that in 1994 became the Carolina Panthers. Charlotte was about to become the exciting place that Slug and I had long hoped it would be.

Once in Ithaca, I felt lost. Suddenly I was a nobody. Park Communications kept a low profile in a town dominated by Cornell University and Ithaca College. Being Roy Park's assistant was more menial than advertised, and almost nothing I did seemed to please him. He had little interest in the cities where he owned a newspaper or a radio or television station. He had bought those properties, each a pillar of its community, and turned them into profit machines. Every Saturday and Sunday, I got the mail from our post office box, took it to his home office, and went through it with him. As we looked over some of the newspapers, I suggested ways they might be improved, but he paid no attention.

Not all was discouraging. One morning I answered the phone in my office saying, "Good morning. Park Communications," only to hear the voice on the end of the line say, "You shouldn't be saying Park Communications. You should be saying Charlotte *Observer.*" The caller was Jim Batten, phoning from Moscow where he was attending a conference. He said that on the flight to Russia he had read my *Observer* history and marveled over it, claiming that he could not have sustained a narrative that long. His remarks about my writing and grasp of Charlotte history were a welcome affirmation at a time when I needed a lift.

None of the excitement that greeted the publication of *Discovering North Carolina* meant anything to Roy Park, who seemed to resent the stature I had achieved in North Carolina. When officials of the Carolinas Carousel, Charlotte's annual Christmas parade, asked me to ride as the marshal for the 1990 procession, Park wouldn't permit it, saying, "That's something *I* do, not what you do." I pointed out that as the parade marshal I would strengthen the Park Communications brand before thousands of Carolinians attending the parade, many of them from the six neighboring towns where Park owned newspapers. That didn't seem to matter.

A couple months later when UNC Charlotte asked if I would speak at its 1991 commencement, he said the same thing—"That's something *I* do, not what you do." When I protested, Park still said no, then promised to think about it. Finally, he grudgingly consented to let me off that weekend to make the trip to Charlotte.

During the commencement, held before twenty thousand people in the Charlotte Coliseum on Tyvola Road, the university awarded me an honorary doctor's degree, citing my contributions to the city and state. Afterward, I spoke about the history of the university, citing obstacles it had overcome. I challenged the 1991 graduates to follow the university's example in pursuing their careers.

Roy Park's sister, who happened to attend the commencement for other reasons, phoned him the next Monday to exclaim over the "thunderclap" of applause that greeted my honorary degree and the standing ovation that followed my speech. Sitting next to Park's desk, I heard every word she said over the speakerphone, but Park never said a word to me about it.

I worked with Park through three dismal winters, countless snowstorms, and his glowering disapproval. My job was to read several daily newspapers and weekly magazines, looking for stories he should know about and to come up with ideas for improving our newspaper, television, or radio operations.

No suggestion I made was ever accepted. The repeated tongue-lashings from Park, endless workdays, and lonely nights left me disillusioned.

Until my wife could sell our Charlotte home and join me, I lived alone in an apartment five miles out of town, cooked meals for one and, after going through mail with Roy Park, spent what was left of my weekends buying groceries and doing laundry. When I called home, my wife seemed to be overwhelmed by the demands of moving to New York.

Our interests had changed. With the birth of our children, she had left newspapering to be a full-time mother. When the children entered school, she earned another degree and began teaching the fourth grade. After that, most of our conversations seemed to be about education. I felt we were living in different worlds.

As my first Thanksgiving in Ithaca approached, I persuaded Roy Park to let me have that weekend off to visit my family for the first time since early September. After working late on a Wednesday afternoon, I drove seven hundred miles and arrived bleary-eyed in Charlotte at four in the morning on Thanksgiving Day. I was greeted by a dark and cheerless house. No one was awake to welcome me, nor was there a note left in anticipation of my arrival. Even as I climbed into bed beside my wife there was no recognition of my presence. It was a reminder that our marriage had become an empty arrangement.

By the time she joined me in Ithaca on New Year's Eve, I was weighing whether to seek a divorce. In letters with my former high school and college sweetheart I felt a renewal of our old romance. With our children grown—my son was working and my daughter was finishing law school at Georgetown—I discussed my situation with Slug, who listened without sympathy. He put great emphasis on families and reminded me that none of our brothers and sisters had been divorced. Finally, he conceded that I had to do what I had to do, but he made it clear it would be without his blessing.

I wrestled for months over the decision, then in March 1991 I made up my mind: I wanted a divorce. My wife took the news as if she had anticipated it. "Christmas will never be the same," she said. We agreed to wait until Labor Day, when our daughter would have finished law school and passed the bar exam, to tell our children we were separating.

About a year later, Roy Park suddenly appeared in the entrance to my office, which he rarely visited. He leaned heavily against the doorjamb, looking ashen and unsteady. He asked if I would drive him home. I dropped everything, got his hat and briefcase, led him to the elevator, then to his car, and drove him home. Later that evening I learned that an ambulance had been summoned to the Park residence and that Roy had been admitted to a hospital. I dropped by the hospital and was told that Park had suffered a small stroke.

After that, he no longer came to the corporate headquarters. As we worked from his home office, he seemed to mellow, occasionally even complimenting me. I felt free to start a monthly newsletter within the sprawling, coast-to-coast company to strengthen corporate identity and create a feeling of belonging among its far-flung employees.

After Park's death in 1993, I stayed with the company another year while his widow sold the entire operation. Through his will he made grants to UNC Chapel Hill and NC State. His widow established the Park Foundation and the Park Scholarships at NC State.

After a long separation from my wife, a divorce was granted in 1994, during my final year at Park. As I was leaving, about twenty-five members of the corporate staff took me to lunch and presented me with a Steuben glass owl in recognition of the wisdom I had brought the corporation.

I returned to Charlotte as director of public relations at UNC Charlotte. On my first day on campus, I visited Bonnie Cone at her home nearby. We talked and laughed about Charlotte College days, but she was still as bright-eyed and enthusiastic about UNC Charlotte as she had been at that 1961 picnic in the old dairy barn. Four months into my work for the university, with Slug present as a witness, I married my high school sweetheart.

"Slug was an extraordinary person, a once-in-a-lifetime personality, a sterling ambassador for the city that had raised him."

CHAPTER
33

A Brotherhood Renewed

People respond to defeat in different ways. Some are so wounded they curse their luck and retreat into sour isolation. Others take heart, pick up the pieces, and try again. Slug took a different course. He tried never to look back or fret over what might have been.

It was a difficult path. His financial struggles—days and nights of burning the candle at both ends—had left scars on his health. He had developed diabetes, requiring regular insulin shots. Years of smoking had produced a chronic obstructive pulmonary disorder that left him short of breath and dependent on bottled oxygen. Failing eyesight and poor hearing forced him to give up driving. To avoid going up and down steps, he and JoAnn downsized to a one-floor condominium where he could watch two television screens at a time. For someone who had flown as high as the Slugger, it was like coming back to earth. It signaled that within him the old entrepreneurial zest was gone.

In the face of all that, he might easily have retired to the plump leather chairs in his pine-paneled den and turned inward, but he didn't. Buoyed by an ever-triumphant spirit, he found other ways to enjoy life, one day at a time. According to his daughter Priscilla, "He willed himself happy."

He had good reason. JoAnn, the love of his life, was there to attend his every need. Around him constantly were his adoring children and grandchildren, whom he greeted tenderly. He had twin grandsons who looked so much alike he couldn't tell them apart, but as they sat on his lap he whispered secrets that would make them laugh. The whole attentive crowd showed him he was beloved.

On my visits I witnessed that affection. Having always emphasized family life, he made family relations the cornerstone of his retirement. His children and grandchildren helped. Remembering vacations at the beach, counting cadence on mountain hikes, or the excitement of excursions to New York, they *wanted* to be around him. He was still fun.

Remarkably, his loving manner was extended to me. We often dined together, either at my house or his. At either place there was a warmth in his tone that I hadn't felt since we were boys. Our old arguments over politics and *Observer* editorials were forgotten. The older-brother-younger-brother rivalry still flashed occasionally, but he let me know in backhanded ways that he was proud of the voice I had in community affairs. Occasionally he would say, "I wish I could have written editorials about..." whatever subject was on his mind.

When we were alone, our brotherly relationship sometimes became the topic of conversation, and some of his recollections were startling. He once said, "You don't know how difficult you made it for me, coming behind you in school after all you had done the year before." Several times he said my bylined stories in the *Observer* trumped what he had done on the football field. "Whether we won or lost," he said, "you always had the last word." Whether he meant it or not, that was impressive humility from a guy who was a three-sport athlete and usually president of his class or of the whole student body.

There were limits to his tributes. In 2001 when I was invited to Chapel Hill to be inducted into the North Carolina Journalism Hall of Fame, I made sure that Slug and JoAnn were there. I was admitted along with editors of *USA Today* and *Sports Illustrated*. *Observer* publisher Rolfe Neill, himself a Hall of Famer, presented me for induction. After the ceremony, Slug and I met briefly in the crowded lobby of Carolina Inn and agreed that for a couple of country boys from Jackass Lane, we had done pretty well.

I wanted to talk more, but Slug didn't stick around to ponder and reflect. He had trouble standing for long periods and, wearing hearing aids, disliked being in noisy crowds. People kept coming up to congratulate me until he had heard enough and went off to bed.

By then I also was beginning to feel my years. Having reached age seventy, I gave up my hectic duties as public relations director at UNC Charlotte in favor of calmer, half-time work as assistant to UNC Charlotte chancellor Jim Woodward, mostly writing speeches and ceremonial remarks. While I was there, Chancellor Woodward (an engineer) built on the work of Chancellors Dean Colvard and E. K. Fretwell and pushed the institution to research university status, greatly enhancing its prestige.

The part-time work freed me to accept invitations to write histories of two other Charlotte institutions. One was *The Crown of the Queen City,* the story of the Charlotte Chamber of Commerce. The other, *Of Pleasures and Power,* chronicled the Charlotte City Club's influence in community affairs.

Even in failing health, Slug's enduring good humor was often on display. One summer evening after grilling steaks in the backyard, he tried emptying the dying coals into a ravine behind his condo. In throwing them out he lost his balance and tumbled down the slope. About thirty feet down, he grabbed the trunk of a small tree to break his slide but couldn't get up. JoAnn threw him the end of a garden hose and tried pulling him out. Unable to get traction in the soft ground, Slug kept falling. Finally, JoAnn called 911 and a pair of burly firemen rescued him, but not before the sound of sirens and the sight of fire engines had aroused the neighborhood. As Slug emerged from the embankment, the onlookers gave a small cheer. Slug was equal to the moment. Waving to the crowd he said, "Hey, who said they couldn't put Humpty Dumpty together again?"

Even after shortness of breath and swollen legs forced him to give up playing golf, he sat at home and found golf matches to watch on TV. One of his Mafia buddies regularly dropped by to bring him a golf magazine. When diabetes required him to monitor his blood-sugar count, JoAnn took clinical care of that. With a light touch she also monitored his consumption of vodka. When he asked for a refill, she would say gently, "No, that's all you can have tonight." He didn't complain.

I could appreciate JoAnn's vigilance. At the time, I was also caring for a languishing spouse. In our twelve-year marriage, my high school sweetheart was frequently ill and hospitalized. At my insistence she had stopped smoking, but not before clouding her lungs and acquiring a hacking cough. In the fall of 2007 she was diagnosed with stage-four lung cancer. She died in March 2008.

In keeping a promise to her, I began writing the story of our romance, but try as I might, I couldn't lift it out of the lugubrious. I sought the help of Dannye Powell, a former colleague at the *Observer*, a poet, and a splendid book editor. She read succeeding versions of my manuscript and offered suggestions. At the end of her final critique, she did me an even greater favor. She asked me to meet a friend, Anne Marie Hogan, a retired reference librarian whose husband had died the year before. Would I come to dinner on Friday night, January 2? I said I would.

In meeting Anne Marie my first thought was, "Wow, Dannye really undersold this lady!" She was lovely. Nothing about her matched my image of a retired librarian. She was vital, sparkling, and engaging, wiping away any misgivings I had about meeting a woman at a setup. She had an elegance and a refreshing openness that immediately put me at ease. She was stylishly dressed, had dazzling eyes and the ease and assurance of someone comfortable in her own skin. I was smitten.

As I extended both hands to greet her, she said we had met before, nearly twenty years earlier. I had encouraged the Charlotte-Mecklenburg Library to produce a book profiling Charlotte authors past and present. That assignment, she said, had fallen to her. She said she had called me at the *Observer* for suggestions in writing the grant proposal for the project. My response, she said, was, "We want them to read." I vaguely remembered the incident and immediately felt embarrassed by it. She had obviously done well with the project without my help because it won an award for the best library program in the Southeast.

We sat alone as Dannye and her husband Lew Powell poured drinks in the kitchen. We talked about a recent *New Yorker* article about Dr. Samuel Johnson, the English wit and lexicographer, and his relations with Hester Thrale. Fortunately, I had read that issue of the *New Yorker* and could share her interest in it. As we traded stories about Dr. Johnson, she laughed easily and often. She was highly literate and exuded an appealing warmth and candor. Even after other guests arrived, I knew by the end of that dinner party that I wanted to see more of Anne Marie Hogan. She was the most impressive woman I'd ever met.

The morning after the party, I called her to suggest that we have dinner after Sunday church services. I suggested a restaurant near her home in the Elizabeth neighborhood where I had often played as a boy. At lunch we talked a long time, each of us sharing important moments in our lives. It was a thrilling exchange, both of us exposing our tenderest feelings and making ourselves vulnerable. I felt a strong kinship building between us.

When we went back to her house for a glass of wine, her landscaped yard signaled that she was a sophisticated gardener. Her yellow living room was comfortable and well appointed. Books and art lined the walls. She also had a big, black dog, Lucca, who seemed to like me. We talked for another hour. Just before leaving I said, "I am looking for someone to share my life with. May I call on you?" She said, "Yes."

Over the next few days I hardly let her out of my sight. We dined, went to movies, lunched, and took long walks. Later that week I had an appointment with an eye doctor who would dilate my pupils and make driving difficult. She offered to drive me to his office and bring me back.

After a long examination, the doctor recommended that to retard macular degeneration I take an injection behind my left eyeball. I asked the doctor's aide to summon Anne Marie from the waiting area. She accompanied me to the treatment room and held my hand as the doctor inserted the needle. Her compassion so impressed him that he asked whether she was "a clergyperson," causing us both to laugh.

At a lunch later in the month, I introduced her to Slug and JoAnn, both of whom found her refreshing. The conversation flowed freely, and Slug kept finding nice things to say to her. During a bathroom break, he confided, "At last you've found a woman worthy of you."

Four months after our meeting, Anne Marie and I were married on May 9, 2009, at Caldwell Presbyterian Church, which I had attended as a boy.

The ceremony was led by the Rev. John Cleghorn, son of Reese Cleghorn, my former editor on *Observer* editorial pages. It was a joyous event, attended by friends and family from both sides of the aisle. Slug and JoAnn were there, smiling approvingly. Slug entered the sanctuary in a wheelchair, jesting about being a "holy roller."

We were frequent guests at Slug's and JoAnn's, usually as part of family gatherings, but sometimes just the four of us. In those intimate settings it was obvious that Slug's health was declining, his hearing poor, and his memory fading. When I would recall something we had done as boys—for instance, crawling through storm-drain culverts under the Central High athletic field to get into the dank cavern beneath the armory auditorium, a space like something from "The Phantom of the Opera"—he had trouble remembering. He would smile at my account of the boxing-gloves Christmas, but I didn't think he actually recalled that incident.

He always wanted to talk with Anne Marie and would motion for her to sit close to him so he could hear. He would tell her how much he appreciated her being part of our family and constantly thanked her for "putting up with my brother."

He also mellowed in his politics, which for most of his life had been hard-line conservative. He didn't like Democrats, didn't like government, hated regulations, and didn't like liberals, though his daughter Priscilla was an outspoken one. They argued often, but not angrily. In the 2008 election, when Barack Obama became the first Black American to win the Democratic nomination for president, Slug confessed that at the last minute he had voted for him.

Watching his decline over the next three years was distressing. I could see him failing but couldn't do anything about it. As weeks passed, he grew less responsive. JoAnn needed help in caring for him. When she could no longer lift him from his favorite lounge chair, she sought assistance from hospice. On my last visit he seemed to be hardly there, yet he rolled over in his bed, looked at me through the same sad eyes I had known since boyhood, and, in the same gregarious tone I had heard so often, asked, "How ya *doing*?"

Even with a morphine drip numbing his pain and dimming his consciousness, he was still the resolute host and dispenser of hospitality. On his last night, with his son Clay standing next to his bed, he looked up through misty eyes, waved a pudgy hand and said, "Clay, go find that young couple a window seat," as if they were still running the Thirtieth Edition. The next day, JoAnn called to say he had died in his sleep. He was seventy-nine. I felt as if I had lost half of my life.

When Slug's obituary appeared on the front page of the next morning's *Observer*, many people in the community responded. Though it had been fifteen years since Slug had run restaurants, the telephone calls, cards, and letters overwhelmed his widow and children. Many of the calls and cards came from people they didn't know. The same was true at my house. Though it had been twenty years since I had a voice in public affairs, the phone rang constantly with calls from people I hadn't heard from in years. All expressed a sense of loss.

The visitation at the funeral home brought a great outpouring of love. In the waning light of a cool March evening, the line of mourners stretched out the funeral home door and for a block down the road. More than five hundred people signed the registration book. Many waited more than an hour to speak to the family.

Among them were people from all parts of the city, community leaders as well as people who washed dishes or bused tables. Former mayor Richard Vinroot was there along with Rolfe Neill. Both waited in long lines to speak with the family, as did Jim Woodward, the retired UNC Charlotte chancellor who recalled that Slug was the first Charlottean he and his wife had met on a secret visit to Charlotte to look over the city and UNC Charlotte before being interviewed by the university trustees as a possible chancellor.

Richard Foard, a star running back and Shrine Bowl player on Central High teams of the mid-1940s, was there to remember that he was among those who had worn jersey number forty-one before the Slugger. Roy McKnight Jr., son of the doctor who sewed up Slug's lip when he was kicked in the mouth during football practice, was there to reminisce and chortle over fond memories of the Slugger.

Most endearing were the remarks of Slug's former employees and patrons. They said such things as, "Slug gave me my first job," or, "Slug taught me to be a waitress," or, "Slug was always so much fun, or, "Slug set a new standard for dining," or, "Slug was a great asset to our city." One woman said, "Slug was my neighbor and the most generous person I ever knew." In truth, Slug's restaurants had broken the old meat-and-potatoes mold of Charlotte dining traditions by opening new paths to new dining delights, a movement that continues today.

At a memorial service the next day, the sanctuary of Sardis Presbyterian Church was full. The preacher talked movingly of Slug as an exemplar of Christian hospitality, of bringing people together for food and fellowship in the tradition of Christ's feeding the five thousand with loaves and fishes.

I spoke a brief eulogy saying a man's life should be measured by his character, by the family he nurtures, by his impact on friends and colleagues, and by his service to the community. By all those standards, I said, Slug was an extraordinary person, a once-in-a-lifetime personality, a sterling ambassador for the city that had raised him. I added, "For me he was a special blessing. He graced both my boyhood and my adult life and enriched my experience of Charlotte. Everybody," I said, "should have a brother like the Slugger." And so should every city.

"Clearly, our boyhood wish for growth and opportunity had been fulfilled beyond anything we might have imagined"

Epilogue

By the time Slug died in 2012, Charlotte barely resembled the town that had welcomed us seventy-five years earlier. All of the landmarks that once defined Independence Square in the heart of the city were gone. The uptown area, once limited to Tryon and Trade, Church, and College Streets, had spilled more than six blocks in all directions to cross the Brookshire and Belk Expressways, which under the Odell plan had defined the center city.

The central business district had exploded as if a roaring tsunami of urban expansion had wiped out everything in its path. The skyline bristled with soaring glass and steel towers that sparkled with lights. Everything seemed to gleam with life. Though as boys we had grown up with the city, our relations to Charlotte had withered. Most of the streetscape seemed new to us.

In the years between 1990 and 2010, when Slug and I were withdrawing from civic activity, the city had bulked up with new banks, new businesses, new institutions, new apartments, and new restaurants. A light rail system ran twenty miles from Pineville in the south to UNC Charlotte in the north. The city had acquired an NBA team, an NFL team, and a triple-A baseball franchise. Its corporate limits stretched to the county line. You could no longer tell where Charlotte stopped and one of the six county towns—Matthews, Mint Hill, Pineville, Huntersville, Cornelius, or Davidson—began. Clearly, our boyhood wish for growth and opportunity had been fulfilled beyond anything we might have imagined.

Not all the growth had been welcomed. In the first decades of the twenty-first century, Charlotte's rapid expansion sapped much of the old intimacy and personal feel of the smaller city. There was a new sense of busyness. With wider worlds to conquer, corporate leaders showed less interest in local opportunities or problems. As my old *Observer* colleague Jerry Shinn once put it, "Charlotte has become the place we always wanted, but now I don't like it."

Even so, despite a lack of pedestrian appeal—no show windows to peer into, no movie house placards to ponder, no pool rooms to entice the imagination—the central city still drew large crowds to its restaurants, art galleries, museums, sports arenas, and concert halls. Hotels dotted its street corners and visitors clotted its sidewalk. Many marveled over the city's "newness," its cleanliness, its lush tree cover, and the glories of surrounding neighborhoods. I still felt a deep personal affection for the place.

In combing my memory for these stories, I was repeatedly astonished at how often our Charlotte connections opened doors elsewhere for the Slugger and me. It was as if an unbroken thread of hometown ties ran through the events of our adult ventures. Our lives would have been far different without the Moseley brothers, Zeke Stinson, Jim Crockett, Jimmy Anderson, Dick Pierce, Wilton Garrison, Vince Bradford, Bill Brannin, or Bob Allen. My life would have been far more difficult without Elizabeth Napier, Wink Locklair, Pete McKnight, Jim Babbor dozens of others who shaped our careers. We learned valuable lessons and gained a sense of self-worth and glimmers of promising possibilities. Charlotte still offers all that.

Though the old intimacy is gone, there is something more powerful in its aura. The stone and steel streetscapes breed ambition. The tall buildings and twinkling lights feed aspirations. The traffic and constant motion represent energy. The pace of activity signals action, adventure, and possibilities. Charlotte is all the things I wanted it to be as a boy, and its best days may lie ahead.

Slug's death reminded me how much we owed the city, but it also left a gaping hole in the diminishing immediate Claiborne family whose members Slug had always convened for reunions. Now it seemed we were gathering only for funerals. We had flown to Memphis in 1999 to attend a memorial service for our oldest sister Alice, who died at age eighty-two. We met in Florida for the funeral of our brother Harold, who died in 2010 at eighty-six. Our sister Phyllis died in 2010 at eighty-nine, and our sister Anne in 2015 at eighty-seven, leaving me the sole survivor, now in my nineties.

I am grateful to live in the same Elizabeth neighborhood of my youth, within easy contact with Slug's widow JoAnn Claiborne and her children—Priscilla Claiborne and her husband James MacIntyre, and Clay Claiborne and his wife Elaine. Sadly, Slug's daughter Patty died in 2015, leaving two children, Bailey and Travis.

When we attend festive family gatherings, we have the great pleasure of being with Slug's grandchildren Rachel, McCrea, Davis, and Carter and now with his great grandchildren, Kennedy, Holden, Mason, and Leo. When we are at one of those gatherings, it is thrilling to see the husbands of the grandchildren (Justin and Troy) manage and care for the children.

When I married Anne Marie, I not only got the wife of my dreams but also got her loving sons John and Michael. John and his wife Andrea found Boca Bay, and we eventually followed, making it possible for us to live a very good part of our life on a marsh on Topsail Island off the Atlantic coast and, most importantly, near the three of them. Michael is indispensable in keeping our life running smoothly and our conversation stimulating. He can fix anything, looks at the world through an economist's lens, and cooks like an international chef. Andrea and the exuberant John make all occasions special and everyday life more rewarding. Through their alerts we do not miss gorgeous moonrises or sunsets or bald eagles on live oak branches.

My son Jacky has surpassed all expectations. It has been a hard but rewarding journey from his diagnosis of autism at age four. He has pursued his love of music by writing and recording his own songs and performing them with aplomb before appreciative audiences. Drawing and coloring his own imaginary world gives him hours of pleasure, and he has developed his very own style. Any of his renderings could only be described as "Jacky Claiborne's." In addition to his artistic pursuits, he has put his stamp on his own apartment and excelled at his long-time part-time job as a dishwasher for the Cypress retirement village.

No one exemplifies a good family member more than Margaret Louise's husband, John Campbell. He has been by Jacky's and her side all the way. There is probably nothing more meaningful in Jacky's life than his music and his performing his own music in front of an audience. John Campbell has worked to find venues for Jacky's concerts in both Charlotte and Atlanta. With great appreciation he has watched Jacky grow and always looks out for ways to make Jacky's life better, from cars to computers. Margaret has been an exceptional sister to Jacky, from being by his side when needed in junior high and high school to tirelessly advocating for his needs as an autistic adult.

When John and Margaret had their first child, Anna, I immediately drove to Atlanta and held their beautiful girl when she was only hours old. Her remarkable talents and abilities continue to amaze me. A fluent speaker of French, she is studying linguistics and anthropology at the University of Pennsylvania. In addition to her academic excellence, Anna is an accomplished baker (Earl Grey and lavender shortbread and even her own bagels) and skillful cook. Her adventurous streak has always been apparent from strapping her ukulele on her back for her high school study abroad in France to practicing screenwriting in the summer in Michigan. Like her mother, she is always looking for ways to help.

My grandson Charles (known in the family as "Chick") has amazed me with his contemplative mind and his gentleness. When still in high school he returned from a family trip to China and right away began teaching himself Japanese. First, he made flash cards for building a vocabulary, then had tutorials in Atlanta, then attended Japanese language camp in North Dakota. Today he is a junior at the University of Virginia, studying world affairs and foreign policy. Like his sister, Chick can cook and, also like his sister, provides out-of-the-ordinary meals for his family and friends. When he was about eight, he made me one of my favorite desserts, banana pudding, with his flourish of browned meringue on top.

My beautiful daughter, Margaret, has delighted me from the beginning. When she was months old, she held her head up over the bumper guards of her crib looking with her big brown eyes for me to give her a two-in-the-morning feeding. I loved teaching her to ride a bike and play tennis and saw her off to Chapel Hill and Georgetown Law and accompanied her down the aisle when she married John Ray Campbell III. Always thoughtful and willing to help, she has become the environmental lawyer for Delta Airlines after a successful career as a partner at a major international law firm. She was meant to soar and has. The Campbell family, including their dog, Farley, gives me deep satisfaction.

Altogether, the entire clan offers a diversity of ideas and experience that affords Anne Marie and me a richer quality of life than we might ever have imagined.

Slug and I knew early on that we would have to work to achieve our aspirations. We did work and, with lots of help on the way, achieved lofty goals. There were disappointments for both of us, but in the end it was Charlotte and our families that gave us the opportunities to thrive. After seeing that Roosevelt rainbow over Memorial Stadium, it was our mother who had the courage to move us to the city and hold the family together and our brother Harold who enabled us to finish school and go to college. I can only hope our story inspires others to seize the opportunities that Charlotte offers. So long as there are boys and girls like the Slugger and me, there will be youngsters looking, not for a handout but for a hand up.

"You may have been a good husband to three wives, but your first love was Charlotte"

—Anne Marie Claiborne

Acknowledgments

This memoir was inspired a few years ago when I heard Judy Goldman, a Charlotte poet and novelist, read from her memoir, *Losing My Sister*. The relationship she described moved me to write the story of me and my brother Slug. After hearing me talk about some of our boyhood experiences, my wife Anne Marie suggested that I widen the scope to include tales of Charlotte. "You may have been a good husband to three wives, but your first love was Charlotte," she said.

I have great memories of our family but needed lots of help from others. One was my late sister Anne, the family genealogist, who filled me in on the wonderful story of how my parents met and married. I am also indebted to my late sister Alice for the story of finding the Fifth Street house and our move to Charlotte. I am indebted to my late sister Phyllis for details about our Derita house, our father's funeral, and the trip there and back. And, of course, I am indebted to my late brother Harold for so many things, including his stories about our life at Newell.

I am beholden to Slug's wife JoAnn, his daughter Priscilla and son Clay for many memories, including Slug's final days and the memorable story about putting Humpty Dumpty together again. Clay's descriptions of Slug's operating procedures were invaluable.

I owe to the highly literate Linda Ashendorf the vision of Slug's riding into the mock political convention on the back of an open convertible with a pep band playing and confetti raining down.

A number of other people read the manuscript at various times and made helpful suggestions. They include my novelist neighbor Jennifer Hubbard, the Charlotte poet and critic Peg Robarchek, my high school classmates Jim Babb and Murray Whisnant, my historian friends Dan and Mary Lynn

Morrill, and my fellow book club members, George and Susanne Sawyer. I am grateful to all of them.

As a full-circle history moment, I'm grateful to our publisher, SPARK Publications, led by Fabi Preslar, for helping make this book a published reality. Located in Charlotte, they were also the design firm on my book *Crown of the Queen City*, published over 20 years earlier.

My deepest thanks go to the staff of the Robinson-Spangler Carolina Room of the Charlotte Mecklenburg Public Library for generous help in looking up names, dates, census data, and Charlotte events, especially President Roosevelt's visit to Charlotte (I was there but was only four years old).

Most importantly, this memoir could not have been written without the steadfast support of my wife Anne Marie, who saw value in the story and encouraged me to write it. She read the manuscript through its many revisions and made perceptive suggestions for warming its tone and widening its perspective. When I wandered off course, she would remind me to stick to the narrative of Slug and me, saying. "This is not the history of Independence Boulevard."

Other than that, all other information was drawn from my memory and my impressions of Charlotte, past and present. Any errors of fact or emphasis are attributable to me.

Index

Author Bio

Jack is a Charlotte native, a graduate of Central High, the University of North Carolina at Chapel Hill, and the University of Chicago. He entered journalism as a high school sportswriter for the *Charlotte Observer* and over the next forty years became a reporter, an editor, a Washington correspondent, an editorial writer, and an associate editor. He completed his career as vice president and assistant to the chairman of Park Communications in Ithaca, New York, and as director of public relations and assistant to the chancellor at UNC Charlotte. He is a member of the North Carolina Journalism Hall of Fame. This is his eighth book. Jack lives with his wife, Anne Marie, in the Elizabeth neighborhood within a mile of where he grew up.

Keep Up with Jack

Use this link to order more copies and discover more of Jack Claiborne's work

JackEClaiborne.com

Some of Jack's past work includes the following titles

The Charlotte Observer: Its Time and Place, 1869–1986
Discovering North Carolina: A Tar Heel Reader
27 Views of Charlotte: The Queen City in Prose and Poetry
Crown of the Queen City: The Charlotte Chamber from 1870 to 1999
Of Pleasures & Power: The Story of the Charlotte City Club
Jack Claiborne's Charlotte

9 781953 555649